Conversations with Allen Ginsberg

Literary Conversations Series
Monika Gehlawat
General Editor

Conversations with Allen Ginsberg

Edited by David Stephen Calonne

University Press of Mississippi / Jackson

The University Press of Mississippi is the scholarly publishing agency
of the Mississippi Institutions of Higher Learning: Alcorn State University,
Delta State University, Jackson State University, Mississippi State University,
Mississippi University for Women, Mississippi Valley State University,
University of Mississippi, and University of Southern Mississippi.

www.upress.state.ms.us

The University Press of Mississippi is a member
of the Association of University Presses.

First printing 2019
∞

Library of Congress Cataloging-in-Publication Data

Names: Calonne, David Stephen, 1953– editor.
Title: Conversations with Allen Ginsberg / edited by David Stephen Calonne.
Description: Jackson: University Press of Mississippi, [2019] | Series:
   Literary conversations series | "First printing 2019." | Includes
   bibliographical references and index. |
Identifiers: LCCN 2019013803 (print) | LCCN 2019022033 (ebook) | ISBN
   9781496823526 (epub single) | ISBN 9781496823533 (epub institutional) |
   ISBN 9781496823540 (pdf single) | ISBN 9781496823557 (pdf institutional)
   | ISBN 9781496823502 (cloth) | ISBN 9781496823519 (pbk.)
Subjects: LCSH: Ginsberg, Allen, 1926–1997—Interviews. | Poets,
   American—United States—Interviews. | Beats (Persons) | Poets,
   American—20th century—Interviews. | Beats (Persons)—Interviews.
Classification: LCC PS3513.I74 (ebook) | LCC PS3513.I74 Z46 2019b (print) |
   DDC 811/.54—dc23
LC record available at https://lccn.loc.gov/2019013803

British Library Cataloging-in-Publication Data available

Books by Allen Ginsberg

Howl and Other Poems. San Francisco: City Lights Books, 1956

Kaddish and Other Poems 1958–1960. San Francisco; City Lights Books, 1961.

Empty Mirror: Early Poems. New York: Totem Press in Association with Corinth Books, 1961.

The Yage Letters (with William Burroughs). San Francisco: City Lights Books, 1963

Reality Sandwiches. San Francisco: City Lights Books, 1963.

The Change. London: Writer's Forum, 1963.

Prose Contribution to Cuban Revolution. Detroit: Artists' Workshop, 1966.

Wichita Vortex Sutra. London: Housmans, 1966.

T.V. Baby Poems. London: Cape Goliard Press, 1967.

Scrap Leaves. Sri Ram Ashram, Millbrook, NY: The Poets Press, 1968.

Airplane Dreams: Compositions from Journals. Toronto: House of Anansi, 1968.

Ankor Wat. London: Fulcrum Press, 1968.

Wales, A Visitation. London: Cape Goliard, 1968.

Planet News 1961–1967. San Francisco: City Lights Books, 1968.

Indian Journals. San Francisco: Dave Haselwood/City Lights Books, 1970.

Notes after an Evening with William Carlos Williams. New York: Portents, 1970.

The Moments Return. San Francisco: Grabhorn-Hoyem, 1970.

Ginsberg's Improvised Poetics. Edited by Mark Robison. Buffalo: Anonym Press, 1971.

Declaration of Independence for Dr. Timothy Leary, July 4, 1971. San Francisco: Hermes Free Press, 1971.

Open Head/Open Eye. Melbourne: Sun Books, 1972.

New Year Blues. New York: Phoenix Book Shop, 1972.

The Fall of America: Poems of These States, 1965–1971. San Francisco: City Lights Books, 1972.

The Gates of Wrath. Rhymed Poems 1948–1952. Bolinas, CA: Grey Fox Press, 1972.

Bixby Canyon Ocean Path Word Breeze. New York: Gotham Book Mart, 1972.

Iron Horse. Toronto: Coach House, 1972.

Allen Verbatim: Lectures on Poetry, Politics, Consciousness, ed.Gordon Ball. New York: McGraw-Hill, 1974.

The Visions of the Great Rememberer, with Letters by Neal Cassady. Amherst, MA: Mulch Press, 1974.

Gay Sunshine Interview with Allen Young. Bolinas, CA: Grey Fox Press, 1974.

First Blues: Rags, Ballads, and Harmonium Songs. New York: Full Court Press, 1975.

Chicago Trial Testimony. San Francisco: City Lights, 1975.

Sad Dust Glories. Berkeley: Workingman's Press, 1975.

To Eberhart from Ginsberg: A Letter about Howl, 1956. Lincoln, MA: Penmaen, 1976.

As Ever: The Collected Correspondence of Allen Ginsberg and Neal Cassady, ed. Barry Gifford. Berkeley: Creative Arts, 1977.

Journals Early Fifties Early Sixties, ed. Gordon Ball. New York: Grove Press, 1977.

Mind Breaths: Poems 1972–1977. San Francisco: City Lights Books, 1978.

Careless Love. Madison, WI: Red Ozier, 1978.

Mostly Sitting Haiku. Paterson, NJ: From Here, 1978.

Poems All Over the Place, Mostly 'Seventies. Cherry Valley, NY: Cherry Valley, 1979.

Old Pond Song. Cambridge, MA: Firefly Press, 1979.

Composed on the Tongue, ed. Don Allen. Bolinas, CA: Grey Fox Press, 1980.

Straight Hearts' Delight, Love Poems and Selected Letters, with Peter Orlovsky. San Francisco; Gay Sunshine, 1980.

Plutonium Ode and Other Poems 1977–1980. San Francisco: City Lights Books, 1982.

Allen Ginsberg on Tour. Wuppertal: Lichtblick, 1984.

Many Loves. New York: Pequod, 1984.

Collected Poems 1947–1980. New York: Harper and Row, 1985.

Howl: Original Draft Facsimile, ed. Barry Miles. New York; Harper and Row, 1986.

White Shroud Poems 1980–1985. New York: Harper and Row, 1986.

Old Love Story. New York: Lospecchio, 1986.

Your Reason & Blake's System. Madras and New York: Hanuman Books, 1988.

Allen Ginsberg Photographs. Altadena, CA: Twelvetrees Press, 1990.

Visiting Father and Friends. Louisville, KY: White Fields Press, 1993.

Snapshot Poetics: Allen Ginsberg's Photographic Memoir of the Beat Era. San Francisco: Chronicle Books, 1993.

Cosmopolitan Greetings: Poems 1986–1993. New York: HarperCollins, 1994.

Mind Writing Slogans. Boise, ID: Limberlost, 1994.

Beat Legacy, Connections, Influences. Louisville, KY: White Fields Press, 1994.

Journals Mid-Fifties 1954–1958, ed.Gordon Ball. New York: HarperCollins, 1995.

Illuminated Poems—paintings and drawings by Erik Drooker. New York: Four Walls Eight Windows, 1996.

Selected Poems 1947–1995. New York: HarperCollins, 1996.

Luminous Dreams. Gran Canaria: Zasterle Press, 1997.

Death and Fame: Last Poems 1993–1997, ed. Bob Rosenthal, Peter Hale, and Bill Morgan. New York: Harper Flamingo, 1999.

Deliberate Prose: Selected Essays 1959–1995, ed. Bill Morgan. New York: HarperCollins, 2000.

Family Business: Selected Letters between a Father and Son, ed. Michael Schumacher. New York: Bloomsbury, 2001.

Spontaneous Mind: Selected Interviews, ed. David Carter. New York: HarperCollins, 2001.

The Book of Martyrdom and Artifice: First Journals and Poems 1937–1952, ed. Juanita Lieberman-Plimpton and Bill Morgan. New York: Da Capo Press, 2006.

Collected Poems 1947–1997. New York: HarperCollins, 2006.

The Yage Letters Redux (with William Burroughs), ed. Oliver Harris. San Francisco: City Lights Books, 2006.

The Letters of Allen Ginsberg. Edited by Bill Morgan. New York: Da Capo Press, 2008.

The Selected Letters of Allen Ginsberg and Gary Snyder, ed. Bill Morgan. Berkeley: Counterpoint, 2009.

Jack Kerouac and Allen Ginsberg; The Letters, ed. Bill Morgan and David Stanford. New York: Viking, 2010.

Beat Memories: The Photographs of Allen Ginsberg, ed. Sarah Greenough. Prestel, 2010.

The Essential Ginsberg. Edited by Michael Schumacher. New York: HarperCollins, 2015.

I Greet You at the Beginning of a Great Career: The Selected Correspondence of Lawrence Ferlinghetti and Allen Ginsberg 1955–1997, ed. Bill Morgan. San Francisco: City Lights Books, 2015.

Wait Till I'm Dead: Uncollected Poems, ed. Bill Morgan. New York: Grove Press, 2016.

First Thought: Conversations with Allen Ginsberg, ed. Michael Schumacher. Minneapolis: University of Minnesota Press, 2017.

The Best Minds of My Generation: A Literary History of the Beats, ed. Bill Morgan. New York: Grove Press, 2017.

Television Was a Baby Crawling Towards That Deathchamber. London: Penguin Classics, 2018.

Don't Hide the Madness: William S. Burroughs in Conversation with Allen Ginsberg. New York: Three Rooms Press, 2018.

Iron Curtain Journals: January–May 1965, ed. Michael Schumacher. Minneapolis: University of Minnesota Press, 2018.

Contents

Introduction

Allen Ginsberg (1926–1997) loved the art of conversation. Among Beat generation authors, he was the most generous by far in granting interviews to journalists, academics, television or radio personalities and virtually anyone who wished to speak with him. Ginsberg was not averse to publicity. Indeed, one should remember that one of his first jobs was in market research—he had learned how to gain the attention of audiences—and he would become a tireless advocate on behalf of several colleagues including William S. Burroughs, Gregory Corso, Jack Kerouac, Philip Whalen, and Gary Snyder in placing their manuscripts with publishers and promoting their careers. The conversations in this book span four decades from the sixties to the nineties and provide a compendium of cultural and intellectual history during these sometimes apocalyptic times. A notable feature of these interviews is Ginsberg's unflagging intellectual curiosity and enthusiasm concerning a capacious range of subjects. We witness his gift for speaking intelligently and provocatively on gay rights, the relationship between music and poetry, nuclear disarmament, censorship, Gnosticism, the spiritual history of India, the major themes in literary masterworks he admires. Readers will also be dazzled by his articulate virtuosity in speaking about political matters—for example regarding drug control or the history of censorship in the media—and by Ginsberg's seemingly effortless recall of specific references and documentation to support his arguments: it is evident when he speaks of controversial issues that he has done his homework.

Allen Ginsberg was born in 1926 in Paterson, New Jersey—the town which would attain literary renown due to the poetry of William Carlos Williams. Williams became a literary mentor for the young Ginsberg, contributing the introduction to his book of early poems, *Empty Mirror* (1961). Allen's childhood was marked by the influence of his father Louis, a poet and English teacher. Although they disagreed about politics—Louis was anti-Communist, supported the war in Vietnam, anti-Fidel Castro, vehemently pro-Israel, and an advocate for a strong US military, all positions diametrically opposed to those taken by Allen—father and son would however remain close throughout their lives. Louis was often a jokester who enjoyed making terrible puns, and indeed his son Allen was also gifted with an often wild, outrageous, and surreal sense of humor as we see in several of his poems as well as in the 1970 interview in which father and son have a wide-ranging discussion. Allen's mother Naomi's existence was much more fraught: her mental instability caused her to be periodically institutionalized. Their tortured relationship is chronicled in Ginsberg's great elegy "Kaddish" in which he depicts Naomi as a profound source of his poetic genius as well as the nexus within his own creative imagination between madness, suffering, and inspiration. In a sense, Ginsberg's own struggles with mental illness, poetic ecstasy, and the search for the tran-scendent coalesced in the primal episode in his spiritual life which occurred in Harlem in July, 1948. Ginsberg recalled that one evening he "opened my book of Blake . . . and had a classical hallucinatory-mystical experience, i.e. heard his voice commanding and prophesying to me from eternity, felt my soul open completely wide all its doors and windows and the cosmos flowed thru me, and *experienced* a state of altered apparently total consciousness so fantastic and science-fictional I even got scared later, at having stumbled on a secret door in the universe all alone."[1]

Following this visionary episode, Neal Cassady—his friend, lover, and hero ("Dean Moriarty") of Jack Kerouac's *On the Road*—composed a thoughtful letter to Ginsberg in August, 1948: "But, beyond all this, you stand head and shoulders above any one man I've ever known—that, in itself, is love—calls for love. Again, look at yourself as Prince Mischkine [sic]—the idiot—you manifest more of the mystic, the Dostoievskian reli-gious, the loving Christ, than does anyone else." Cassady had read Fyodor Dostoevsky's *The Idiot* (1868–9) in 1943 while in reform school.[2] Ginsberg responded to Neal: "I long more to go to God than to you, and perhaps you are a temptation rather than an angel. Yet you have a star in your forehead; that is why I long ago was happy to think with you that our lives were bound together."[3] Dostoevsky's Prince Myshkin merges with Ginsberg's roots in Jewish mystical traditions. Robert Duncan remarked in *The Truth and Life of Myth: An Essay in Essential Autobiography*: "In the belief in the Hidden Zaddik, the divine wisdom that the least of men may be illumined by, the Chassidic masters speak not only to the Jewish community but to our com-mon humanity. In the fairy tales of every people there are stories of those who will not recognize in the wretched and contemptible even, the pres-ence of a divine life." Like Myshkin, Ginsberg's otherworldly temperament marks him as a Zaddik whose fervent desire is to attain union with God.

Kenneth Rexroth believed the prophetic poet of "Howl" was "in the direct line of the *nabis*, those wild men of the hills, bearded and barefoot, who periodically descended upon Jerusalem, denounced king and priesthood, and recalled the Chosen People to the Covenant. If any writer is true to his tradition, it's Ginsberg. Behind him stretches away for generations the prophetic, visionary and orgiastic tradition of Hassidism. He is a Zaddik." Ginsberg was born of Jewish parents but they were non-practicing and his mother's political commitments to Leftist causes—Naomi was affiliated with the Communist Party—greatly influenced him. However, in poems like "Howl" and "Kaddish" the themes and style of the Hebrew Bible, the prophets, as well as the Kabbalah on Ginsberg's sensibility is evident.[4] *Tikkun olam*—in Hebrew "repair of the world"—the notion that one should work ceaselessly for the welfare of humanity is central to Ginsberg's political vision. A recurring theme throughout these interviews is the struggle for equality and social justice, and a truly communal world in which each person is respected. In the Lurianic Kabbalah, the importance of ethical action is stressed, and Ginsberg familiarized himself with Kabbalah as we see in his famous line from "Howl": *who studied Plotinus Poe St. John of the Cross telepathy and bop kabbalah because the cosmos instinctively vibrated at their feet in Kansas.*

The visionary poetry of William Blake, combined with Ginsberg's tendency towards frenetic psychological states and "Hassidic" devotion to the Dostoevskian saintliness of Prince Myshkin were thus significant sources of inspiration as his career began. Ginsberg would spend the next several years reading widely and obtained his "highs" as frequently from his unquenchable appetite for literature and philosophy as from entheogens. For example, he wrote to Neal Cassady on May 20, 1949: "I read & got great kick out of mad novel by mystic P.D. Ouspensky, short, almost like bill [William S. Burroughs] in condensation and single-trackness. Called the *Strange Life of Ivan Osokin*. I will mail it to you as you may find it useful. Reading it gets you on mystic high, almost physical. But mail it back."[5] This novel by Ouspensky (1878–1947)—the Russian mathematician and pupil of the Armenian-Greek guru G.I. Gurdjieff (1866–1949)—depicts Ivan Osokin who in an illustration of Friedrich Nietzsche's idea of the eternal recurrence lives—and subsequently relives—his life in the same way, but this second time with prior knowledge of his past mistakes. Throughout these interviews, we continually encounter Ginsberg's enthusiasm upon encountering writers and ideas which excite him, and we witness his increasingly intense interest in Buddhist philosophy. For example, five years after his Blakean revelation,

Ginsberg began to study D. T. Suzuki's *Introduction to Zen Buddhism* and in a May 14, 1953 letter to Cassady narrated a number of koans, describing the moment of *satori* or illumination as "a specific flash of vision that totally changes" one's perception of reality. Ginsberg finds the Zen idea of God fascinating for Zen Buddhists "refuse to have a theology or admit that one exists, or anything verbal at all. That's the point of these anecdotes; to exhaust words. Then the man sees anew the universe."[6] In contradistinction to the more cerebral Buddhist traditions, Zen seeks an instant radical change in perception through two modes: in *zazen,* or meditation while sitting, the mind is cleared of all extraneous stimuli and the practitioner concentrates on their posture and breathing. In the second method, the *koan* is utilized to break the student's habit of logical, rational analysis. There is a famous "visual koan" known variously as the "Ten Oxherding Pictures" or "Ten Bulls"; Ginsberg also studied these with keen enjoyment and then sent the book to Cassady as a birthday present. The drawings emerged in twelfth-century China and would influence the school of Chan Buddhism as well as the American composer John Cage. Enlightenment in the ten drawings is illustrated by the struggle to tame the bulls. At first, the bull and tamer are antagonists; in the following four panels, tamer and bull gradually ignore each other; and in the final two, first the bull disappears and then the tamer. The final drawing is of a completely open circle: both bull and tamer have vanished. It is a marvelous allegory of the illusory nature of tamer, bull and existence itself, and the final enlightenment is to return again to the place from which one began.[7]

As we see throughout these interviews, Ginsberg hungered for deeper knowledge of the hidden reaches of the mind and consciousness. He investigated many philosophies and sought answers not only in books, but through worldwide travels, and during the fifties and early sixties journeyed widely in continuous pursuit of wisdom. In Mexico in 1954 he read the fourteenth century mystical text *The Cloud of Unknowing* and composed "Siesta in Xbalba." The following year on October 7, Ginsberg premiered "Howl" in San Francisco and on October 13 Lawrence Ferlinghetti sent him the famous telegram which echoes Ralph Waldo Emerson's prediction for Walt Whitman: "I GREET YOU AT THE BEGINNING OF A GREAT CAREER [stop] WHEN DO I GET THE MANUSCRIPT OF 'HOWL'?"[8] During the late fifties and early sixties, Ginsberg experimented widely with entheogens—another recurring theme in the interviews—and recorded his experiences in his poetry. In 1960 he journeyed to South America in search of *ayahuasca* or *yage.* And Ginsberg would ultimately desire—like Henry David Thoreau and Ralph Waldo Emerson who had read the *Bhagavad Gita* and ancient Sanskrit texts—to return to the primal source of transcendental thought in India. The sixties would be marked by a fervent philosophical search among American youth for alternatives to the monotheistic religions. Indeed, Hugh McLeod entitled his book on this period *The Religious Crisis of the Sixties*, for the decade charted a powerful shift away from the accepted pieties of the past. Ginsberg took this quest seriously, spending more than a year and a half in India, visiting the famous historical sites associated with Buddha and writing *Indian Journals* (1970). Here we find him in the first interview with R. Parthasarathy from 1962 discussing poetry with Indian poets and three decades later in 1993 describing in rich detail in an informative interview with Suranjan Ganguly his deep relationship to India's great spiritual traditions. One of the results of this journey may be seen in the poetics which Ginsberg evolved during the sixties for he began to chant Hindu and Buddhist mantras, memorizing an impressive number of ancient sacred texts. The Beatles made an important trip to Rishikesh in northern India in February, 1968 to study transcendental meditation with Maharishi Mahesh Yogi and George Harrison learned to play the sitar (the distinctive sound of this instrument began to be featured in his compositions). It is perhaps no accident that The Beatles gave themselves a name containing the word "Beat," since a song like John Lennon's "Imagine"—with its exhortations to live a life without addiction to materialism and to peaceful unity with nature without the mind shackles of ideology—seems at once an embodiment of the ideals of Eastern wisdom as exemplified in Lao Tzu's classic *Tao Te Ching* as well as the American Beat philosophy of life. There was indeed a clear mutual relationship between Beat fascination with Asian thought—Kerouac had compiled *Some of the Dharma*, a huge manuscript on Buddhism during the fifties (published posthumously in 1997)—and the turn in popular culture towards non-Western paths towards enlightenment.[9]

Ginsberg's interviews of the sixties are marked by the intense political, social, ecological, sexual, and artistic upheavals of that apocalyptic decade. During the early sixties, writers became aware a shift was occurring away from the jazz and bebop of the fifties towards folk music and rock and roll and that music was winning the battle for the attention of young people. The poet Brother Antoninus—William Everson—pointed out that during the sixties, the shamanism of the Beats had "now been largely taken over by the rock band. . . . We Beats were a manifestly poetry-oriented generation, whereas the voice of the succeeding one is indubitably rock, so that poetry is relatively unemphasized right now."[10] Ginsberg's meeting with

Bob Dylan in 1963 opened new possibilities for his own creativity. Dylan had given an autoharp to Michael McClure to accompany his poetry and Ginsberg also began to devote more time to chanting, singing and set himself to learn some rudiments of musical theory and performance, acquiring finger cymbals and a harmonium. As Ginsberg points out in his interview with Suranjan Ganguly, the harmonium—like the autoharp which has chords already built into the mechanism of the instrument, knobs which are easily pushed down by the fingers and strings strummed by hand—is an instrument a child can play. Clearly Ginsberg—although not a talented musician or vocalist (although it must be said that the voices, for example, of Bob Dylan, Tom Waits, and Leonard Cohen are not "beautiful" according to our usual standards of evaluating singing)—became increasingly curious about exploring the connections between poetry and song and to set the poems by his "guru" William Blake. Ginsberg saw the emerging folk music/protest/spiritual/apocalyptic/lyrical mode of Dylan as a continuation of the Beat traditions of speed, intensity, spontaneity, and energy that he and Kerouac had explored during the fifties. Dylan's genius in creating imaginative metaphors, his wide range of allusions to literary, esoteric (the *I Ching*, the Chinese book of divination, and Tarot cards for example), Biblical and philosophical sources, his surreal flights of fancy, the gathering intensity of his ballads which moved non-stop over several minutes, and his "chains of flashing images"—as Ginsberg described them—all were convincing evidence that Dylan was indeed a Beat poet for the sixties.

The popularity of The Beatles also skyrocketed in the United States following their appearance on the Ed Sullivan television show in February, 1964, and Ginsberg would become acquainted with both John Lennon and Paul McCartney. In his 1970 interview with Robert Head, Ginsberg traced the ways rock and roll derived from African music which induced voodoo-like trance states, stimulating overwhelming feelings of erotic abandon and the impulse to practice Dionysian dancing which he had witnessed among young people in England: "And there was also trance states or ecstatic possession in Liverpool, you know, girls going into a trance state for George or John Lennon . . . wetting their pants or whatever . . . going into an hysteric trance, which wasn't just a hysteric trance, it was an actual possession state . . . exactly as in Voodon or in Shango dancing people go into trance states . . . and then the actual circle of dancers and the shuffle step is exactly the same, or was the same, in Cuba in 1965 and I guess I saw it in 1967 in Liverpool, which is a real simple step, one two three four, one two three four, so it was just a shuffle step."

The sixties interviews also track Ginsberg's extensive travels throughout the world. Following his trip to India, in 1965 he journeyed to both Cuba and Czechoslovakia. He vividly described to David Widgery his experiences in Prague where he was crowned "King of May" but was investigated by the police and ejected from the country. And while he was in England, journalists misreported what had actually occurred during his meeting with the poet Edith Sitwell: "I learned a lot about mass communications at this point, because I could see the difference between what is being reported and what isn't. If there's such a gap in my case, then imagine that blown up on a larger scale with reporting on China or Russia. In other words, the structure of reality presented to everyone is completely fabricated. Not consciously I mean; these people don't know the difference. Of course it may be in the nature of mass communication itself, because as soon as you abstract yourself from the event, you are no longer dealing with it." Ginsberg was prescient in his awareness that we have entered a period mediated by print and electronic "control systems" by means of which "the structure of reality presented to everyone is completely fabricated," a subject which would preoccupy Ginsberg's friend William S. Burroughs and which forms the theme of the popular science fiction film *The Matrix* (1999). Burroughs emphasized that what the Hindus call *maya* defines the illusory nature of reality as moderns experience it. Ginsberg's clarity of perception, his *seeing through* the falsity and meretriciousness of canned, consumer, media-controlled reality may be seen as an example of what psychiatrist R. D. Laing meant when he spoke of the wisdom of supposed "madness"—that the "unbalanced" person in the contemporary world is often the one who sees most clearly because their blinders have been removed and they perceive the *constructedness* and repression of the "reality show" we are presented with on a daily basis.

Ginsberg turns in his interview with *The Cottonwood Review* to the question of literary influences and his favorite writers. He had read extremely widely in world literature and cites Guillaume Apollinaire, Ezra Pound, William Carlos Williams, Arthur Rimbaud, Antonin Artaud, Sherwood Anderson, Louis-Ferdinand Celine, Jean Genet, Henry Miller, Buddhist sutras such as the *Prajnaparamita*. We know from his letters—as we have seen above—and allusions in his poetry and prose that he had also read deeply the works of Fyodor Dostoevsky, the *Bhagavad Gita*, a variety of Zen texts, William Blake, T. S. Eliot, St. John of the Cross, St. Teresa of Avila, the Neoplatonic philosopher Plotinus, Pseudo-Dionysius the Areopagite, and the Roman love poet Catullus, among scores of others.[11] For Ginsberg, the spiritual and literary quest are connected for he sees literature not as a purely "aesthetic" activity to be pursued apart from one's own psychological struggles, but rather as a means to record one's own deepest philosophical insights and quandaries. In this respect, Ginsberg shared many similarities with the so-called "Confessional" poets such as Robert Lowell, Theodore Roethke, John Berryman, and Sylvia Plath who made their poetry directly out of autobiographical experience. Furthermore, due to his political commitments to gay rights, pacifism, and ecology, Ginsberg saw literature as a way to engage directly in the struggle for justice and social change.

It is also interesting to witness the ways Ginsberg's spiritual search was connected to his experiments with entheogens—substances which literally stimulate the sensation that one is directly encountering the divine, or in ancient Greek, *theos*. After his many investigations in the late fifties and early sixties and participation in research studies with Timothy Leary at Harvard and Gregory Bateson at Stanford, Ginsberg began to proselytize for widespread use of psychedelics in order to bring about an expansion of consciousness which might create what his hero William Blake called the "New Jerusalem" in America. However, a provocative exchange occurred during the interview recording Ginsberg's 1968 meeting with A. C. Bhaktivedanta (1896–1977), the leader of the Hare Krishna movement:

> SWAMIJI: You have not had LSD, Allen?
> GINSBERG: I have had it.
> SWAMIJI: It is dependence, Allen.
> GINSBERG: It's like a car—a mental car—to resolve inner things.
> SWAMIJI: Krishna Consciousness resolves everything. Nothing else is needed.

There was widespread debate during the sixties concerning whether employing entheogens could provide an "authentic" mystical experience: the distinguished Oxford professor R. C. Zaehner argued in *Mysticism Sacred and Profane* against Aldous Huxley's thesis in *The Doors of Perception* (1954) that psilocybin provided access to more profound awareness than could be experienced through "natural" means.[12] Throughout the interviews we witness Ginsberg discussing this issue in a variety of contexts.

One of the characteristic features of the sixties was the proliferation of the underground press, and Ginsberg's work appeared widely in these publications.[13] For example, in 1968 a Ginsberg interview appeared in John Bryan's Los Angeles-based *Open City*, an important newspaper devoted to countercultural topics where Charles Bukowski would publish his famous "Notes of a Dirty Old Man" column which brought him to fame: two years later in 1970, Ginsberg was interviewed in Robert Head and Darlene Fife's *Nola Express*, another significant New Orleans underground newspaper. 1968 was of course a pivotal year in American cultural and political life. Ginsberg discusses in his interview with John Bryan the campaigns of Eugene McCarthy and Robert Kennedy and also devoted serious consideration to the racism and violence which marked the late sixties, advocating a pacifist approach to demonstrations being planned for the Democratic National Convention to be held in Chicago in August:

> Because of this kind of thinking they were even foolishly attacking Martin Luther King for continuing his Washington plan. But what King said is correct. If the non-violent thing doesn't work in Memphis, it should be given a full-scale try in Washington. He believed the same thing as Gandhi. And Gandhi made a Himalayan mistake when he said that the Indian people weren't ready for non-violence. People have got to be helped to be non-violent.
>
> I guess the theme at Chicago should be protection and good feeling as a model to show society what we should be trying to do. We need that good feeling between white and non-white people.
>
> I don't know what to do, though. I ain't got no answer. Just keep going.

This interview was conducted in April, 1968 and of course Ginsberg's hope for a non-violent protest in Chicago—he marched with Jean Genet, William S. Burroughs, Norman Mailer, and Terry Southern—would prove to be unfulfilled, for there was a full-scale police riot in the streets of Chicago during which many demonstrators were severely injured. Along with the growing movement against racism and the Vietnam War, the sixties were also marked by the beginning struggle for gay rights and here as well we witness in the interviews Ginsberg's efforts to fight for gender equality as well as against censorship of films and literature.

Some scholars refer to the "Long Sixties" which argues that the decade of the sixties should not be understood simply as being ten years in length, but rather a period of powerful historical change stretching from the mid-to-late fifties all the way to 1973. Thus many of the key issues of the "Sixties"—gender equality, gay rights, ecological awareness—continued to preoccupy Ginsberg during the early seventies. In his interview with the *Nola Express*, for example, he continues his discussion of Bob Dylan, his meeting with the Beatles, Jim Morrison's collaboration with Michael McClure on a play, sexuality and communal life, and ongoing philosophical interests. In 1970, an important event occurred when Ginsberg met the Tibetan Buddhist guru Chogyam Trungpa (1939–1987). Although he did not realize it at the time, after Trungpa died, Ginsberg located a photo of himself while in India with a youthful monk who turned out to have been Trungpa who was then in the Young Lamas School. He would be asked by Chogyam Trungpa to create a poetics program at Naropa University in Boulder, Colorado, which became the Jack Kerouac School of Disembodied Poetics. Ginsberg recruited many authors to teach and lecture at Naropa including Gregory Corso, Robert Duncan, Diane di Prima, William S. Burroughs, and Robert Creeley. Ginsberg had always been in search of a guru, and he found a charismatic one in Trungpa, however his teaching methods were not without controversy. An uncomfortable situation developed during Trungpa's fall 1975 Seminary at Snowmass, Colorado when the poet W. S. Merwin and his partner Dana Naone took their leave of a party because they refused to remove their clothing along with the other Seminary members as instructed by Trungpa. Trungpa then sent in his "Vajra Guard" to bring them back to the gathering and forcibly strip them of their clothing. The episode of course raised questions concerning the cult-like atmosphere that may develop around the "guru"—or indeed any religious or political leader—and the consequent dangers to free speech and thought.[14]

During the eighties, the interviews reflect Ginsberg's attention to American involvement in Nicaragua, as well as his new publishing contract with HarperCollins to publish his *Selected* and *Collected Poems*. This was an important development in Ginsberg's career, charting his increasing visibility in moving from the countercultural press scene as represented by City Lights to a commercial New York publisher. Over the decades, Ginsberg toured countless college and university campuses and in his 1986 interview with the *Harvard Crimson* he declares that he sees himself as a member of the true, "hermetic" American "Establishment" represented by Henry David Thoreau, Walt Whitman, and William Carlos Williams; he speaks of his latest volume of poetry *White Shroud* which contained graphic sexual descriptions; he condemns the efforts of the attorney general Edwin Meese "to ban erotic life and persecute it." In other conversations, Ginsberg reveals that he was not only widely read in world literature, but was also a lucid commentator on the writings of his fellow authors in the Beat movement. In 1987, Jeffrey Dunn conducted a fascinating interview with Ginsberg in which he explored the curious teacher/student, father/son relationship he had with Burroughs in which their roles seemed often to reverse: as in any intense love relationship, they learned from each other. Ginsberg also comments here with a great deal of acumen on Burroughs' *oeuvre* and recently an entire volume has been published—*The Best Minds of My Generation: A Literary History of the Beats* (2017)—in which Ginsberg considers—among other authors—John Clellon Holmes, Peter Orlovsky, Carl Solomon, Corso, and Kerouac.[15]

During his final decade, Ginsberg returned to many of the themes which had driven his political life as well as poetics. In his 1990 interview with *The Monthly Aspectarian* he discusses his collaborations with the composer Philip Glass on *Hydrogen Jukebox*. We also note that Ginsberg continued to be impressively well-informed concerning the intersection between governmental power, free speech and the various contradictions and paradoxes which inform American political life, proving himself well-prepared to argue effectively, giving appropriate facts and figures to support his case. For example, his discussion concerning the legalization of marijuana in *The Aspectarian* seems eerily prescient. Many of his arguments of three decades ago have now been implemented in the liberalization of marijuana laws throughout the United States. He also cites the glaring contradictions inherent in the pro-alcohol and tobacco lobbies and the ways they have been influenced by corporations such as Adolf Coors'—of the famous beer company—support for the conservative Heritage Foundation. Ginsberg also remained intellectually incisive and curious, even as his last years arrived. Just four years before his death in an informative interview with Sunjaj Galuly from 1993, Ginsberg enumerates his wide reading in the literature of India over the decades which included Ramakrishna, the *Vedas*, the *Mahabharata*, the *Bhagavad Gita*, and the *Upanishads*.

During his final years, Ginsberg also continued to pursue his experiments with the spoken word in relation to music. For example, in his interview with Harvey Kubernik, Ginsberg speaks of the musical setting of his poem "The Ballad of the Skeletons" which was composed as a response to the conservative drift of American politics during the eighties and the reactionary "Contract with America" released by Newt Gingrich in 1994 during the Republican Party's Congressional election campaign. Ginsberg also reveals here his musical collaboration with Paul McCartney as well as the help he gave McCartney in writing his own poetry. In addition, Ginsberg considers Bob Dylan's *Renaldo and Clara* to be an underappreciated film which explored the concept—familiar to us from Buddhism—that the self has no fixed identity. And in one of his very last interviews, conducted by Australian Stuart Coupe less than a month before his death, we learn that Ginsberg was caught up in a plethora of creative projects until the very end.

Thus we can see in these interviews the wide range of the intellectual and aesthetic preoccupations of one of America's greatest twentieth-century poets and his desire to be constantly reading, seeking, teaching, and learning. Ginsberg was at the vanguard of the gay rights movement, the struggle against censorship, the legalization of marijuana, the protests against the war in Vietnam. For Ginsberg, poetics, sexual freedom, the quest for expanded consciousness, ecological awareness, and spiritual exploration were all of a piece. The reader witnesses him moving easily among all these topics and in so doing emphasizing their essential interconnectedness. Ginsberg was constantly in motion, illustrating the dictum of his hero William Blake that "energy is eternal delight." It was virtually impossible to have been born in the fifties in America and not encountered Allen Ginsberg over the next five decades in his many incarnations: making literary history reading "Howl" in 1955 in San Francisco; appearing in the film of Bob Dylan singing "Subterranean Homesick Blues"; at the "Human Be-In" in San Francisco; in the audience on William F. Buckley's television show "Firing Line" as his friend Jack Kerouac and Ed Sanders held forth on the counterculture; marching in the Chicago streets at the Democratic National Convention in 1968; reading his poetry and prose in the underground newspapers and magazines; witnessing his poetry readings at college and university campuses; seeing his photographs of his Beat colleagues; hearing his settings of *Songs of Innocence and Experience*. He was no ivory tower intellectual, but rather was willing—as he memorably declared it in his poem "America" from 1956—to put his "queer shoulder to the wheel" to change our country and the world for the better.

DSC

Notes

1. On Allen and Louis, see *Family Business: Selected Letters Between a Father and Son: Allen and Louis Ginsberg*, ed. Michael Schumacher (New York: Bloomsbury, 2002); Allen Ginsberg, "Prose Contribution to Cuban Revolution," in *Deliberate Prose: Selected Essays*, ed. Bill Morgan (New York: HarperCollins, 2001), 138.

2. *As Ever: The Collected Correspondence of Allen Ginsberg and Neal Cassady*, ed. Barry Gifford (Berkeley: Creative Arts Book Company, 1977), 38.

3. Ibid, 45.

4. Robert Duncan, *The Truth and Life of Myth: An Essay in Essential Autobiography* (Fremont, MI: The Sumac Press, 1968), 34; Kenneth Rexroth, "Allen Ginsberg in America" in *With Eye and Ear* (New York: Herder and Herder, 1970), 206–7. In

an interview, the great scholar of Kabbalah Gershom Scholem recalled his pleasant meeting with Ginsberg whom he described as "a likable fellow. Genuine. Strange, mad, but genuine. I took a strong liking to him." See Gershom Scholem, *On Jews and Judaism in Crisis*: *Selected Essays* (New York: Schocken Books, 1976), 40.

5. *As Ever*, 62.

6. Ibid, 141–42.

7. Ibid, 146. For a reproduction of the sequence, see Paul Reps and Nyogen Senzaki, *Zen Flesh, Zen Bones*: *A Collection of Zen and Pre-Zen Writings* (Boston: Tuttle Publishing, 1998), 163–87.

8. *I Greet You at the Beginning of a Great Career*: *The Selected Correspondence of Lawrence Ferlinghetti and Allen Ginsberg, 1955–1997*, ed. Bill Morgan (San Francisco: City Lights Books, 2015), 1.

9. Hugh McLeod, *The Religious Crisis of the 1960s* (Oxford: Oxford University Press, 2007); Paul Saltzman, *The Beatles in India* (San Rafael: Mandala Publishing, 2018).

10. David Stephen Calonne, *The Spiritual Imagination of the Beats* (New York; Cambridge University Press, 2017), 102. On Ginsberg, Dylan and the Beatles, also see Simon Warner, *Text and Drugs and Rock 'n' Roll*: *The Beats and Rock Culture* (New York: Bloomsbury, 2014).

11. On Ginsberg and Catullus, see Matthew Pfaff, "The Invention of Sincerity: Allen Ginsberg and the Philology of the Margins" in *Hip Sublime*: *Beat Writers and the Classical Tradition,* eds. Sheila Murnaghan and Ralph M. Rosen (Columbus: The Ohio State University Press), 73–96.

12. On Ginsberg's experiments with entheogens, see Marcus Boon, *The Road of Excess: A History of Writers on Drugs* (Cambridge: Harvard University Press, 2002), 160–62; 261–62.

13. See John McMillan, *Smoking Typewriters*: *The Sixties Underground Press and the Rise of Alternative Media in America* (New York: Oxford University Press, 2011).

14. Fabrice Midal, *Chogyam Trungpa*: *His Life and Vision* (Boston and London: Shambhala, 2004), 277; Tom Clark's interview with Ginsberg concerning the Trungpa episode appeared in the *Boulder Monthly*, March, 1979 and is reprinted in Clark's *The Great Naropa Poetry Wars* (Santa Barbara: Cadmus, 1980).

15. Allen Ginsberg, *The Best Minds of My Generation*: *A Literary History of the Beats*, ed. Bill Morgan (New York: Grove Press, 2017).

Chronology

1926   On June 3, Irwin Allen Ginsberg born in Newark, New Jersey. Allen's brother, Eugene, was born five years earlier and named after the famous activist in the Socialist Party of America, Eugene Debs (1855–1926). Allen's father Louis Ginsberg, composed poetry and taught high school while his mother Naomi, nee Levy, was also a teacher and supporter of the Communist Party but was forced to quit teaching due to her periodic bouts of debilitating mental illness.

1930   The Ginsberg family moves to 83 Fair Street in Paterson, New Jersey. Over the next ten years, Allen's mother Naomi is treated for mental illness at the Bloomingdale Asylum and Greystone Park Psychiatric Hospital.

1931   Ginsberg begins first grade at P. S. 1 in Paterson.

1933   The Ginsbergs move to 155 Haledon Avenue in Paterson. Louis' teaching positions in various places causes the family to move frequently.

1938   Age twelve, Ginsberg attends a lecture on yoga in Paterson.

1939   Begins high school at Central High School in Paterson where his father Louis is a teacher. Ginsberg works part time at the Paterson Public Library. After two years, he transfers to Eastside High School. While living at 288 Graham Avenue, he works as a volunteer for the Democratic Party until 1942.

1940   The Ginsbergs move to 288 Graham Avenue on the east side of Paterson. In June, Ginsberg writes a column for the *Paterson Evening News* concerning events in his high school. He also joins the *Tatler*, his high school newspaper.

1942   In the fall, Ginsberg campaigns for the Democratic candidate for the House of Representatives, Irving Abramson.

1943   Graduates from Eastside High School. Enrolls at Columbia University where Lionel Trilling is one of his professors. Through his classmate Lucien Carr, he meets William S. Burroughs.

1944   Meets Jack Kerouac. Carr murders David Kammerer who had pursued him sexually. Professor Raymond Weaver at Columbia gives Kerouac and Ginsberg a list of books to read including Gnostic texts.

1945   Expelled from Columbia for inscribing supposed "obscenities" on his dormitory window and moves to 419 West 115th Street. Herbert Huncke introduces Ginsberg, Kerouac, and Burroughs, as Ginsberg later recalled, "to floating population hustling & drug scene Times Square." Begins composing "long poems about a last voyage looking for Supreme Reality. Which was like a Dostoevskian or Thomas Wolfeian idealization or like Rimbaud." Reads Oswald Spengler's *Der Untergang des Abendlandes—The Decline of the West.* Smokes marijuana for the first time and takes morphine with William S. Burroughs. In April he works for a month as a spot welder—his job title is "helper shipfitter"—in the Brooklyn Navy Yard and enrolls in a six-week Merchant Marine training course.

1946   Returns to Columbia and meets Neal Cassady through Hal Chase, a Columbia student who had met Cassady in Denver, Colorado.

1947   In June, moves to Denver in pursuit of Neal Cassady. Visits William S. Burroughs, along with Herbert Huncke and Neal Cassady, at his farm in New Waverly, Texas. Enrolls in Merchant Marine, sailing to Dakar on a fifty-day voyage aboard the S. S. John Blair from Freeport, Texas. Mother Naomi is hospitalized at Pilgrim State Hospital. Ginsberg signs papers to have her lobotomized and the operation is performed on November 14.

1948   Experiences on a July evening in Harlem an auditory hallucination during which he encounters William Blake reciting the poem "Ah! Sun-flower" and "The Sick Rose." Immerses himself in mystical literature including the Kabbalah, St. Teresa of Avila, T. S. Eliot's *Four Quartets,* Plotinus, St. John of the Cross.

1949   On April 21, Ginsberg is arrested after stolen goods are left in his apartment by Herbert Huncke, Little Jack Melody, and Vickie Russell. Instead of jail, Ginsberg spends eight months—from June 29, 1949 to February 24, 1950, at the Columbia Presbyterian Psychiatric Institute. Here he meets Carl Solomon who will figure in Ginsberg's "Howl." Solomon shares with him several books he obtained in Paris by Antonin Artaud, Jean Genet, Henri Michaux, Lautreamont, and Henry Miller.

1950   Ginsberg lives with father Louis in Paterson where he writes essays on Cezanne and Dante, telling Neal Cassady in a letter that he is "trying to *fix* my mind—but to no avail." Meets William Carlos Williams as well as Gregory Corso at the Pony Stable bar in Greenwich Village, following his release from the Clinton Correctional Facility at Dannemora. Works in market and opinion research for the next four years in Manhattan.

1951   In August, Ginsberg leaves New York and drives with Lucien Carr to Mexico City to visit William S. Burroughs. Burroughs is out of town, so Ginsberg tours Mexico with Burroughs's wife Joan. Upon returning to the US, he learns on September 7 from a newspaper report that Joan has been killed by Burroughs during a game of "William Tell."

1952   Period of voracious reading which included—among many other authors—D. H. Lawrence's *The Plumed Serpent*, Franz Kafka's *Diaries*, Hermann Hesse, Thomas Hardy's *Jude the Obscure*, Jean Genet, William Faulkner, Robert Lowell. Ginsberg sends his poems to William Carlos Williams and gives Carl Solomon the manuscript of Burroughs' *Junky* which Solomon's uncle eventually publishes.

1953   Works as a copyboy at the *New York World Telegram.* In fall, collaborates with William S. Burroughs on editing their correspondence which will become the *Yage Letters* and the manuscript of *Queer*—not published until 1985—at Ginsberg's apartment at 206 E. 7th Street between Avenues B and C, Lower East Side Manhattan. They go together to the Museum of Natural History and Metropolitan Museum of Art and view Carlo Crivelli's (ca. 1430–1495) "Dead Christ Supported by Two Angels," the Mayan Codices and ancient Egyptian sculptures. Spends time with Kerouac at State Island Ferry dock, walking under the Brooklyn Bridge where they, as Ginsberg recalled, exult in singing together "rawbone blues & shouting Hart Crane's 'Atlantis' to the traffic above."

1954   Travels to Mexico, spending six months visiting Merida, Chichen Itza, Xibalba, and Palenque and during his travels reads the famous fourteenth-century mystical text, *The Cloud of Unknowing.* Works eight to ten hours a day on a long poem entitled "Siesta in Xbalba" which he completes the following year. In June, spends three days in San Miguel de Allende. In her home in San Jose, on August 20, Carolyn Cassady finds Ginsberg in bed with Neal and removes Allen from their house, depositing him in North Beach in San Francisco. In San Francisco, Ginsberg obtains a position at Towne-Oller in market research with a salary of fifty-five dollars a week. Meets Kenneth Rexroth, Michael McClure, Kenneth Patchen, Robert Duncan, and Peter Orlovsky—who will become his lifetime companion—through the artist Robert LaVigne.

1955   Writes Part I of "Howl" at 1010 Montgomery Street, San Francisco. Attends the premiere of Robert Duncan's play *Faust Foutu*, at the conclusion of which Duncan took off his clothes in front of the audience, a practice Ginsberg would continue on October 31, 1956 when he was faced by a booing spectator in Los Angeles: Ginsberg disrobed, announcing "A poet always stands naked before the world!" In August, Ginsberg meets Lawrence Ferlinghetti who founded City Lights Bookstore in 1953. Enrolls in classes for fall semester at UC Berkeley and moves into a cottage at 1624 Milvia Street. On October 7, Ginsberg reads "Howl" at the 6 Gallery where Philip Lamantia, Gary Snyder, Michael McClure, and Philip Whalen also appear, with Jack Kerouac in the audience shouting "Go" and passing around a jug of Burgundy.

1956   Ginsberg takes hitchhiking trip with Gary Snyder and Philip Whalen in January and February to Pacific Northwest, gives readings with Snyder at the University of Washington in Seattle and at Reed College. In San Francisco, works at Greyhound Bus Terminal for fifty dollars a week. Ships out with the Merchant Marines on the USNS Sgt. Jack J. Pendleton, returning in September. "Howl" is published by City Lights. Friendship with Robert Creeley. Mother Naomi dies and "Howl" is banned as obscene. Ginsberg spends two weeks with Kerouac in Mexico City where Kerouac begins writing *Desolation Angels*.

1957   In January, visits William Carlos Williams with Jack Kerouac, Peter Orlovsky, and Gregory Corso at his home in Rutherford, New Jersey. Visits Burroughs in Tangier, Morocco, helps him edit *Naked Lunch* and meets Brion Gysin and Paul Bowles. Kerouac retypes the "Interzone" section of the novel. On June 3, City Lights Bookstore manager Shigeyoshi Murao is arrested by two undercover police inspectors—later Lawrence Ferlinghetti will be as well—for selling copies of "Howl." They are released on bail. Judge Clayton Horn rules during the "Howl" obscenity trial that the poem is not obscene. In July visits Venice, Italy. Moves to

Paris, registers with Orlovsky and Corso to stay in the famous "Beat Hotel" at 9 Rue Git-le-Coeur. Begins composing "Kaddish," "fueled by "an injection of amphetamine plus a little bit of morphine, plus some Dexedrine later on to keep me going," which he completes two years later.

1958   Meets Louis-Ferdinand Celine and Henri Michaux in Paris. In July, returns to New York from Paris. Ginsberg gives a reading at Muhlenberg College in Pennsylvania and on November 24 at Yale University in Harkness Hall. Also reads at Harvard, Columbia, and Princeton. He meets D. T. Suzuki and Thelonious Monk, giving the latter a copy of "Howl" who upon being asked later what he thought about the poem replied that "it made sense." Over the next few years experiments with laughing gas (nitrous oxide), ether, mescaline, yage (ayahuasca), LSD, heroin and describes their effects upon him in several poems.

1959   In January, gives benefit reading for *Big Table* magazine in Chicago which had been ruled obscene and seized by the US Post Office for publishing a section from Burroughs' *Naked Lunch*. In May, with John Kelly and Bob Kaufman, Ginsberg publishes the first issue of the literary magazine *Beatitude* in San Francisco. Appears—along with Corso and Kerouac—in Robert Frank's film *Pull My Daisy*. Makes a recording of "Howl" for Fantasy Records. Visits the house where Walt Whitman lived at 328–330 Mickle Boulevard in Camden, New Jersey. Takes for first time LSD as part of study conducted by Gregory Bateson at the Mental Research Institute at Stanford University. Visits Robert Creeley in New Mexico and spends May-August in San Francisco.

1960   In January, attends writers conference at the University of Concepcion, Chile with Ferlinghetti. Ginsberg remains in South America for six months visiting Argentina, Bolivia, and Peru searching for *yage—ayahuasca*. His experiences with William S. Burroughs will appear in *The Yage Letters*. Meets the occultist and musicologist Harry Smith at the Five Spot in New York. Reads his poems on entheogens at The Group for the Advancement of Psychiatry and meets Humphry Osmond who supplied Aldous Huxley with mescaline. Ginsberg, on Osmond's recommendation, then meets Timothy Leary who is working at Harvard's Center for Personality Research. Along with Peter Orlovsky, William S. Burroughs, and Charles Olson, Ginsberg participates in Leary's research program by ingesting psilocybin and also gives the entheogen to Thelonious Monk and Dizzie Gillespie. Ginsberg meets Fidel Castro when Castro visits New York in September at a reception at the Hotel Teresa in Harlem. Receives $1,000 grant from The Poets Foundation.

1961   Ginsberg travels to Paris where he sees Corso, and to Tangier where he visits William S. Burroughs, then on to Greece and Israel. *Kaddish and Other Poems* published by City Lights.

1962   Travels with Peter Orlovsky to Kenya and then through India where he spends eighteen months. Stays in Calcutta and Benares, meets up with poet Gary Snyder and his wife Joanne Kyger, making pilgrimages to Bodhgaya, where Buddha attained enlightenment meditating under the Bodhi tree and to Sarnath, where Buddha delivered his first sermon. Meets the Dalai Lama.

1963   Travels to Bangkok, Saigon, Angkor Wat in Cambodia, composing a long poem about the famous temple. He visits Gary Snyder in Kyoto, Japan in June and participates in a four-day *sesshin* at the temple and meets Nanao Sakaki. On March 4, William Carlos Williams dies. On the train from Kyoto to Tokyo on July 17, he has epiphany that he needs to cease looking for ultimate answers to life's unanswerable questions and composes the poem "The Change: Kyoto-Tokyo Express." Ginsberg reads at the Vancouver Poetry Conference at the University of British Columbia, July 24—August 16—an important symposium which included Denise Levertov, Philip Whalen, Margaret Avison, Charles Olson, Robert Duncan, Bobbie Louise Hawkins, and Robert Creeley. He begins to employ mantras as part of his performance using finger cymbals and also begins chanting Hare Krishna. On October 28, Ginsberg protests the visit of Vietnam's Madame Nhu in San Francisco. *The Yage Letters*—a collection of Ginsberg's correspondence with William S. Burroughs—is published by City Lights. Meets Bob Dylan.

1964   Works on screenplay for "Kaddish" with Robert Frank. Ginsberg joins Ken Kesey and his Merry Pranksters on a bus driven by Neal Cassady during the journey to Timothy Leary's psychedelic research center in New York, Millbrook. In October meets the psychiatrist R. D. Laing.

1965   Arrives in Havana, Cuba in mid-January. In February, he meets the Argentinian poet Miguel Grinberg and is expelled from Cuba for openly speaking of homosexuality, capital punishment and freedom of speech. Czech students name him "Kral Majales"— "King of May"—in Prague, and is also expelled from Czechoslovakia for his supposed "subversion." In London, Bob Dylan introduces Ginsberg to the Beatles at the Savoy Hotel. In an alley behind the hotel the next day, Dylan makes film of "Subterranean Homesick Blues" with Ginsberg chatting with Bob Neuwirth in the background. On June 11, reads with Gregory Corso, Lawrence Ferlinghetti, Alexander Trocchi at the International Poetry Incarnation at Royal Albert Hall in London. Visits Cambridge University to see the William Blake manuscripts at the Fitzwilliam Museum. From July 12–24, he participates in the Berkeley Poetry Conference along with Robert Duncan, Robert Creeley, Charles Olson, Gary Snyder, Jack Spicer, and Ed Dorn. Ginsberg receives a Guggenheim grant, using some of the award to purchase a VW bus. Ginsberg takes a camping trip for a month with Gary Snyder in the Pacific Northwest where Crater Lake in Oregon makes a deep impression on him. He also visits Reed College with Snyder. On August 22, he goes to hear the Beatles with Snyder at the Portland Coliseum and during the concert John Lennon cheers Ginsberg's presence in the audience. On October 15, participates in the Vietnam Day Committee's teach-in.

1966   Gives readings at the University of Kansas in Witchita and in Lincoln, Nebraska. Visits Robert Creeley in Placitas, New Mexico. Testifies in front of a Senate Subcommittee on Drugs. Meets Swami A. C. Bhaktivedanta in New York.

1967   In January, appears at the "Human Be-In" in San Francisco with Snyder, McClure, and Ferlinghetti. Meets the great historian of religion Mircea Eliade in Chicago in February. Gives reading at San Francisco State University. Participates in a benefit in Santa Monica, California to support Ed Sanders due to the obscenity charges brought against his magazine *Fuck You: A Magazine of the Arts.* Meets his father Louis and stepmother Edith in Italy. In September in Milan, Italy, works with his Italian translator Fernanda Pivano on translations of his poems. Meets poet Giuseppe Ungaretti and Ezra Pound, singing for him the *Hare Kirshna* and *Prajnaparamita Sutra.*

1968   On February 4, Neal Cassady dies in San Miguel de Allende, Mexico. Ginsberg reads in Appleton, Wisconsin with The Fugs.

In March, Ginsberg appears at the Buffalo Festival of the Arts along with Robin Blaser, Robert Duncan, and Louis Zukofsky and in June at the international poetry festival at Stony Brook. Participates in mass demonstrations during the Democratic National Convention in Chicago with Abbie Hoffman, Jerry Rubin, David Dellinger, Tom Hayden, Rennie Davis, John Froines, and Lee Weiner—the famous "Chicago Seven." Begins to make musical setting of William Blake's *Songs of Innocence and Experience*. In August, Ginsberg purchases for nine thousand dollars the ninety-acre East Hill Farm near the village of Cherry Valley in upstate New York which features an old eight-room house where Lawrence Ferlinghetti visits him in December.

1969   Gives reading with his father Louis at the Marine Stadium in Miami. Jack Kerouac dies on October 21, and Ginsberg attends his burial at Edson Cemetery on Gorham Street in Lowell, Massachusetts. Visits the University of Arizona where he engages in a strenuous argument concerning homosexuality with a news reporter. Testifies on December 11–12 in defense of the "Chicago Seven" in conspiracy trial. All of the convictions were finally reversed.

1970   Charles Olson dies on January 10 and Ginsberg travels to Gloucester to be a pallbearer at the funeral. In May, joins the Mobilization Committee to End the War movement in a march to the Washington Monument. Gives a reading on May 1 at Yale University during the student strike which was then in progress and chants "OM." Meets Chogyam Trungpa on the streets of New York as well as Swami Muktananda who gives Ginsberg mantras and sitting exercises.

1971   Visits Calcutta and camps for refugees in East Pakistan. At the Fitz Hugh Ludlow Memorial Library in San Francisco, Ginsberg composes his "Declaration of Independence for Timothy Leary." Works on creating musical settings of a second group of Blake poems and makes recordings with Bob Dylan. In April, Ginsberg appears with Robert Duncan for a reading and lecture at the Creative Arts Festival at Kent State University, Ohio.

1972   On April 20 at Notre Dame, Ginsberg takes part in a symposium with Robert Duncan and Diane Wakoski. Corresponds with Paul Metcalf, great-grandson of Hermann Melville concerning Gnostic thought. Demonstrates in Miami during the Republic National Convention with Peter Orlovsky and spends three days in jail.

Attends Chogyam Trungpa's Buddhist seminary retreat in Teton Village, Jackson Hole, Wyoming where he takes LSD and meditates. Reads at the Adelaide Arts Festival in Australia. Takes psilocybin mushrooms and takes photograph of himself on March 24, "on top of Uluru, Ayers Rock, near Alice Springs, central Australian desert aborigine sacred waterporous sandstone monolith." Viking Press commissions Ginsberg to contribute an introduction to Jack Kerouac's *Visions of Cody.*

1973   In June, attends the National Poetry Conference at Thomas Jefferson College in Grand Rapids, Michigan. Participates in poetry conferences in London and Rotterdam, travels in Scotland and England. Visits Burroughs in London.

1974   Chogyam Trungpa founds the Naropa Institute, the first Buddhist college in the United States. Jack Kerouac School of Disembodied Poetics is founded by Ginsberg and Anne Waldman. Wins National Book Award for *The Fall of America.* On March 18–22, Ginsberg attends the "City Lights in North Dakota" conference at the University of North Dakota along with Michael McClure, Gregory Corso, Kenneth Rexroth, Gary Snyder, and Lawrence Ferlinghetti. Spends time with Gary Snyder and Peter Orlovsky working on building a cabin in the Sierra Nevada which he hopes to use as a retreat. Ginsberg becomes a member of the American Academy and Institute of Arts and Letters. Ginsberg's friend Harry Smith makes recording of Ginsberg's first musical composition, *First Blues.*

1975   In April, Ginsberg, Orlovsky, Burroughs, and Corso read at Columbia University. During the summer at Naropa, Diane di Prima, Ed Sanders, John Ashbery, Ted Berrigan, Philip Whalen, and William S. Burroughs are visiting faculty. In the fall, poet W. S. Merwin and his partner Dana Naone attended Chogyam Trungpa's Vajradhatu Seminary retreat and a scandal involving their forced stripping occurred. Travels with Bob Dylan on the Rolling Thunder tour and in November Ginsberg and Dylan journey to Lowell, Massachusetts to pay their respects at Kerouac's gravestone at Edson Cemetery. They read choruses from Kerouac's *Mexico City Blues,* a scene included in *Renaldo and Clara,* a film by Dylan which appeared in 1978.

1976   Reads with William S. Burroughs at the Corcoran Gallery in Washington, D.C. Records *First Blues* album. Ginsberg's father Louis dies on July 8.

1977	In April, Ginsberg appears with Robert Duncan at Colorado State University and in October speaks at the East-West Convergence Conference in Hawaii. At St. Mark's Poetry Project, Ginsberg reads with Robert Lowell. Attends University of California at Santa Cruz Conference on LSD and visits Kauai.
1978	On August 9, Ginsberg is among sixty protestors arrested for protesting the Rocky Flats Nuclear Weapons Plant in Colorado. Participates in Whole Earth Day with Stewart Brand and Peter Orlovksy. *Mind Breaths* published. Influenced by Hans Jonas' *The Gnostic Religion: The Message of the Alien God and the Beginnings of Christianity*, Ginsberg composes "Plutonium Ode." Ginsberg gets help from the scholar of Jewish mysticism Gershom Scholem with the kabbalistic terminology employed in the poem. Beginning November 30, Ginsberg participates in the three-day Nova Convention in New York with Frank Zappa, Patti Smith, Brion Gysin, John Cage, and Ed Sanders to honor William S. Burroughs.
1979	Receives a fellowship from the National Endowment for the Arts. In March, begins teaching three-month course in creative writing at Brooklyn College. Tours Europe with musician Steven Taylor, performing at Oxford, Tubingen, Heidelberg as well as International Poetry conventions in Rome, Genoa, Paris, Amsterdam, Rotterdam, and Cambridge.
1980	Participates in Rome International Poetry Festival. Ginsberg reads at the poetry festival in Bisbee, Arizona. In July, he appears at the D. H. Lawrence Festival which took place in both Taos and Santa Fe and featured a number of writers including Stephen Spender, Derek Walcott, William S. Burroughs, and Thom Gunn.
1981	August 9, travels to Mexico City for the International Poetry Festival with Andrei Voznesensky, W. S. Merwin, Gunter Grass, Octavio Paz, and Jorge Luis Borges.
1982	Travels to Managua, Nicaragua for poetry festival. Ginsberg's two-album *First Blues* is released which contains original songs. During the summer, there is a twenty-fifth anniversary celebration of Kerouac's *On the Road* at Naropa in Boulder, Colorado.
1983	Visits Copenhagen, Oslo, Stockholm, Helsinki, and Germany. Begins teaching at Brooklyn College. In Maine and New York, meets with photographer Berenice Abbott.
1984	Attends with Gary Snyder "The Source of Inspiration" conference in Beijing and spends two months in China. At Naropa during the

summer, Norman Mailer and William S. Burroughs participate in a roundtable discussion with Ginsberg. Establishes contract with Harper and Row to publish his *Selected* and *Collected Poems* as well as three other volumes.

1985   *Collected Poems* published by Harper and Row. Performs at Miami Bookfair International. His first photography exhibition, "Hideous Human Angels" opens at the Holly Solomon Gallery in New York and the photos are exhibited later in Boston, Dallas, and Washington. Up all night, August 1, 1985 on ecstasy powder in Boulder, Colorado. On September 13, visits with his step-mother Edith and William de Kooning at his studio at Springs, East Hampton. In November, visits Russia where he reads his poetry in Moscow and also travels to Tbilisi where he meets the great Armenian film director Sergei Parajanov.

1986   Participates in International PEN conference in New York. Begins teaching at Brooklyn College. Lecture tour of Poland, Yugoslavia and Hungary.

1987   In March, Philip Whalen lectures in Ginsberg's Brooklyn College class "Literary History of the Beat Generation." In April, Ginsberg with his stepmother Edith and esotericist and musicologist Harry Smith visit the University of Mississippi in Oxford, the Southern Folklore Center Blues Archive, and also journeys to Clarksdale and Holly Springs. Chogyam Trungpa dies on May 28. Ginsberg attends the funeral services in Barnet, Vermont, composing the poem "On Cremation of Chogyam Trungpa, Vidyadhara."

1988   From January 5–28, teaches a course at Camera Obscura School of Art in Tel Aviv on "Photographic Poetics" with Robert Frank and Steven Taylor. In May, visits Gary Snyder at his house Kitkitdizze on San Juan Ridge, California. Attends demonstration in Tel Aviv to protest treatment of Palestinians. Collaborates with Philip Glass on *Wichita Vortex Sutra* which premieres at Lincoln Center. Readings in Tokyo, Osaka, Seika, and Kyoto and gives the Charles Olson Lectures at State University of New York, Buffalo.

1989   Gehlek Rinpoche establishes the Jewel Heart Buddhist Center in Ann Arbor, Michigan, where Ginsberg frequently visited during the 1990s. Exhibitions of Ginsberg's photographs in Chicago, Vienna, Los Angeles, Hamburg.

1990   *Allen Ginsberg: Photographs* is published. Ginsberg attends forum of the Federal Communications Commission's Bar Association and reads a list of works affected by the new "obscenity" rulings including Edward Albee's *Who's Afraid of Virginia Woolf,* James Baldwin's *Another Country* and Normal Mailer's *The Naked and the Dead.* Participates in Majales celebration in Prague with Nanao Sakaki and Vaclav Havel. Attends party for *Zap Comix*—the celebrated underground magazine which featured the art of Robert Crumb—at Psychedelic Solution Gallery at St. Mark's Place in New York City.

1991   Receives Harriet Monroe Poetry Award from the University of Chicago. Gives reading at Herbst Theater in San Francisco.

1993   Receives the *Chevalier des Arts et des Letters*—the Order of Arts and Letters—from the French Minister of Culture.

1994   In October, Ginsberg sells his archive containing 174,061 items—not only letters, manuscripts and journals but also laundry lists, bus tickets, calendars, and T-shirts—to Stanford University for a million dollars which enables him to purchase a loft on East 13th Street. *Holy Soul Jelly Roll* which contains four CD's of his singing and poetry recitations released by Rhino Records. In November, Ginsberg travels to Arkansas to attend the Hot Springs Documentary Film Festival where Jerry Aronson's *The Life and Times of Allen Ginsberg* was being shown.

1996   In April, the National Portrait Gallery in Washington, D.C. sponsors the "Rebel Poets and Painters of the 1950's" exhibition. Ginsberg reads along with Jonathan Williams, Gregory Corso, Lawrence Ferlinghetti, and Michael McClure. On his birthday, June 3, he stays home and works on the proofs of *Selected Poems 1947–95.*

1997   In March, goes to New York's Beth Israel Hospital emergency room and is diagnosed with inoperable liver cancer. On April 5, dies of complications from hepatitis in New York City.

Conversations with Allen Ginsberg

Meeting Allen Ginsberg

R. Parthasarathy[1] / 1962

Writers Workshop, May-August, 1962, 65–66. Reprinted with permission.

I first met Allen Ginsberg, Beat Poet (*Howl and Other Poems*, City Lights Books, San Francisco, 1956; *Kaddish and Other Poems*, City Lights Books, San Francisco, 1961), at 31 Dongersey Road, Malabar Hill. When I rang the bell at 31 Dongersey Road on a Sunday afternoon, I was ushered in. I was told *they* were resting, i.e. Ginsberg, Gary and Joanne Snyder, and Peter Orlovsky.

Half an hour later, Ginsberg walked in, followed by the Snyders and Orlovsky. After the usual introduction, we sat down on the floor. I noticed Gary had crossed his legs and assumed the *padmasana* pose. He had spent two years in a Buddhist temple in Japan, practicing Zen Buddhism. Ginsberg was relaxed. Physically unimpressive and slight of build, a little bald, Ginsberg, thirty-six, is the son of a Russian émigré. He was born on 3 June 1926 in Paterson, New Jersey. He wrote his first poems some fifteen years ago.

Contemporary American poetry, of which Ginsberg and Gregory Corso are the leading practitioners, is unconventional. It's a slap-in-the-face of genteel English and American poetry. Witness the following passage from "Death to Van Gogh's Ear" [from *The Fall of America*]:

> But I walk, I walk, and the Orient walks with me, and all Africa walks with me, etc.

Said Ginsberg: "The roots of this kind of poetry go back to the Red Indians and to Jazz, which is the one original flower of American civilization." Speaking of influences, he mentioned William Carlos Williams. "Technically, he is a major literary influence. We have learned a great deal from him, especially his use of long and short lines."

It may be said the technique employs neither rhymed nor free verse. Its idiom is typically American, racy, and non-literary, spiced generously with four-letter words, e.g., c***, p***, s***. It is highly experimental and shock-ingly naïve. Its subject-matter is unlimited.

Ginsberg was critical of traditional prosody. "I see no use for it," he remarked. "What we are trying to do in America today is to create a new prosody." The lines on the printed page of a Ginsberg poem resemble a musical score. The lines are uneven in length. One set of lines is counter-pointed and balanced against another. To get down to the actual notation, Ginsberg said, he merely let himself go, physically. He demonstrated how this was done by wriggling his hips and arms about as Dionysiac as Twist.

"Another technical innovation," Ginsberg went on, "is the cut-out method introduced by William Seward Burroughs. A whole set of lines from one part of the poem is transposed elsewhere in the body of the poem. This is done to counteract any conscious arrangement of the lines in a poem." When I interrupted to ask if this did not violate the understanding of the poem, Ginsberg threw his hands up and exclaimed, "Well, if the poem has anything to say, if it is written from an inner conviction, it has to come off."

On the following Wednesday, Ginsberg, Snyder, and Orlovsky read their poems to a small gathering on the terrace of E. Alkazi's flat on Warden Road. Nissim Ezekiel introduced the poets. The California Renascents were a queer lot that day. Ginsberg appeared in shorts, red socks and tennis shoes, which he removed before reading. Peter Orlovsky's hair was a bird's nest. His trousers were rolled up, and throughout his reading he kept on puffing at a *pilahathi* cigarette. His shrill voice intoned in a monomanic frenzy. Afterwards it was a relief to listen to the cool and gentle lyricism of Snyder, who was the only one respectably dressed among the three.

Ginsberg began his reading with some early poems. They were brief and often witty. But the *piece de resistance* was the long poem *Kaddish* [kad-dish is a Jewish mourner's prayer], a ceremonial elegy on his mother, Naomi Ginsberg. Later, when I congratulated Ginsberg on his excellent reading, he told me he never read this poem out aloud as it affected him deeply. It was too personal, he said. I also learned that Ginsberg had not given a public reading of his poems since the last three years. He had been travelling a great deal, Israel, Africa, and India. He hopes to be in India for at least a year.

The reading over, we walked down Warden Road to Nissim Ezekiel's flat at 67 Breach Candy. After a round of drinks and *chikki,* we settled down for another session of poetry reading. The poets were Adil Jussawalla, [whose poems *Land's End* have recently appeared under the Workshop imprint, Rs 6], Lancelot Ribeiro, R. Parthasarathy, and Nissim Ezekiel.

"We would like to know what Indian poets writing in English are like," said Ginsberg. When the reading was over, Peter thrust his head forward and said, "If we were gangster poets, we'd shoot you." Not a bad epitaph, I thought, for Indian poets writing in English. The reading raised the inevitable question of Indians writing in English. Ginsberg commented that Indian writing in English was literary and derivative. He said there was no sense in aping English poets. They were equally bad. He considered writing in English for an Indian to be impossible. As he said, "The English used in India is too polite and genteel. There is no Indian English like there is an American Negro English . . . Contemporary English poetry is played out. The only English poets who interest me are Christopher Logue and Charles Tomlinson." He added it was more profitable to learn from the eccentric than from the established poets. He mentioned in this connection Christopher Smart and Emily Dickinson. Ginsberg brought the evening to a close with a remark, which I suppose he meant to be taken as prophetic. "The future of English and American poetry," he said, "is only in the hands of eccentric poets." Which is to say, with Allen Ginsberg. Bravo.

Notes

1. R. Parthasarathy is a poet and translator. He is author of *Rough Passage*, a long poem, and has edited *Ten Twentieth-Century Indian Poets*, an anthology, both published by Oxford University Press, New Delhi. His translations include *The Tale of an Anklet: An Epic of South India* (from Old Tamil) and *Erotic Poems from the Sanskrit: An Anthology*, both published by Columbia University Press, New York. He is professor emeritus of English at Skidmore College in Saratoga Springs, New York.

Conversations With . . .

David Widgery / 1965

U: Inter-University and College Magazine, Vol. 3, No. 7, October 1965, 7–13.

The following interview is put together from a series of tape-recorded interviews with Allen Ginsberg during his recent visit to England. They were made at parties, in flats and in taxis. I only hope they express the complexity and gentle intelligence of this very deep man.

Allen Ginsberg: I don't think it's a good idea to be sponsored by the State Department on tours. It's the same as being sponsored by the Writers' Union, or by a professor at a university. As soon as you get involved with the institutional structure you have to accept the ground rules of institutional existence. I mean, if some nice guy in the State Department says: "Well, you're not really our material but I love your poetry, so I'd love you to go out . . ." Then if you take off your clothes in Hungary in front of the son of the Minister of Culture he gets into trouble, or the Writers' Union that invited you gets into trouble. So the best thing is to go around like a lonely ghost. I manage better that way. Lots of people manage that way—hitch-hiking around.

Editor: But you don't seem to have had to. You've been in America for a long, long time.
Ginsberg: No, I left America in 1961 and went all the way around the world. I was a year and a half in India, then in Japan, Saigon, Bangkok, Ankor Wat. This year I've been away for six months. I was only in America for one year actually.
　I have money next year—I have a Guggenheim Fellowship next year.

Editor: How much is this?
Ginsberg: I'm not sure, I haven't had the formal . . . I just read about it in the *New York Times*. It may be six thousand dollars, I don't know, for one or two years.

Editor: Will you do anything besides travel?

Ginsberg: I applied for the Guggenheim to go live a year in Russia, but maybe I'll see if I can go to China instead.

Editor: Will they know you at all in China? Does it worry you that you wouldn't be welcomed with red carpet?

Ginsberg: In this situation, no. I think it's too dangerous. In Prague I was too well-known and got bounced by the police. I went there from Cuba and did lots of readings. The official weekly of the Czech Writers' Union, *Literati Noveni* introduced me as the most characteristic representative of non-academic American poetry. In fact, I lectured on "The Development of American Poetry"—you know, Beat and the changes in prosody and meter with Creeley and Olson, and then the New York movement.

Editor: Real academic stuff?

Ginsberg: Of course. I AM the Academy.

Then I was in Moscow and got drunk every night with Yevtushenko and Voznesensky. They've translated Kerouac, and they're just publishing my poems, translated very well by a young Russian poet.

Editor: But you were deported from Prague?

Ginsberg: Only because I became King of the May. You see, the Student May Day festival is traditional, but they haven't had it for twenty years, so the last couple of years the students have been going up to a statue of some poet in a woodsy park overlooking the river and the city, and having big demonstrations of five or six thousand students, and fighting with the police, and the police would be coming out with dogs and tear gas.

This year the Government decided to organize it and let them have their demonstration, so what they did was, they elected me May King. That was a much better manifestation of what they felt than hitting a policeman. And it apparently shook the government more too. I was on this huge chariot covered with roses, with beautiful girls lying round me and everyone crying and screaming. I stood there shouting, "On your left, Comrade, is the actual house where saintly Franz Kafka lived and cleaned his teeth and wrote his huge novels which your comrades have not even published. . . ." until '57, I think. He lived in a wonderful old room with one window looking directly into the nave of an old, holy church. By the time the procession was properly in Prague, there were about 120,000 young people there.

I've got this summary of the Prague Press, May 17th, made for a creepy capitalist organization called Radio Free Europe:

"Czechoslovakian Communist Party daily, *Rude Pravo* has accused American beatnik poet Allen Ginsberg of having abused Czechoslovakian hospitality and grossly violated the norms of decent world behavior. The accusations were made one day after *Czedeka*"—that's the Czechoslovak Press Service Association—"reported that Ginsberg had been expelled from the country"—that was on May 7th—"because of his negative influence on young people. Last Sunday *Czedeka* also had quoted Communist Youth Organization daily *Malda Fronta,* which printed excerpts from his personal diary. *Rude Pravo* claimed that the documents printed by *Malda Fronta* testified to the fact that Ginsberg is a person with a sexual deviation and to narcotics addiction. They alleged that in his notebook Ginsberg described *in detail* sexual orgies he staged in various places with young men. Ginsberg's character is completed by the notes in which he speaks with disdain of our Republic and of the citizens whom he met and with whom he talked. The number of those who had taken their guidance from Ginsberg has not been negligible, the paper said, adding that after the publication of the facts about his moral character all have the opportunity to correct their own critical feelings.

Last Sunday's editorial of *Malda Fronta* said that, "at the request of his friends, Ginsberg participated in the May Day programme of the Prague students."—That's an understatement—"On the nights of May 3rd and 5th he was apprehended by a police patrol for creating a disturbance,"—I was attacked in the street by the police, and literally knocked down—'was questioned and subsequently brought to his hotel.'—On May 3rd I was drunk, that's true, but I was singing Tibetan hymns on the street. Actually the only reason they took me in was that I didn't have my passport on me. The hotel had my passport.—"*Malda Fronta* says that in his diary we find insults to representatives of our State, our Party and our people. The diary was found by a citizen and handed over to the police." I figure I lost it at a concert.

After I got elected plain-clothes cops followed me. Finally they picked me up in a restaurant on the outskirts of town and said, "We have your diary. If you come down and identify it we'll give it to you, and you will be back with your friends in half an hour." As soon as I had signed the paper saying it was mine they said, "Now we wish to inform you that we are keeping it, because on a sketchy perusal it looks as if you have written illegal writings in this book, and so we will hand it over to the Public Prosecutor to determine if there is anything illegal." I don't think they did it legally, even by their own law.

Editor: How did the American Embassy view all this?

Ginsberg: Well, when I got elected King of May they didn't know what to make of it. The secretaries came up and congratulated me. They were nice little girls, making tea at tea-time, gossiping about shoes. I got on well with the young kids. Lots of young kids.

Finally, the President of Czechoslovakia got up and attacked me. This is a dispatch from Vienna, from a newspaper two days ago, June 2. "Deliberate Corruption of Czechoslovakia's Youth is the latest charge made against the West by the Czech President Anton Novotny." About two Sundays ago he went on the air and explained why I was bounced, because one hundred thousand people elected me, and now the Government has to bounce me. It's not very democratic, so they have to go around explaining it.

Editor: Yes, but right or wrong, it's not going to do much good. It fouled everything up.

Ginsberg: It's terrible. I was trying to get out of the Cold War, not in it.

Editor: I remember reading a very bad report in the "Esquire" about India . . .

Ginsberg: It was all lies. This nice girl, one of the editors came out there for a week, and she wore high heels so she couldn't walk with us in the burial grounds or by the rivers. She scribbled some notes and then when she got home she got dysentery or flu or something, and she couldn't write her own story. So she gave it to another editor, some smart, slick professional journalist from New York who turned it into a machine job and couldn't read her notes right either. It was literally full of bad journalistic nonsense.

But most journalism is very inaccurate, that's why it's not prose or poetry. I've been dealing with journalists for some years and the principle I adopted was not to manipulate them, that is to say, deal with them as you would another human being, and then if it comes out bad it's their karma not yours, because you have attempted to communicate completely. You can't attempt to control them from your side, or tell them in advance, you just have to trust them. I've found, at least in America, that ninety-nine percent are not honorable, or just not smart enough to understand. So the stories are stereotyped.

Like the time *Life* magazine reported that Edith Sitwell had insulted us and told me that I smelled bad and that I had offered her some heroin cigarettes or something. And she had said, "Oh no, it makes me come up in spots all over. You do smell bad don't you?" So I wrote them and said, "That isn't what happened, that isn't fair," and one of the editors wrote back and said, "I'm sorry but we trust the informant who gave us this story as accurate." Then she wrote to them and they still didn't believe it. But their whole psychology or personal being is such an unlovely universe that that's the only thing they could imagine.

I learned a lot about mass communications at this point, because I could see the difference between what is being reported and what isn't. If there's such a gap in my case, then imagine that blown up on a larger scale with reporting on China or Russia. In other words, the structure of reality presented to everyone is completely fabricated. Not consciously I mean; these people don't know the difference. Of course it may be in the nature of mass communication itself, because as soon as you abstract yourself from the event, you are no longer dealing with it.

Editor: What do you think of England now?

Ginsberg: Liverpool was good. A special sort of awareness. The dances have ceased to be specific . . . you know, boy-girl opposition. I saw them dancing in a circle doing these very strange hip and foot movements as a sort of ceremony. But these movements are identical to the ritual dancing in Indian tribal religions. So the young people of Liverpool have their own religious ceremonies. Freedom of vision in this case is being achieved through music and the sensuality of African rhythms and sometimes through drugs or beauty . . . the end of the dictatorship of convenience and convention. There's a lot of activity . . . I hope I might come and live here.

But we had terrible struggle last time I was here. Gregory Corso and I went up to read at Oxford. First of all most of the academic group weren't very friendly, though the poets were. Edith Sitwell was there and she was wonderful. The students were still very dumb at that time. That is, the poets were still tied up in the accentual English prosody so they still hadn't opened their own lungs or breath or body. They still thought it a great accomplishment to write a villanelle. . . . They were at the primary stages of technique and the more hip students hadn't yet been able to smoke pot so they didn't know much about that aspect of consciousness—exploration. And they were a little politicized: They were interested in banning the bomb, which was nice, but Gregory read a great poem called "Bomb," which was a hymn of praise to the bomb. It's neither for or against the bomb, it just reduces the bomb to insignificance because the poem is greater than the bomb. But they misunderstood and thought it was pro-bomb and someone threw a shoe at him while he was reading it. They were real angry youngsters, and I realized that they're not the people who are going to bring about peace. They were angry, they wanted to fight—they wanted to fight poetry. This was the primary stages of awakening in England. Nobody had long hair in those days.

Editor: That's what's done it? Long hair and topless dresses?
Ginsberg: Yes, apparently topless dresses and high style of this kind always comes with periods of joyous liberation. It happened, apparently, during Elizabethan times. *"Naked human form divine"* that's what it's all about really. That's quoting Blake.

Editor: Is this happening in America?
Ginsberg: Yes, but under more disadvantageous circumstances.

Editor: Because the mechanics of civilization have gone further?
Ginsberg: Yes. The buildings in New York are too tall. Here's it's like a great park. We were walking today around Hyde Park and Charing Cross and talked to some French beatniks in Trafalgar Square, and people were standing around at leisure in the sun. But it was a city where the buildings were to be used, whereas in New York the buildings dominate and unless you have your own souls completely in your own possession you get pushed around quite a bit by the specters around you—the concrete and the wire and chromium, and steel and the messages coming through from every direction, tell you who you are and what to do. And there's a police problem in New York. The police are unloved, that's the problem.

The police in New York are all paranoid . . . they were so hateful for so long that everybody got to hate them, and that just accumulated and built up. The only answer to viciousness is kindness. Sooner or later everybody's got to realize that. The people in the United States are scared of the police. There was even a poem by Williams in the twenties when Sacco and Vanzetti were electrocuted, saying that it was a trauma, that people would be frightened when the police stopped them. The problem with the younger kids is that they still haven't learned that you've got to make love to the police in order to solve the police problem, so they're still provoking them, which is a mistake. Even in Czechoslovakia the kids are provoking them. I mean, it doesn't solve the problem. The problem is un-love or un-feeling.

For the demonstrations calling for the legalization of marijuana, in America, we introduced the singing of Tibetan and Hindu mantras in order to calm both the picketers and the police, and it worked very well. There was a great cry of *"om om"* going right through the circle, and the police would become somnolent and more friendly. The vibration hits them somewhere in the abdomen, where it feels good. So we didn't have any violent trouble, because you can't hit a man over the head with a billy-club when he's saying *"om om"!* Also if you have an activity like chanting mantras on the part of the picketers, all the frustrated energy for self-expression finds a way of release so it becomes a satisfactory experience and thus the frustration-violence is avoided. Everybody has a chance to express themselves as gods for that moment.

Editor: But how do you force this love on people?
Ginsberg: Make love to them.

Editor: Yes, but it is a practical problem—there are an awful lot of people.
Ginsberg: I know. It's going to take a long while but it's a lovely project.

Editor: You need highly trained squads of love-makers rushing about.
Ginsberg: Well, through the discipline of poetry, because poetry is a religious medium. Say, in India, poetry is a form of yoga or adhana, as a path of discipline, equal to or as yoga. So your *guru* can be Blake or Whitman. One of the Holy Ladies in Brindaban told me to take Blake as my *guru.*

I have no simple answer to the whole scene. Either how to deal with the great post-Stalinist bureaucracy in Russia, where twenty million Russians were arrested and about fifteen million disappeared, according to gossip around Moscow; and so you have the hangover from that last bureaucracy, and all the people responsible are still alive, and you have the younger generation coming up, that abhors what happened. Or this great predatory capitalist scene going on all over the world, emanating from America with a huge bureaucracy and everybody brainwashed and regimented. I can't figure out any way of getting around it. And now the two groups look like they're going to destroy each other with atom bombs. It's a very weird situation. I have no prescription.

Editor: Are American students very concerned about this sort of thing?
Ginsberg: Something is happening in the universities. For one thing the professors are waking up. They are beginning to answer back to the State Department. Of course, McCarthyism was very bad on the campus, too. It blacked out any activity for years and now it's just waking again: poetry and politics and everything, slowly.

For instance a lot of students are going down South—carrying copies of *On the Road* apparently too. In that way poetry can have an effect: it has the sympathy. Not the ideals or the inspiration, but simply the experience of the human spirit flowering, showing that it is possible for the human spirit to flower. So you either go out and cut your hair and take some job and work your way up and eat shit all your life and make a living, or you can try to remain tender and gentle and aware of the wonderful complexity of everything.

And the walls of the white intellectual worlds of the west are being penetrated by all sorts of interesting influences. Zen, which is Chinese really, Buddhism from India, that kind of exploration of human consciousness is taking over from the rigid rationalism of the west. On another level you have the experiments in sensorial perception, dreams, and drugs. People are able to have visions again, either on their own or with LSD, or with sensory-deprivation experiments, or by getting a spaceship and looking at the earth, seeing colors that were not seen by the eye before. The Space Age has opened up consciousness also. Just as there was a shift of consciousness in the Copernican-Galilean period with Man's perspective in terms of the Universe. Then, the Earth was no longer the center. Now the Sun is no longer the center, the Self is the center.

You'll find all the young intellectuals in America affected to a great extent by influences from South American Indians, Mexican peyotel and mushroom Indians, and negro church-rites and that's had a terrific effect on painting and poetry. And now the Tibetans are dispersed over America and Russia. Then you've got the Yoruba and Congo religions permeating into the West, and jazz taking over painting and poetry . . . and mathematics, finally. It's a revenge of the irrational, in a sense, of the oppressed. They're supposed to be primitive, and they're taking over French poetry and European painting. And what they're bringing; they're not returning with the body, but with the divine—the divine as defined by the ecstasy which the Being is equipped to experience and transmit. The enlargement of the consciousness to include a consciousness of all the different centers instead of just one portion of the brain.

The following discussion, between Allen Ginsberg, Gregory Corso, and U editor David Widgery took place a few days after the poetry reading at the Albert Hall on June 11th.

Ginsberg: At the Albert Hall poetry covered itself with urine. Would that something beautiful had happened! There was an opportunity there to present the lung-breath of English poetry and the poets were lacking. There were all these lousy second-rate English poets coming on like semantic beatniks.

Editor (*to Corso*): Why didn't you read properly? You ran away like a kind of crated dehydrated chicken.

Gregory Corso: I did not run away like a crated dehydrated chicken. I ran away as I is and am, by God. No, really I didn't feel it at all that night. It wasn't the audience, I've faced audiences . . . it was the way the evening was going and I was bugged about it earlier. I thought I'd be reading with the poets. None of them were poets but the five Americans. Nationalistic, yes. There are some English poets, but they weren't there.

Editor: But there were five thousand people there, and it should have happened.

Ginsberg: I, Allen Ginsberg, accept full responsibility . . .

Corso: Why are you jumping on me? I was in Paris and I was told to come to the reading at the Albert Hall, and when I thought of the Albert Hall then I said that it's under the auspices of responsible people. It sounded like a responsible business with Neruda, Allen, myself, Ferlinghetti, and Fernandez. I thought, wonderful, it's historical. I haven't read in three years and I wasn't going to read again for some time. The new poems I have are not readable aloud. Why couldn't I just read a straight poem that I did . . .

Editor: But you just sat there and mumbled into microphone. I couldn't hear you. Why?

Corso: Why? Because first of all I told you I was dehydrated—no, you said I was dehydrated. The big WHY is why didn't that reading come out with the poets reading that I thought would be reading when I came here to London.

Editor: Why didn't Voznesensky read?

Corso: Because it was a big hodge-podge of a nightmare. He was sitting there watching it . . . the madness going on there, the nightmare. He saw some very strange scenes outside of the poetry. Perhaps that's why he didn't get up and read.

But today he did. When he saw that the poetry was there and that the poets were giving out with the poetry he could feel it. And he read in Russian and the people felt the poem. He did not have a translator for today. They felt it and it was real.

Editor: But this means poetry is a kind of silent cinema . . . words have no meaning.

Corso: NO. The sound . . . the rhythm and the sound. Words have meaning, because he gave a literal translation, which is the best you can give. Why have a translation into Russian? In English it's just not like the Russian. Voznesensky himself speaks English a little, so he gives you a literal translation and then reads the poem which is much finer.

Ginsberg: Because he reads poems with a fantastic rhythm. A great profound Kremlin Bell sound that came forth from the belly.

Editor: But why does this happen for two hundred people and not for five thousand?

Corso: Because of the people reading that night. It was disorganized. It had nothing to do with the crowd. You said that five thousand is better to relate to than two hundred. I don't know too much about that, but I came here believing that five people would read and it seemed that fifteen people read, and there wasn't enough time to go round.

Editor: There was a terrible end with voices booming out saying, "Go back to your homes, if you have any."

Corso: They did four hours and it was right for them to say something if they felt that they did not get anything out of it. You should have had an organizer who would have known just what poets would be there and it would not have been still or awkward like that, but a beautiful reading, by everyone being in rapport with it. But you just have to have one clown get up there . . . the guy who started the evening was clowning, so that was the keynote for the nightmare. So I looked at it later and said, "Oh hell, it's happened." Looked at objectively it's almost a comical thing. That's what they came for, maybe, and that's what they got.

That was the first reading ever in my life that I read like that. Allen knows how I used to read. . . I used to go with it, and read poems that related to the audience. That's why my head was bowed, reading my poem mainly to myself and to the poets in the circle. It could have been saved.

Ginsberg [Parts One and Two]

William D. Knief / 1966

Cottonwood Review, Vol. 1, No. 2 Spring, 1966, 3–10 and Vol. 1, No. 3, November, 1966, 3–11. Reprinted with permission.

Interviewer: The first thing I want to ask you is, what poets have influenced you particularly in your poetry and your poetic style?

Allen Ginsberg: Guillaume Apollinaire, a French poet, 1910 or so; Ezra Pound; William Carlos Williams . . . Primarily, however, above those, Jack Kerouac, who I think is the greatest poet alive, but is not well-known as the greatest poet alive. William Burroughs, a prose poet. Christopher Smart, an eighteenth-century friend of Dr. Johnson. Blake more than anyone, from spiritual points of view; an Indian poet named Kabir, another Indian poet who is called Mirabai, as well as an American poet who's called Emily Dickinson. And Whitman. A little Poe on account of the crankiness in it, and the spiritual isolation . . . a little of Vachel Lindsay . . . a little bit of Robert Creeley. Charles Olson. A lot of Shelley, and a lot of Rimbaud and Antonin Artaud, then Laforgue, a Frenchman, and Chuang Tzu, who is a Chinese philosopher-poet who said "I am going to speak some reckless words now and I want you to listen to them recklessly." And, um, a little bit of Milarepa, who is a Tibetan poet. And then a couple of other people, let's see, who else—Gary Snyder occasionally, recently, influenced me a little, and Gregory Corso has influenced me a lot. And Orlovsky because I live with him, and listen to his conversation all the time, and his humor all the time, and his goofiness, influences my writing style a lot.

Interviewer: What is your opinion of what seems like the most widely accepted conventional poets at this time? I am thinking in particular of Sandburg and Frost—

Ginsberg: Accepted by whom? The question is, accepted by whom. Really, literally, it is a question of being accepted by whom.

Interviewer: Then you wouldn't accept them?

Ginsberg: No, I think they're fine poets. I don't think they're the best poets we've got around. Well, Frost is dead; Sandburg is a fine old man—is he dead or alive?

Interviewer: I think he's still alive.

Ginsberg: Yeah, I think he's still alive, and he's a fine old poet, too; however, they're not necessarily the best poets that we've produced in this century. Like Pound was incomparably a better poet than Frost. William Carlos Williams was a much better poet than Frost. As far as my feelings and my uses are concerned, I can find more use for Williams and Pound that I could for Frost. And even if you stacked the work of Frost against the work of a younger poet like Gregory Corso, after one hundred years I think we'll all find a lot more use of Gregory Corso than we will have found out of Frost.

Interviewer: What fiction writers do you most admire? You mentioned poets, primarily.

Ginsberg: I'm not so much interested in fiction as I am in prose. And I do make that distinction, because fiction is a vaguer term, and prose means something. Prose means somebody interested in the composition of syntax, composition of a sequence of language that does reflect some actual process of verbal phenomena going on in the consciousness. So—whereas fiction writers are interesting in writing stories to sell for movies or something, a prose writer is interested in composition, in the sense that Gertrude Stein, who was a great prose writer, spoke of composition as creation. So the prose writers I am interested in are—in America, you mean?

Interviewer: Well, let's start there.

Ginsberg: Kerouac, primarily, who continues into the sixties to be the most interesting composer of prose sentences, and also the most sincere and spiritual reporter of the phenomena of existence, and probably the wisest reporter, because he is one of the very few who realizes that the universe doesn't exist. And second, William Burroughs, who has written a whole series of prose books that are affecting a lot of people, mainly the young, in the sense of altering their own sense of consciousness. And Hubert Selby Jr., who wrote a book called *Last Exit to Brooklyn*, who has the virtue of being able to write a sentence in which three or four different people are speaking in different accents, and he doesn't use punctuation marks, but you could tell that there are three or four distinct people individually speaking. He's that wise and canny about accents and diction.

Another prose writer that I am in love with, Herbert Huncke, who is about fifty years old and never published anything except this year for the first time his journals were published by a small press in New York, and the book is called *Huncke's Journal*. About seventy pages of that have been published. And I think in a hundred years, we'll look back on Huncke as the great creator of Americana, in the sense that Sherwood Anderson was. Huncke is the big ex-thief-junkie-hustler-faggot-charmer who's influenced a lot of people in New York. He's had a big influence on me and my poetry— I left him out when I was talking about influences. He also had a big influence on Burroughs and Kerouac. But he never published anything and he never collected his writing. He just wrote little notebooks and nobody paid any attention to it until a few people began typing them up in the last few years, and now something's being published. The only place you can get that is through the City Lights Bookstore in San Francisco at 261 Columbus Avenue, or through the 8th Street Bookstore, 17 West 8th Street. If there's anybody interested in prose composition and wants to examine *Huncke's Journals*, they have to get ahold of them there, in those places.

Interviewer: What do you think of the—
Ginsberg:—Other prose writers. We haven't finished with other prose writers, like Genet, and more importantly, Louis-Ferdinand Celine, who wrote a book called *Journey to the End of the Night*, and *Death on the Installment Plan*, and *Guignol's Band*, all of which were published by New Directions, as well as *Castle to Castle*, another book of his—let's see— who else is good in prose? Robert Creeley's prose is interesting, the book *The Island*— LeRoi Jones' prose is interesting. There's a novel by Michael McClure, of Wichita, which is interesting but has never been published— all about fucking and drinking and riding around in the night mist with neon lights on the streets of Wichita when he was seventeen. And then another half of the novel is the same thing except it takes place when he is twenty-seven and he's married.

And there's an unpublished book by a guy by the name of Kirby Doyle Jr.: *The Happiness Bastard*, which is a great piece of prose also. There's a very great composition by a young kid about being a happiness bastard in America.

Henry Miller's prose is important. Sherwood Anderson's prose is important. William Carlos Williams's prose is important to me as specimens of real composition.

And going back before that, Gertrude Stein's prose is important. She's really, in a sense, the mother of prose composition. She was the first one to try to write prose without having any idea in mind as to what she was supposed to write; she wrote what was in her head at the moment of writing, where the writing itself was the primary activity, where the terms of the writing were the immediate consciousness of the moment *while* writing, whereas everybody else was looking into their memory—or looking into space or looking into the future or looking into some imaginary project. She was the only one who looked into her head and the visible eternity around her while she was at the desk writing. And that was a big experiment and discovery, just like Einstein's Theory of Relativity.

Interviewer: You mentioned Sherwood Anderson. Hemingway, who was writing at about the same time and place as both Stein and Anderson, has said that he was profoundly influenced by these two. What do you think of Hemingway?

Ginsberg: Well, Hemingway was a nice guy, but he should have been sucking cocks for a while to get rid of the excessive necessity of being a man . . . because he had too formal an identity with being a masculine mammal. And that's not worthy of our species. Our species is much more variable and ample than that, which is something that Sherwood Anderson understood. Not that Anderson was a fairy, or anything like that, it's just that Anderson was a much more open soul to reflect the loneliness of the middle American scene, and the extremes of desire which grew like sunflowers in the middle of whatever state Anderson was from. Whatever lonesome earth he walked upon. See what I mean? Now Hemingway was a very, very great technician, and a good head and a real sharp mind, and basically a very sympathetic person. Especially toward his death. Especially in his prose of his last years he is much underestimated, I think. But Hemingway did have this problem of being too proud, with capitals PROUD—like too proud!—a desperate man. He had a nice beard—

Interviewer: Do you see any particular direction in modern American poetry today?

Ginsberg: Yeah. Toward reproduction of the actual consciousness of the poet, and communication of that, which is going to be the communication of the kind of consciousness which is just like the consciousness of the people listening. Meaning that he ain't gonna lie no more, meaning he's going to talk about the hairs around his asshole.

Interviewer: I noticed that there seemed to be a difference between your poetry and Whitman's; that you seem to have more of your own consciousness in your poems. Would you agree with that, or not?

Ginsberg: Whitman was constantly reflecting his subjective nature, and if you read Whitman aloud, it's pretty shocking. And he also had to deal with the repression of the time, and I don't. We have fought against that and beaten it down. So now we have free speech according to our American constitution, so that at this point a poet is constitutionally, legally, empowered to communicate to the public anything he wants to communicate. Whereas previously there was an isolation of constitutional rights by police, judges, publishers, district attorneys, mayors, newspapers, media of mass communication, where they all were conspiring to suppress individual expression, which occasionally affected emotional or political life in what Whitman would call "these states." The Supreme Court has now said that you can't stop anyone from saying what he wants about *persons*. You see how that sentence ends. Persons—meaning in the sense of persons, rather than objective Object. Someone can say something about feeling being the being who feels, and has imaginations and fantasies. So, anybody can say what he wants, now, about that, without being told that he's not supposed to have fantasies when they border on areas people want to repress, like sex. Or God.

Interviewer: Am I correct, then, in assuming that you consider sex and God fantasies?

Ginsberg: Everything is a fantasy; the whole universe is a fantasy. The universe doesn't exist.

[Here, someone in the group of people around us asked, "Can you talk a little louder?"—and Mr. Ginsberg replied]

I have to think while I'm talking and I can't orate. It's hard to think as it is, without having to talk louder. It alters the syntax if I have to scream. You see, it becomes abnormal if I have to talk *that* much louder. It's not normal any more. It would be interesting to have to satisfy the conditions of the microphone and the conditions of the ears. That's normal.

"We could ask the people to stop playing the guitars."

No, it's normal that they're playing. . . . Guitar strings in the background —.

Interviewer: People have described your style of writing as being anything from obscenity to actual written music. How would you describe it?

Ginsberg: That's a good enough description.

It depends on who I was describing it to. As far as I'm concerned, like if I'm describing it to someone I know well and trust as a writer, like Kerouac, or Peter Orlovsky, or Corso, or Robert Creeley, or Charles Olson, I just say I'm scribbling whatever comes into my head, because that's really where the action's at. I'm not trying to write poetry. I'm not interested in poetry, I'm not interested in art. I'm interested in like reproducing the contents of my consciousness in a succinct, accurate way, trusting that the contents of my consciousness, as the contents of anybody else's consciousness, have symmetry and form and rhythm and structure and—lack-of-logic like anybody else's. Like the whole universe, in fact.

After structure, before we got to lack of logic, there's a dash in the prose transcription of this sentence. You understand? Structure and—lack-of-logic—to indicate a *shift* of thought. See, that's what I'm concerned with, the sudden shifts of thought; the sudden contradictions of mental activity, the *shifts* of thought which have a beautiful structure of their own, and if you try and eliminate those shifts and eliminate the rhythm of those shifts, you eliminate the music of thought and speech, and you eliminate the truthfulness of the way people communicate. So my writing, if it's going to be called writing, is actually simply a model of the consciousness which is manifest in language—rather than a substitute or a denial of that consciousness. By substituting an artificial model. Like a model of "syllogistic" discourse.

Interviewer: Why do you write? What is the purpose of—
Ginsberg: Because I'm lonesome. I want to get laid.

Interviewer: Does the poet have a responsibility to his society, or his public, or to anyone he is writing to?
Ginsberg: If the universe doesn't exist, how could anybody have any responsibility for anything?

Interviewer: Then he writes simply out of and for himself?
Ginsberg: He isn't really writing. "The hand was not there that moved." And there's a lot of people that want the hand to be there and want responsibility and want the universe to be there, so they're going to be stuck with that on their deathbed, too, as it vanishes away from their grasp—nobody's got no responsibility for nothin', in that sense. Not in the sense that you asked the question, so there's no responsibility at all. The only thing you might call responsibility, if you want to be highfalutin' about it and use that kind of bullshit terminology, as "responsibilities," is that he does have

the responsibility to reproduce the actual contents of his feelings and consciousness rather than the supposed contents or the contents that would please other people who have power to save him from the electric chair.

Interviewer: Technically, *how* do you write?

Ginsberg: I write in a little notebook like the one I have in my pocket now, called "Record," which is an 89c notebook I get at Walgreen's or wherever I can buy it, and it has little lines in it, and I scribble in it wherever I can. And when I retype it I follow the exact *form* that I wrote it in the first time, to note that the exact traces of the composition are left there in the poetry.

Interviewer: Do you ever rework a poem?

Ginsberg: Never, never.

Interviewer: Then it's absolutely spontaneous?

Ginsberg: It's not really even spontaneous; I either write it and it's there, as a record of that passage of time, a cut of time—and that's something I learned from Kerouac, who is a genius at that, and like unalterably advanced into an area where what he has written he has written, and therefore how can he change it? In other words, if I walk down the street, how can I go back and retrace my steps and say I walked a different way? So actually, revision in his view is lying, because it's trying to cover the traces of mental activity or cover what seems to be embarrassing or too revealing. What's *really* important is like to reveal, not cover the revelation, so sometimes the revelation turns out dopey, or stupid, or uninteresting, so then I don't publish it, but what I do publish is whatever I have written that I don't have to change that really was there, when I was in a coherent, conscious mood while composing—so that means you gotta write a lot. Which is the big discipline. You gotta write all the time, every day a little bit—five minutes, at least.

Interviewer: How long did it take you to write "Howl"?

Ginsberg: Oh, a couple of hours. I wrote it in three different times; three different parts. I revised a little, not much.

Interviewer: When did you first start writing?

Ginsberg: I don't remember. I guess when I was eighteen, or something, like anybody else. Puberty, when I sprouted hairs around my pubis.

Interviewer: Do you consider your formal education to have helped you, to have been important to your writing?

Ginsberg: It blocked me from writing completely. In fact, in my formal education, I was taking a creative writing course at Columbia College, and started writing a piece of prose about my actual life and actual existence, and the creative writing instructor who was the head of the English Department, a man named Prof. Steves, took it down to the dean of Columbia College, a man named Nicholas McKnight, and they forbade me to continue writing it. So as far as I can see, at least at that time, 1945 (we've moved things around and changed things since then), the academy was not only indifferent to writing, it was actually a venomous, vicious, vitriolic, malevolent, jealous enemy of any kind of composition from nature.

When I was hanging around in school, I was hanging around with Burroughs and Kerouac, and they were teaching me how to write. Not the professors—professors have changed a little bit, like they recognize their own weaknesses now, so things are a little bit better off. I don't know if that's true in the provinces, but that's true in the centers of intellect, supposedly, like Columbia, Harvard, Berkeley. At this point I'm a professor, like I go around and teach.

Part 2

The first part of this tape-recorded discussion appeared in the second issue of the *Cottonwood Review*, in the spring of 1966. The interview itself, uncut and uncensored, was obtained at a party in a home located just off the University of Kansas campus earlier that winter. We sat on the floor huddled over the tape recorder, Mr. Ginsberg and I, in a room filled with people who had come to see him. And so we taped with "guitar strings in the background," as he put it. For nearly an hour this went on. He spoke in a quiet, unhurried voice, smoking cigarettes, taking an occasional drink of beer from the can on the floor by his knee. As he spoke, lamplight reflected from his glasses and he leaned over the microphone, concentrating, attempting to express and communicate the synthesis of his consciousness. And when the session was over, Allen Ginsberg was for me no longer the mystic enigma or the rampant wild man that he is said to be. Rather, I found him to be a genuine teacher, a poet, and a man with a great deal on his mind.

Interviewer: You and William Carlos Williams have both been closely associated with the town of Paterson, New Jersey, at one time or another. Is there any reason for that?

Ginsberg: I grew up in Paterson. That's my hometown. And later, when we met, we took walks there together, by the banks of the Passaic River—Can you print all this exactly as said?

Interviewer: Yes.

Ginsberg: Including what might be considered off-color words?

Interviewer: Yes.

Ginsberg: That's nice—if anybody questions it you've got to remember that the implications of this are ultimately political, so that any censorship of this is censorship of political expression, and that kind of censorship is prohibited in the United States Constitution. You see the exploration of consciousness and the manifestations of consciousness in language ultimately affects one's awareness of social conditions and political circumstances. And so the accurate expression of language has direct consequences on political thinking, finally. So that if a poet wishes to speak in a language that he chooses, if anybody tries to alter that language they are attempting to alter a citizen's expression of his consciousness within the society, and the citizen's reflections on the nature of that society, and that in itself is something that is a function of citizenship that is protected by the Constitution. So that anybody who tries to censor anything I say is completely un-American—I wrap myself in the American flag and do declare my soul.

The corollary of what I just said was a statement by Plato: "When the mode of music changes, the walls of the city shake." You can see an absolute, direct thing with the Beatles and Bob Dylan; when the mode of music changes, the walls of the city shake.

Interviewer: Would you mind clarifying the reasons for the "smoke pot" movement?

Ginsberg: Yeah, simple. One, there have been a series of governmental and scientific reports from the last seventy years asserting unequivocally that there is no physiological, psychological, mental, or moral danger to the human being that can be caused by smoking cannabis herb leaves. These reports are: one, the British East India Company report done in the late nineteenth century which concluded that pot was not a problem, but that alcohol was perhaps a problem. Two, the Panama Canal military commission report done in the twenties and thirties and reprinted in the "Military Surgeon" which was a journal of the US Army. Also in the thirties and forties were editorials in that magazine which said that marijuana was not the cause of trouble, crime, degeneration, or disease among the soldiers after the surgeons made an investigation. Some made the recommendation that nothing be done about it.

There was also a report in 1937 by the LaGuardia Committee, which was a group of doctors, who published a report by the President's—I'll give you the exact thing on that [here he took a small notebook from his coat and turned to a quotation]—"The Proceedings of the White House Conference on Narcotic and Drug Abuse" done in the State Department auditorium September 27–28, 1962, page 286. QUOTE: "It is the opinion of the panel that the effects of marijuana per se have been exaggerated and that long criminal sentences imposed on an occasional user or possessor are in poor social perspective." And it continues, QUOTE: "Although marijuana has long held the reputation of inciting individuals to commit sexual offenses and other anti-social acts comma, the evidence is inadequate to substantiate this, period. Tolerance and physical dependence do not develop and withdrawal does not produce an abstinent syndrome."

And there are also editorials in the British journal of medicine called "Lancet" saying there is no harm in pot and therefore proclaiming the opinion of British physicians that they might as well legalize it in Great Britain—actually there are a lot of other scientific things; there is a report done by the Rand Commission, which is the great Army military exercises bureau, a scholarly bureau; that says there's no harm in pot, it's just a cultural difference. And there is the fact that, man, from my concern—that I've lived in India for a long time, and it's legal there; it's part of religious rituals—and I've also lived in North Africa, and there it is a part of commonplace day-to-day meditative relaxation and leisure and recreation of elderly respectable Muslim citizens in their tea houses. So that, to confront the hysteria and terror and police state activity in this area in the United States is a revelation of a shockingly low-grade bureaucratic activity of the Treasury Department. It's just trying to work up business for itself so that the narco department police won't lose their jobs. What's happening in the United States is that when the bureau was created, Anslinger, who was head of the bureau, wanted power, and proceeded to propagandize through the mass media that there was something wrong with pot, on the strength of a lot of unscientific documents and a lot of gossip which had nothing to do with nothing. They never really produced any scientific evidence that there was anything wrong with pot but he somehow managed to swindle and hypnotized some foolish newspapermen and editorial writers that there was a reefer menace, way back in the twenties and thirties, and that mythology has persisted till about ten years ago, when so many people were smoking pot that nobody believed it anymore, and everyone realized that it was just a swindle. The swindle doesn't continue, really, in the sense that the great majority of intellectuals and college students and rock and roll singers and poets and advertising men and newspapermen who have direct contact with pot and who have themselves smoked it, know that it is all a big illusion and a big bureaucratic boondoggle. And an invasion of private consciousness by the officers of the state. Which is also forbidden by the Constitution. So I am merely defending the United States Constitution, again.

Also I think that pot has a positive valuable contribution in enlarging the consciousness. It amplifies the sensing awareness of the individual who smokes it. It makes him more sensitive to aesthetic forms, and to the sensations of the senses, and makes him explore the senses, because he sees how the senses can alter the external universe. So ultimately it has a religious function which it is used for in India as part of Shivite ritual; part of the worship of the god Shiva who is the god of asceticism, meditation, and marijuana—the creator and destroyer of the universe. Shiva is *not* marijuana.

So I was just speaking of the situation of the police state on this, of people getting busted and everybody having anxiety; it's totally unnecessary; it's time that that prohibition era ended just like the old prohibition of liquor ended—*more* justly that the prohibition of marijuana should end because marijuana is less dangerous than alcohol. In fact I'm beginning to suspect that it was alcohol manufacturers who wanted to see pot banned, though I can't prove it. But I bet there's some connection. In the lobbying for the marijuana tax act of 1937 there must have been some liquor money in that one—or cigarette money.

Anyway, I smoke pot all the time—but very rarely, actually, like once a week or once every two weeks. But I smoke cigarettes *all* the time, and I'm addicted to cigarettes. And, like, cigarettes are much more of a definite threat to my metabolism than pot has ever been. In other words the whole anti-pot mythology is a lot of shit. It's about time everybody—revolted—did something about it because it's an imposition on us as citizens.

Oh, yeah, and one more thing. It's not good for the existence of the State itself—State with a capital S—to have unjust laws based on gossip and garbled misinformation and self-interest on the parts of the bureaucracies who have to administer those primitive laws are on the books and are prosecuted because the most sensitive citizens of the State smoke pot. And it's merely destroying the best minds of every generation.

Interviewer: I've heard that line before. You said that pot altered your perception of the universe, and before this you stated that the universe is a fantasy—please explain that.

Ginsberg: Well, according to Buddhist theory and many other theories, probably Einstein, finally, the universe is a series of waves and these waves exist in what? A void? They never even took place; your flesh is a—fake. Existence is a fake, the whole of the earth is a fake, the whole of the solar system is a fake, everything, the entire universe is a *quirk*, a misunderstanding that arose because there was nobody to shut off the light. The universe was originally a big unborn void. So here we are—phantoms of illusion.

Interviewer: Then what are we perceiving?

Ginsberg: Each other, I suppose. We are perceiving our own desire not to be wiped out from the blackboard. But ultimately we are all wiped out. In fact, the whole universe ultimately is wiped out, isn't it? Some day?

Interviewer: For us—

Ginsberg: Well, for the universe itself, I mean that's not going to last forever. So everything's going to be—. So it never was, really. Well, pot gives you a certain amount of perspective into that. Simply because it is a question of the senses—Oh, I'm garbling it all up. It was garbled from the very beginning of the universe anyway [laughter]. So I can't expect to undo the universe in three sentences.

But, say, you take the Buddhist doctrine as expressed in the Prajnaparamita Sutra [he spelled it out]. They say form is emptiness, emptiness is form, form is not different from emptiness, emptiness is not different from form. —Every Buddha depends on highest perfect wisdom, which is the understanding where there is no eye, no ear, no nose, no mind, no touch, no object to touch, there is no consciousness, no world devised, no world of consciousness.

Interviewer: Isn't this closely related to Taoism—

Ginsberg: Yes. It's related to Zen, Taoism, everything. Everything is related finally to the fact that we are all here by accident. It's an interesting accident, and nothing to be scared of, but to take it seriously and try to reinforce it like the police do, and hit everybody on the head to make them believe that the universe is real—is a big mistake which any priest would disapprove of.

Interviewer: Do you find that through your writing and the revealing of your innermost feelings—do you find that this isolates you in any way?

Ginsberg: No. It communicates me more. I get more contact, more attachment with people.

Interviewer: Does Creeley feel this?

Ginsberg: He writes *out* of isolation; he feels that everything is isolation, in a way, but they're little tentative steps toward saying one thing, one word after another, one syllable after another, to bring him into contact with his wife and his kids.

Interviewer: Doesn't he find this a painful experience?

Ginsberg: Not as painful as being *totally* enclosed and not being able to say one syllable—his writing is a way of contact and communication for Robert, not a way of isolating himself.

Interviewer: What do you think about Henry Miller?

Ginsberg: We were talking about him before; I thought he was a great exemplar of authentic composition from the center of the mind, and in that sense an innovator in prose; he said what he actually was thinking—at a time when most people were synthesizing structures for novels and structures of syntax for their sentences which did not reflect the actual process of thinking in their minds or hearts and were mainly built to satisfy an arbitrary idea of literature which they had inherited from their academic studies. Whereas *he* threw all that overboard and started looking directly into the raw material of writing which was his own consciousness. Much as Cezanne begins to paint directly from nature. Or redo Poussin from nature, as Cezanne said.

He was a sort of American Cezanne composing from nature.

Interviewer: What influence do you think T. S. Eliot has had on modern poetry?

Ginsberg: Well, he still has—I'm sorry. Go ahead. I didn't let you finish.

Interviewer: Well, just on modern poetry in general.

Ginsberg: There's different kinds of modern poetry, like there's very different schools and very different styles. But there's still some modern poetry which depends on a previously organized, syntactical construction, and a previously dictated rhythmical construction and a previously dictated rhyme repetition; and a lot of that depends on Eliot. But he wasn't very useful in showing the way to reproduce authentic front brain consciousness on paper—he influenced me a lot, with a swooning, longing religious crooning melancholy which is very charming. He's *charming*, I would say. And everybody finds him charming, even the modern poets. But everybody took him much too seriously for a long time.

Interviewer: What about Dylan Thomas? What do you think about him?
Ginsberg: Well, one thing, Dylan Thomas was writing in an old style in a way, except that he was writing out of his own lungs, and he got back to physiology in a very direct way, and in a very nice way—how come your pupils are so large? Are you on Benzedrine, or something?

Interviewer: No, nothing at all—
Ginsberg: [To the people around us] He has giant pupils.
   Your pupils are bigger than mine. Anyway he got back to physiology, Dylan Thomas [laughter].
   [He paused and reflected a moment, and grinned.]
   If you could reproduce *that*, it'd be great.

Interviewer: I plan to—
Ginsberg: Because that's really prose, see?

Interviewer: Yes, I see—
Ginsberg: I think that's about it, isn't it? We've covered about everything.

Someone in the crowd: The Library wants a copy of this.
Ginsberg: If you can hear it. The wires may have exploded.

Interviewer: What do you think is your best expression?
Ginsberg: Singing, at the moment.

Interviewer: Would you like to put some of that on the tape?
Ginsberg: Yeah, sure. There's too much noise outside, though—it's very difficult to—

Interviewer: We could ask them to be quiet.
Ginsberg: No, I don't want to interrupt the stream that's going.
   What I've been doing is singing—for the last couple of years *learning* to sing—mantras. That's an Indian form of magic religious short-form prayer

formula. Uh, combinations of words mostly in Hindi or Bengali or Sanskrit or Tibetan or Japanese that are supposed to affect the vibrational structure of the universe when they are pronounced properly.

Interviewer: Do you feel that they do?

Ginsberg: Oh, they affect my physiology, so they do affect the structure of the universe. Actually, if you sing out of your belly instead of out of your chest or throat, it affects your breathing and that affects the intake of oxygen, and that affects the chemical composition of your body and that affects your metabolism and that affects what you're feeling, and that affects, as I said, the vibrational structure of the universe in the sense that "the eye altering, alters all." Unquote, William Blake.

Interviewer: Have you seen the movie, *Zorba the Greek*? What you just said sounds something like—

Ginsberg: No, I didn't see the movie. I'll get around to it.

Interviewer: What do you consider your best published piece of poetry?

Ginsberg: I don't know —pieces of "Kaddish," um, pieces of "Howl," pieces of "Over Kansas"—a few lines in that. Um, some stuff I wrote a few weeks ago. I'm just experimenting now with working with a Uher tape recorder, composing directly onto the tape. But I haven't transcribed them yet, so I don't know what they'll be like. I'm more interested in that, son.

Someone in the crowd: Are you afraid of the tape recorder at all—

Ginsberg: No, I carry one around. I've got one here.

Voice: I mean the continuity of thought—

Ginsberg: No, I don't need one; who needs continuity? If it's not there, why force it? I'm just interested in what really exists, not in stitching together some nonexistent entities. If my thought is too discontinuous, well then that's my thought, and so why should I have a continuous thought? But, anyway, how can it *not* be continuous in some way or other? So the problem is to find out how it is continuous, really, and recognize the continuity, rather than saying, well, these things don't seem to fit together so they must be discontinuous. In other words, whatever is real, whatever I really said to the tape recorder, must have some connection with the next thing.

Interviewer: Can this serve as a communication?

Ginsberg: I find most people are talking the way I do, lately. We're all talking the same lately. It's the space age.

Interviewer: I just remembered a line in one of your poems about giving autographs. Has fame—

Ginsberg: What's the line? I don't remember it.

Interviewer: Something about, uh, who really wants to give autographs—

Ginsberg: Oh, yeah.

Interviewer: Has this atmosphere of notoriety had any advantages, any disadvantages?

Ginsberg: Yeah, it's had two definite advantages. Three definite advantages. It's easier to get laid. Four advantages. Two: it's easier to score, for pot or anything I want to score for. It's easier to score; that'd be one and two. Secondly, since I have seen the difference between the actuality of my own subjective phenomenon, which is to say the facts of my own existence as I can see them, and how they are reported from the outside, I've got an ENORMOUSLY useful insight into the operations of the mass media and mass communications. So that I can see the difference between the external image which is projected and the actual thing which I sense and feel with my own—body. And I know that there are a lot of lies being sold to a lot of people, because I know that the whole Public Reality, capital P, capital R, is a shock comma, an illusion comma, a manipulation of consciousness; a mess, see? So that I can see what's the difference between what is me and the image which is reported. I can also see what actually was going on in Vietnam where I visited, and what was reported about it. In other words I can see the difference between Private Consciousness and Public Consciousness. Private reality and public reality. And the only one that exists is private reality; pubic reality is a complete lie that has been invented by people who are trying to protect their interests—or their fantasies.

Interviewer: What would be the ideal world?

Ginsberg: No world at all, I suppose.

Interviewer: Would you elaborate on that because I sure—

Ginsberg: The bliss of the unborn, as Kerouac says.

Interviewer: What's he doing?

Ginsberg: He's living in retirement and isolation in Florida composing ditties.

Interviewer: Is it true that he wrote "On the Road" in one sitting?

Ginsberg: No, not one sitting. In about two weeks. That's quite long for one sitting. He had to sleep occasionally. He didn't revise it though. He just sat down and wrote it. I watched him, so I know. I was there while he was writing. Not every day, but I came by visiting and he read me little pieces, just as it was. On one long roll of paper. United Press teletype roll. The third advantage is—the question of identity, or who am I, which everybody is interested in, searching for. Fame is like an image mirror, an echo, a—pun on identity. So that, if you are originally interested in the problem of identity and then you get famous, it makes the problem in a sense more difficult to solve. In the sense that if you have no insight into the fact that you don't even exist at all, you can then from the image which is projected by other people, assume all sorts of different identities, but if you are firmly affixed in the unborn, and realize that you don't exist to begin with, then the same reproduction of identity makes it easier to understand the illusory phantom nature of all identity. So that actually it's a catalyst to the further understanding of illusions. Unless you get trapped in one or another aspect of illusion.

Interviewer: If you don't exist then how does death fit into your idea of reality?

Ginsberg: An old friend. A letter that was never sent, or Mr. Pzucqrx—that's Corso's phrase, or something similar, maybe XbAJB. Death doesn't exist either. Our old friend doesn't exist. I am drunk and speaking reckless words, so listen to them recklessly—. That's what Chuang Tzu said: "I will now speak some reckless words and I want you to listen to them recklessly." Period. Enough?

A. C. Bhaktivedanta Swami and Allen Ginsberg: A Conversation

A. C. Bhaktivedanta Swami / 1968

Back to Godhead: The Magazine of the Hare Krishna Movement, Vol. 2, No. 2, 1968, 27–28. Recorded by Guru Das Adhikary. Article courtesy of The Bhaktivedanta Book Trust International, Inc. www.Krishna.com. Used with permission.

Swamiji had come to San Francisco in late January, 1967 for the opening of the Krishna Consciousness Temple there, at 518 Frederick Street. Allen Ginsberg had always shown friendly and helpful interest in the Society; and he agreed to attend the giant "Mantra Rock Festival," which the Temple members were planning to hold in the Avalon Ballroom. And so, a few days before that event, the good poet came to early morning Kirtan (seven A.M.) and later joined the Swami upstairs in the apartment his pupils had rented for him.

We were sitting in the glow of this holy man, munching on Indian sweetballs cooked by the Swami, when Allen Ginsberg came through the door, a warm smile on his face. The Swami offered him a sweetball: "Take."

They sat in silence for a few moments, radiating mutual love.

Swamiji: Allen, you are up early.
Allen Ginsberg: Yes. The phone hasn't stopped ringing since I arrived in San Francisco.

Swamiji: That is what happens when one becomes famous. That was the tragedy of Mahatma Gandhi also. Wherever he went, thousands of people would crowd about him, chanting, "Mahatma Gandhiki jai! Mahatma Gandhiki jai!" The gentleman could not sleep.
Ginsberg: [smiling] Well, at least it got me up for Kirtan this morning.

Swamiji: Yes, that is good.

A few days before, the San Francisco Chronicle had published an article called "Swami in Hippie Land," in which the reporter had asked: "Do you accept 'hippies' in your temple?"

The Swami had replied, "Hippies or anyone—I make no distinctions. Everyone is welcome."

Swamiji: Allen, what is this "hippie?"
Ginsberg: The word "hip" started in China, where people smoked opium lying on their hips. [He demonstrates.] Opium and its derivatives then spread to the West, and were looked down upon by the people in power, who were afraid of its effects. As a result, the hip people created their own culture . . . language, signs, symbols.

San Francisco is a spiritual "shivdas" [meeting ground]. The word hip has changed into hippie today. But basically, Swamiji, the young people today are seekers. They're interested in all forms of spirituality.

Swamiji: Very nice.
Ginsberg: The hippies will all fall by at one time or another.

There was some discussion regarding New York's Lower East Side and the Haight-Ashbury in San Francisco—both of which are locations of Krishna Consciousness temples, and are well-known to Allen Ginsberg. Then:

Swamiji: You have not had LSD, Allen?
Ginsberg: I have had it.

Swamiji: It is dependence, Allen.
Ginsberg: It's like a car—a mental car—to resolve inner things.

Swamiji: Krishna Consciousness resolves everything. Nothing else is needed.

Then they discussed the upcoming dance at the Avalon. Allen Ginsberg felt that certain mantras would be more palatable to American ears than others, and that he would like to try his tune at the dance. Swami agreed: "Very nice."

Poet Ginsberg said he was not yet ready to become a devotee, but that he chants the Maha Mantra every day, and will do so until he leaves this Earth. The Swami thanked him for the work he'd already done in spreading the

Kirtan (Krishna Conscious) Movement and assured him that, if he chanted Hare Krishna daily "everything will be perfect."

Allen Ginsberg then prostrated himself, and, touching the Swami's feet, he symbolically wiped the dust from them onto his forehead. Then, with a few sweetballs in a paper bag under his arm, he took his leave.

Allen Ginsberg on Everything

John Bryan / 1968

Open City, April 12–18, 1968, p. 10

Allen Ginsberg, an ebullient ball of hair and good-humored wisdom, last week bounced into the rather heady atmosphere of springtime revolution which now engulfs the campus of Long Beach State College.

He appeared there at noon Wednesday [April 3] to give an open-air reading followed by two longer sessions inside a small theater, followed by an evening class in mantra chanting.

In all, about five thousand students heard Ginsberg. And—of course—he took the opportunity to champion the cause of sculptor Bill Spater whose live-sized masturbatory mannequins had been locked up by the school after a "guerilla" exhibit on the lawn just two days before Ginsberg came to read [see *Open City* #49]. He demanded that the school release a sculpture of a television viewer being blown by a boy/girl "thing" which pokes its head out of a TV set because "it is a revelation of the unconscious that was occurring in the same kind of imagery in a poem I was reading on the campus."

The statue stayed locked up. Ginsberg kept protesting through the day. [Coincidentally, things at Long Beach State really reached a head just a day after Ginsberg's visit. The Black Student Union took over the school's academic senate, refusing to leave until their demands were considered.]

I followed Ginsberg around the Long Beach State campus Wednesday and heard his three readings. Then we sat down for a short interview about nearly everything. He's A. I'm B.

B: What do you think about violent street revolt happening this summer?
A: I'm going to die. Too much trouble. Too much work. I'm lazy. The pain is terrible. Oh, fuck it! It's all an illusion. I'll drown in religious bullshit.

B: Can we just stand there and watch the blacks get slaughtered by the Man?

A: Remember what Stokely Carmichael suggested. He said that if Flower Power has any meaning, let's see the hippies get in between the Negroes and the police.

B: If that kind of street war breaks out, it will mean that every black man will shoot at every white man he sees . . . including me.

A: Well, we'll get shot down. It's scary. But the real problem is more than that. It's the violence inside the white man. Pacify the white man.

B: How much of that have we accomplished so far?

A: Some. Not a lot. The problems are whizzing around us. Electric atmosphere. Remove the threat from the electric atmosphere. In psychological ways. Psycho-guerillas.

B: You're a poet-guerilla.

A: Magic. Well, what is it? Is it magic or is it real? What's happening? Purely psychological.

B: I'm very pleased to see how effective you are. You're invited by dozens of universities to come and fuck with their students' heads quite publicly which is really a marvelous step forward from my point of view. And they even pay you for it. Even for teaching mantra chanting as you're doing here at Long Beach.

A: Which is quite proper because that should be part of the curriculum provided by the state and they're not providing . . . courses in meditation, exploration of inner space. The state—the elders—have failed to provide the proper education for the young. And the young are providing it for themselves with programs like this and in the experimental colleges.

B: Back to politics. What about using ridicule instead of violence to get rid of monster-politicians?

A: Well, it's effective. But it doesn't clear the air entirely. Love isn't the thing entirely either. But there's awareness . . . There's a shift in evaluation going on now. On the American public's part. Like the change of attitude toward Johnson.

B: Who do you think will be elected, McCarthy or Kennedy?

A: McCarthy has a nice presence on television, Kennedy still sounds hard, staccato, like a D.A. But the atmosphere has changed. Even James Reston says so. On TV the other day, they were quoting Fulbright and Mansfield saying that the next time that Johnson gives a speech he should have it written by someone who is more conscious of the artistry of language. Language black magic.

B: You're going to attend the Yippee [Youth International Party] convention in Chicago this August—at the same time the Democrats are having their hoe-down there. What will you propose to the Yippees?

A: The society is wide open for new propositions. And the student society should get out into the society-at-large and apply itself to the problems. We'll see what happens in Chicago. I may chicken out at the last minute if it looks like violence. I don't think Yippee should happen at Chicago if it looks like it's going to lead to violence and provocation. The difficulty is how to keep agents provocateurs of the police and agents provocateurs of the alternative metaphysical interpretation of non-violence from provoking violence and getting everybody's head bashed in by accident. There are groups which feel violence and provocation are necessary. I think it excites them. It's a mirror response to the general violence.

Because of this kind of thinking they were even foolishly attacking Martin Luther King for continuing his Washington plan. But what King said is correct. If the non-violent thing doesn't work in Memphis, it should be given a full-scale try in Washington. He believed the same thing as Gandhi. And Gandhi made a Himalayan mistake when he said that the Indian people weren't ready for non-violence. People have got to be helped to be non-violent.

I guess the theme at Chicago should be protection and good feeling as a model to show society what we should be trying to do. We need that good feeling between white and non-white people.

I don't know what to do, though. I ain't got no answer. Just keep going.

B: There's a lot of menopausal mysticism going around today among the hip population, people determining their lives upon auguries. One *New York Times* writer observed that "hippies will accept whatever defies the test of reason." Your thoughts?

A: There seem to be indices of the unconscious, also. They have a role. Meditation. Forms of meditation. Forms of mental magic. The writer for the *Times* is also subjected to the mental magic of the language factory he works for and the interpretation thereof. So it's no more extravagant. We all have some sort of mythology. Like the middle class and their national mythology, trusting its life to the augury of the war with China. So that's just as tarotesque. Just as far out.

B: Shouldn't we be the reasonable ones, though?
A: Well, you've got to change the augury.

B: It has a lot to do with acid magic, too, that particularly.
A: The acid seems to reveal the environment, to get you out of the box or traps you're in—the war trap, the politics trap, maybe the university trap. The kind of trap McCarthy stands for when he asks his campaign people to cut off their hair.

B: And Kennedy is trying to attract the hip vote.
A: Kennedy said something fantastic yesterday. Rebellion, he said, is a good thing in the universities. But don't try it without permission.

That was the Bad Bobbie talking. That was a strange augury.

B: Why all this about Bobby confessing his mistakes, to create the NEW, Good Bobby?
A: To do that he would have to go through confession of his father's role in Vietnam. If Johnson is proved wrong, as he now obviously is, and Kennedy says he was wrong and Romney says he was brainwashed and Thurston Morton, past chairman of the Republican National Committee, repeated the same kind of brainwash business about what is going on, if they're all freaking out, what about the hippie leaders and black power leaders and A. Ginsberg and J. Rubin and Stokely Carmichael and Rap Brown? How about them freaking out, too?

B: Maybe it's time for some new leaders. Would you, for instance, run for President on the Yippee ticket?
A: At this point anybody could be president. I could be president . . . practically.

B: Would you run?
A: No, too much work.

B: Anything you'd like to add?
A: Ommmmmmmmmm. Ommmmmm. Ommmmm.

Ecology is the thing for me now. I've got land in the country I want to go to, in the hills of New York and the Mountains of California. I want to go plant trees up in the mountains.

An Interview with Allen Ginsberg

Robert Head / 1970

Nola Express, Issue 67, October 30-Nov. 12, 1970, 4–5; Issue 69, November 27–December 10, 1970, 10–11.

Robert Head: Do you feel any kinship with the rock groups that are good with words—Doors, Love, Airplane?

Allen Ginsberg: I know Morrison because Morrison is working with McClure on a play—so I met them. And I know the Band because I put on an evening with them in the Brooklyn Academy of Music—like reading poetry for my stint and their doing their—

H: You worked actually with them?
G: Yeah.

H: How does it work? Can people hear you?
G: No, no, not simultaneously. We put on the evening together—like I read and then they play, or they play and then I read. Like I knew briefly the Beatles in London . . .

H: What I want to know, do you see any way of fusing what electric rock bands are doing and what printed poets are doing?
G: Well, Dylan did that, I think.

H: He did it?
G: Dylan did it, sure. And the Beatles did it. Like the Beatles text for *I Am a Walrus* would not look out of place in any book of early-twentieth-century Dadaist poetry and *A Day in the Life* is just exactly like something by Apollinaire. It's like Apollinaire's own.

H: It hasn't gotten across to our poets yet because you have a lot of fine poets who are sitting around depressed as hell all by themselves out in the country.
G: Now?

H: Yeah, you got . . . and these are poets who have kept their integrity and there's just completely no relationship. They can't get out to the rock . . . they're not out . . . their presence . . . they should be out on stage. I don't know what to do about it.
G: What I've been doing, I've been learning music. The only way you can do it is to learn music, you know. You can't expect a bunch of musicians to come up and be your sidemen, you know, lift you up on a golden chair. So what I've been doing is learning music, learning notation of chords, keyboard a little bit, and actually composing and performing. Except I wound up, not with rock people, but with black jazz. Musicians like Don Cherry and Elvin Jones.

H: Do you rehearse together? For many hours?
G: With Cherry. A couple evenings. They're such great musicians you don't have to rehearse those things. That is, you know, with a studio musician, if you have your tune very firmly in your head and you know what you're doing and you go in and give them a lead sheet which has the tune written down or even sing it to them properly, they can pick up instantly and do, if you're an amateur like me, they can play around you more than you ever dreamed. You know, very pretty, slow . . .

H: It comes out structural? It's not mood music?
G: No, no, it comes out, you know, it's chord changes. They know about chord changes. They know like how many bars. Working with Elvin Jones was fantastic. He took, I sang the tune, it was a tune from Blake's "Grey Monk": "Vain the sword and vain the bow/They never can words work overthrow/The hermit's prayer and the widow's tear/Alone can free the world from fear." So I'd written a long tune, written it out as a lead sheet, he took one look at it, I sang it through while he looked at it, then he took a little piece of paper and he jotted like a shorthand version of the entire song . . . showing it divided into sections like sixteen bars at a time . . . so he divided the song into four or five parts . . . it's like a song of maybe eight or ten stanzas . . . he divided it into four or five parts, not filling in the music but filling in the time . . . with indications for himself with time, then when

we came to record I sang the notes and he was there on time all the time, not only there on time all the time but little literary things that we discussed he was there with also, like "Thy father drew his sword in the north/ With his one thousand strong he marched forth" he was there on time with ta ta ta tah, ta ta ta tah . . . military drumbeat. "With his one thousand strong he marched forth" and then with a line like "The iron hand crushed the tyrant's head" he did cymbals down on "crushed . . ." right on time . . . we even had a little literary discussion should we have the "crushed" on top of the note or the "crushed" right after . . . He was right there completely one hundred percent and he knew the music better than I did within like twenty minutes . . . cause these people are geniuses . . . that's their universal language. . . . whereas to a poet learning. . . .

H: You've learned to write music notes?
G: Yeah, I can notate it.

H: You didn't used to know how?
G: No, just this last year. So in other words, what I'm saying is, you have structure, yes, absolutely, they know structure inside out, upside down, can tell you all about it . . . in six different chords, in twelve different keys, in Lydian mode, in Dorian mode. . . . For what you're asking, I think Dylan did accomplish the transition back to minstrelsy. Remember Pound all along recalled that poetry began with dance and music with the Greek chorus . . .

H: So few people have learned it from Dylan. They're so many good poets that I'm constantly dealing with and they're just demoralized because they can't get out front.
G: There's more chance to get out front now than ever before because there's more mimeograph magazines . . . anybody who writes anything that's readable can get it printed even if he has to mimeograph it himself . . . which is what I did, the first thing I ever put out, when I was younger.

H: I'm not thinking about mimeograph, I'm thinking about the function that rock groups . . . electric rock bands . . . to give people energy . . . say The Grateful Dead . . . I think the poets should be out there doing that.
G: Why?

H: I'm just convinced of that.
G: Yeah, but anthropologically it should be a shaman out there.

H: That's exactly what I've been talking about!

G: But the shaman did not always depend just on literary picture words. He did depend on dance, music, moaning, groaning, shrieking, ecstatic body movement, rhythmic behavior of all kinds, whether verbal mantra of dancing to Shango's drums.

H: I was just going over that the other day. Me and you have arrived at shamans apparently independently because that's what I've been screaming about.

G: I've been talking about it a long, long time. Burroughs says so in print a long time back in *Naked Lunch.* He warns that he is a shaman and one of the things about a shaman is that if somebody disapproves the shaman is likely to crack up and die right there on the spot. He needs total belief. The shaman's art is not necessarily like literary sentences so it would be incomplete for a purely verbal poet to try and perform at all unless he depended very heavily on rhythm as I did or as Dylan Thomas did or as Vachel Lindsay.

H: You have to learn more than one art . . .

G: Yeah, but . . .

H: . . . that's the wrong word.

G: You have to inhabit your body. You have to get into your body very deeply and that would involve the art of chanting or minstrelsy at any rate, I think. The thing I visioned originally was a beautiful naked long-haired cat dancing, chanting language with musicians . . . finally, as an end product, somebody in a state of ecstatic prophesy . . . which really in a way Jagger and Morrison aspire to . . . What there is, is a background for what we got electrically now . . . is dancing and chanting and trance states which take place in Cuba and other Caribbean countries in front of the drums of Shango, Shango being a Yoruba god from Niger represented by a phallus colored red . . . very similar to Shiva the Indian. And in Yoruba ritual as now practiced still in Caribbean countries like Cuba and, I think, in Brazil where Shango is also worshiped . . . the drumming has the same effect as vibrations into your muscles and bones that electric rock machinery does . . . in other words, the original African drum also had that heavy vibration or physical impact on the body . . . especially as practiced in a room about this size . . . maybe twenty feet . . . with a high ceiling . . . packed with maybe fifty, sixty people with three or four guys doing heavy drumming . . . the god Shango being incarnate in the drum itself and the devotees and worshippers dancing in front of the drum, to the drum, are worshipping Shango that way. So that the form of that ritual is very similar to what could be observed around 1965 in Liverpool in the Cave or Sink which was a rock n roll underground night club. . . . literally underground . . . in cellars . . . where there'd be maybe fifty to sixty people dancing in the same way—lined up—in circles or row on row . . . black Afric style . . . in front of the rock musicians who were laying out vibrational patterns that went through the wood of the seats . . . and the tables and the peoples' bodies and bones. And there were also trance states or ecstatic possession in Liverpool, you know, girls going into a trance state for George or John Lennon . . . wetting their pants or whatever . . . going into an hysteric trance, which wasn't just a hysteric trance, it was an actual possession state . . . exactly as in Voodon or in Shango dancing people go into trance states . . . and then the actual circle of dancers and the shuffle step is exactly the same, or was the same, in Cuba in 1965 and I guess I saw it in 1967 in Liverpool, which is a real simple step, one two three four, one two three four, so it was just a shuffle step.

H: In conjunction with this do you see any new viable unit of social life? John Sinclair is trying to build a positive consciousness . . . We are a People. Burroughs wants to get rid of the nation and the family . . .
G: . . . and the tribe too. He wants to get rid of women to begin with . . . Snyder is working in that same area . . . attempting to build a tribe.

H: In conjunction with the shaman thing it seems we've got to somehow prevent a Janis Joplin scene where we've got this person way out there . . . We need a smaller unit . . .
G: The Tibetans have shamans too, you know, who had a classical thing of shamans who would do prophesying and predicting, and to do that, I think, they took a drug that was datura-esque and they had a short lifespan. So classically shamans and often poets and musicians do, as we know, freak themselves out of the universe. It isn't something that I want to do, or did do.

H: It takes a lot of soul.
G: It takes a lot of soul to live too. It takes some courage I guess to go into complete swirling transvestite universes and blow them up.

H: Do you think that ordinary people could learn to live like this without having to depend on Janis Joplin to give 'em some life on Friday night?
G: Yes! Ordinary people always did.

H: The situation you have now, people live off these rock stars, they go there for soul, and that's what they want; it seems to be killing some . . .

G: Some. It's just an extension in large magnification of what went on, say, with Bix Beiderbecke and the great blues singers of yesteryear. What's interesting is to go to Preservation Hall and see the jazz musicians who played with Bunk Johnson who are now very ancient, who are the selected ones who didn't freak out, didn't drink too much, didn't take too much dope, probably didn't even smoke . . . and survived seventy years and they're still playing. There are some ancient musicians, a lot of them have died on the way, but here are some ancient musicians hanging on, still blowing. I wonder, I kept thinking when I was sitting there, whether the dead musicians would accuse them of being finks and bourgeois mediocrity musicians.

H: Do you see any new kind of social unit that could be viable for people? What I'm envisioning is something that combines both politics and friendship when you don't have a political party where everybody pays lip service to something and half the people in them are agents. Some unit of social life for self-preservation and to grow . . . other than the family . . . we've had that problem on the paper.

G: OK, the problem is, the trouble with rock 'n' roll groups, and city hippy families, is that they are alienated from the production of useful foods, and goods, that sustain them, that they are dependent upon the city. Until they get into something basic like garbage collection or food production there'll still be a feeling of uselessness, of disconnection from Mama Earth, so that I keep feeling the most strong form of commune or new family group or tribe group would be one that is connected with either reprocessing garbage, doing something absolutely useful ecologically, or growing their own food organically, or making experiments that are of use to other people. Communal groups have the best chance of having a reason for being . . . aside from their love for each other . . . have their best chance if they're producing something that's of use to themselves and to others.

What I would recommend as political action for everybody henceforth after Leary's flight and statement and Weatherman affiliation is that whatever political action anyone take it should be done on the basis of at least a minimum of one hour daily sitting, meditation, contemplation, of one form of yoga or another with or without a teacher but at least one hour daily best in the morning around dawn. In other words, if we propose to ourselves that we're going to have a revolution and that we've got to be disciplined to have a revolution then the least thing we can do is stick with the original revolutionary illumination which was the universe of soul that everybody discovered either naturally by God's finger's touch or psychedelic drugs, so I think to supplement the drugs and to make that trip a little more solid, and to augment the drugs and make the psychedelic illumination more steadily integrated with the daily body, or even to replace the drugs if one wants to do that, the universal medicine, universally applicable in the United States right now, and traditionally classically universally applied by American Indians, by Indian Indians, by any tribal groups that had to sit long hours waiting for animals or gods to come into their consciousness. Sitting. So I think we ought to all start doing that. It will provide a bodily base for any further actions that need to be taken during the day, of either a revolutionary nature, of a political nature, of a communal nature, of a productive nature. But a politics that is not based on absolute spirituality is the same old draggy politics that will drive everybody up the material walls screaming with the heebie-jeebies again, which everybody is at this point anyway.

The medicine for the immediate hysteria which you can see reflected in the horrible pig-mantra chanting in all the underground newspapers, the remedy for that is I think, the physical effort of relaxing for exactly one hour every morning, in total silence. Everybody at this point has been in contact with one swami or another, one religious group or another, in order to get any specific practical meditation exercise started. If nobody's been in contact with them, you can sit for an hour every morning, back straight, in a comfortable position, and say Om with each breath in and out, or Hare Krishna with each breath in and out, or any word that particularly pleases you. Pronouncing any mantra that you know that you like. The point of the mantra is just to focus the mind somewhere, preferably to say, though, silently in the heart area while breathing easily. I've been doing it now ever since Leary left jail. That precipitated my decision, you know. . . . decision for Christ [laughter]. That precipitated decisive things. I've been thinking a lot about meditation and I had done some in the past but I had never like stuck fixedly to it as a medicine path. That's my news, and that's my proposition for the entire American left. Sit down an hour every morning from now on. Otherwise there will be a growing credibility gap between inflated revolutionary violent rhetoric and the so-called spiritual revolution which is also part of the inflated violent revolutionary rhetoric.

So if we're going to have a spiritual revolution we better have the means and the tools and the weapons of a spiritual revolution. And finally, if everybody is going to get so *serious* about guns then they might as well get *serious* about spiritual sitting.

The net effect of Leary's alliance with the Weathermen on me so to speak has been to move me further left into actual practice of research into inner space.

H: It's happening in New Orleans too.
G: It's logical and it isn't anything new or anything shocking because after all that was the premise originally from beatnik times to hippy times to be in times of entire change of consciousness and alteration of mind. The original premise was alteration of consciousness as part of whatever was going to take place to change the world. And like it has to be stuck with faithfully. Else we get trapped in the world of our own heads, just as illusory as any capital investment.

H: Are there any Russian poets we should know about? I'm interested in Russia because of the similarities [with America] in the state apparatus.
G: I was in Moscow in 1965 and met with a couple of guys in madhouses— in jails. Alexi Ginsberg from Moscow published a magazine called *Syntax* in the early sixties which like stole and printed—mimeographed—poems by respectable poets about Stalin, like a poet named Shlutsky—Shlutsky's sonnets on Stalin, which are attacks on Stalin, embarrassed Shlutsky who is a member of the Writers Union, so the Russian police couldn't get Alexi Ginsberg in jail on grounds of mimeographing on account of a mimeograph machine is protected by the Soviet constitution, so they interviewed all his friends, like two hundred people, until they found something on him, which was that he lent his university luncheonette card to a friend and they put him in jail for two years for that. So the surveillance and technical legal nit-picking jail-horror scene is very similar there to here. Though the thing that must be remembered, which I think the left has not remembered, is something that many of the poets told me in Moscow which is that between 1935 and 1953, twenty million Russians were arrested, and fifteen million didn't come back. And the guys that did that are all sitting as they say in their chairs in the bureaucracy still. Still clinging to their chairs in the bureaucracy. So what the Russian poets and the intelligentsia are trying to climb up out of now is a total police state horror-massacre scene which is much heavier than anything we've seen here. And much more depressing.

H: I read where they found a Russian underground paper in the engine room of a nuclear submarine being run by the engineers.
G: That's possible. I've heard of people dropping acid in American Polarises.

There's another Russian poet named—the bastard son of Yesenin—Yesenin Volpin—whom I saw with Alexi Ginsberg in Moscow and he was interested in having people send him books on British Constitutional law because, see, their whole battle there is to make the government stick to the constitution. Just like here. With them it's like a wit fight, to get an advantage verbally in public or in private, to force them by mind-force to obey the constitution.

H: That's what we've been trying to do.
G: So the situation is very parallel.

H: Have you seen *Suck*, the underground erotic paper out of Amsterdam, run by Jim Haynes—he can't get it into Russia, England, or Spain.
G: Anti-grass, anti-sensory awareness, anti-sex forces in right-wing America and police-bureaucracy-wing Russia are identical persons, so to speak. The mentality is almost identical. That's why there's a war, there's these two power groups, totally identical, fighting each other, with everybody else caught in the middle.

H: Do you see any way we could get the Russian police and the American police to wipe each other out?
G: Hum. No, you see, the funny thing is, they're using us as pawns. They're using the populace as pawns to wipe each other out.

H: I've often wondered, by the very nature of the police, that they always obey orders, if we couldn't take advantage of this fact?
G: Yeah, you might tell 'em to walk into the ocean [laughter].

H: You got any ideas about what UPS papers ought to be doing? In the way of intellectual initiative?
G: Yeah. There should be more pragmatic spiritual recording and reporting in the underground papers. There should be regular columns on inner search and yoga.

H: I see all these rock groups and they're out there in front—and I think poets should be out there speaking intelligible words too.
G: I don't think you can separate the words from the music.

H: I agree.
G: So then what you're asking is for greater rock groups, or greater poets in the rock groups.

H: Right.

G: Or greater minstrels. But that is coming anyway, because this is the first generation of such minstrels, that is ten years now. And there's still second generations coming. You know, this generation, which grew up, invented rock minstrelsy out of, for the whites at any rate, though it had always been there as a mode for the blacks, in fact the whites stole it from the blacks in a sense, or adapted it for their own use from blacks, watered it down from blacks, but the next generation of whites is going to have grown up with that form . . .

[Part Two]

G: What were we talking about?

H: We were talking about . . .

G: . . . shamans . . .

H: . . . what I saw.

G: Yeah, what were you dreaming of?

H: I was just dreaming of some sort of viable social unit that's organized around production where people can sustain their own soul.

G: OK, now, Snyder has proposed that; I've proposed it and am working on it in terms of farming.

H: You're doing your own farming now?

G: Yeah, we produce. The farm that I'm on is a commune, we produce, the people there produce enough food. Maybe they've canned something like two hundred cases of vegetables. That's eight quarts a case. So, you know, they've been working all summer. They get their own milk and they get their own eggs. We're just experimenting around. We have a hydraulic ram to push the water uphill, instead of a gas pump. You work it on gravity, and we're experimenting with electricity.

So the poets are proposing like a return to nature, to put it in an attackable way. Or at least proposing a return to production. It doesn't solve the problems of the large cities at all but the large cities problems may be beyond solution at this point.

One thing I know is that the bureaucracies, like the welfare bureaucracy and the health bureaucracy in the large cities—the city hall bureaucracy in New York is completely broken down *within itself.* Everybody is rushing around, overloaded with papers and answering too many telephone calls and no one knows how to respond because too many things are happening at once. They're just doing patchwork.

H: You got any ideas about what UPS papers ought to be doing? In the way of intellectual initiative?

G: Yeah. There should be more pragmatic spiritual recording and reporting in the underground papers. There should be regular columns on inner search and yoga.

For instance, I went down to Texas checking out on a certain swami that was visiting Dallas and called up the *Notes* there because I was checking up on their repression and their problems with the police, and I asked them, incidentally, did they have any interest—there was a swami in town teaching a little—did they have any interest in checking him out, or did the Houston people have any interest. And the Houston . . .

H: *Space City.*

G: *Space City News.* And they said no. And I said, What's the underground press papers coming to? It's a big weird kundalini swami visiting Texas like a real rare scene and the so-called long-haired hippy paper really is so hung on bomb politics or fear politics that they're no longer interested in other spirit news. Gee, what kind of revelation, what kind of revolution is that?

H: I've had a hard time trying to find good writers in that field. We tend to get a lot of gobbledy-gook mysticism.

G: I know but you don't need a good writer: you send out your regular reporter, you know, if you've got a so-called holy man coming through town you send out your regular reporter.

So, actually, there's a minimum of art coming out now, it's all slanted politically in a very narrow way. From LNS and in the underground papers, except when, you know, there's a local talent or a special production. There's a lot of slush bad revolutionary poetry being published. Just because it's revolutionary sentiment. But it's poetry that would be shameful and shocking according to the criteria of real solid human actual speech rather than abstract hysteria speech.

H: You have anybody particular in mind?

G: No, I don't wanna mention no names here.

There's a lot of slush being published under the guise of revolutionary poetry, or translations from foreign revolutionary poetry. The only really good revolutionary poetry I've seen is some translations from Ho Chi Minh a little while back. That one about: I've been in all the jails of the government for months and how charming of them to give me board and lodging and feed me so well.

H: Vallejo . . .

G: Well, you see, Vallejo is another matter. But there is a lot of bad poetry published. They're not out looking for poetry. You see like the underground newspapers haven't been circulating around with all the interesting poets, like Olson before he died, asking for texts. The one great thing they've done is published a lot of Burroughs. That's because Burroughs somehow got into a groove and he *answers*, you know, every request from anybody you know mimeograph or underground. So he cooperates.

H: Let me ask you one more question: A lot of people look to you as having the answers to everything . . .

G: Hum, boy, they're gonna sure be torn up in the eyeballs by the lion jaws of death when they come out and get us all, man, cause we don't know the answers.

H: What I want to know is, how can people teach themselves to think? Burroughs is always talking about deconditioning from past mal-education . . . new techniques and methods of learning how to think . . . Everybody looks to other people for answers, always wanting a famous figure to tell them, you know . . .

G: Well there are some very specific practical suggestions that can be made, though obviously no guru-like answer that I can give. One thing, for deconditioning and for education and for general heart-understanding that I propose is that everybody sit down every morning for an hour. Really, like as a programmatic thing for the entire younger generation, and older generation, in America. As a serious political proposition, now and henceforth forever.

The other is follow your heart in political matters. The communal consciousness that everybody is concerned with is, I think, a real thing but it has to come from—it can't be forced—and it can't be on the basis of fear or hysteria.

Like the communal consciousness of the Panthers in New Haven at the time of the Rackley affair was based to a great extent on intimidation and fear and confusion rather than on clear-heartedness and clear-sightedness and that's where they all got into difficulty. Because they were taking things for granted on the basis of fear rather than the basis of trust. So, in a way, any political conclusion that you come to is a result of a process of intimidation by your best friend.

H: . . . is fatal. The politics of guilt is fatal. Everybody knows that.
G: . . . is obviously not a community.

G: The problem is that the planet may be so vast and degenerated at this point that all we're experiencing in terms of our own violence and government violence is a by-product of that. That all the small political riots and sit-ins and so-ons that we get involved in are just the result of atmospheric poisons and land-mass groanings and species disappearances and ocean poisonings. The *NY Times* editorial, mid-October, was quoting scientists as saying that available information now indicates that the oceans will be as dead as Lake Erie by the end of the century. Thirty years. So if the upper middle class is accepting that as fact that's really very serious. In a way that the revolution is not taking it seriously, or the so-called revolutionary groups here.

Another thing that I feel is the revolutionary groups are fighting among themselves so badly. By the way, you know, like insulting each other so badly.

H: Need a little more joy, no doubt about it.
G: Not only need more joy, you need more unity . . . The same left groups that are fighting among themselves, what would they be like if they had power?

. . . And yet there is a commonality throughout the left on a kind of humane change of consciousness, new human heart, earth-adaptation. I think that's the most widespread understanding: the most widespread understanding is change of consciousness and a return to a new relationship with nature.

H: In the communes that you've had experience with, have you seen any new sexual models that you thought were worthwhile?—as opposed to the family.
G: The one thing I've noticed, it may be that I'm getting older, is a diminution of sexual spirituality and ecstasy and interest—because everybody is losing their hard-on on account of the seriousness of the revolution, the violence, and the ecological catastrophe—is what *I'm* noticing. I don't know if other people are getting into that but it's more difficult to take body

pleasure, romantic body pleasure and intimate one-to-one personal sexual relation seriously when in the back of the shadow of the mind is the fact that like the earth is coming to an end anyway, and anyway, you know, all my old loves died a decade ago, and anyway, *sigh of grief,* I slept with almost every beautiful boy and girl I always wanted to and now why continue *that?* You know, what good is, you know, where is that getting? And anyway, maybe kundalini yoga is more interesting. Or Hare Krishna. Or revolution. Or organic gardening. Or, you know, what is sex? And then, with the sex revolution, you see, the sex revolution might wind up dethroning sex as being so important as the Catholics had insisted as it should be. It might all along have been, you know, like a religious plot to keep everyone hooked to sex.

H: I sometimes doubt if the sex revolution has taken place at all.
G: I know I don't get into joyous body scenes as much as I used to, partly my own preoccupations, and paranoias, but, also, it doesn't seem as urgent a form of prayer as it used to. Silence seems almost a more beautiful form of prayer than lovemaking.
H: Let us have silence.

Louis and Allen

Michael Scharfman, Howard Mandel, and Sam Hemingway / 1970

The Daily Orange, Vol. 69, No. 25, October 30, 1970, 1, 6–7. Reprinted with permission.

Daily Orange: Many people just know—beatnik, Allen Ginsberg, poet. And that's it. I know that you got a degree in advertising from Columbia.
Allen Ginsberg: No, English, and economics. I worked in advertising in the fifties and marketing research which is basically the technology of brainwashing, that is, picking people's brains for money.

DO: You got a master's, right?
Allen: No. B.A.

DO: Will you just say what your formal education was?
Allen: I went to grammar school in Paterson, New Jersey, and Central High School in Paterson. Then I was transferred to East Side High School in Paterson. When I was sixteen, I went to Columbia. I got kicked out of Columbia on and off, and finally got a B.A. in '48, having entered in '43.

DO: When did you go across country?
Allen: I didn't do much traveling until 1950.

DO: Until after you got out of college. When did you start writing poems?
Louis Ginsberg: Allen was always saturated with poetry at home, Shelley and Keats and so on. I wouldn't be surprised if some lines sort of floated up later on, a little bit transmogrified by his own ingenious . . .
Allen: I wrote my class poem . . . my first poem was "Once upon my window sill a sparrow hopped and then stood still" . . . I went into advertising after I got out of the bughouse. I think it was forty-eight or nine, and I couldn't get any other jobs, so I got a job, originally in public opinion research,

questionnaires and then grading and coding them and analyzing that was for University of Chicago, political research. Then I got a job for advertising companies doing the same thing. I was writing books; the first book I published was written before that.

They wanted to know about the cold war, at that time. "Is Truman handling things right or not?" The opinion was just as mushy as it is now, you see, all those things depend on how you put the question: if you say, "Is he handling foreign affairs wrong?" everyone says, "Yeah, I guess he's handling them wrong." The questions always suggest the answers; it takes a lot of will power for someone who's asked a stereotype kind of question to transform the question around to fit his own individual thought. Surveys distort opinions. Surveys condition the opinion, the answer, the syntax, the diction of the question determines the political syntax and diction of the answer. So if you ask a honky middle class question to a black or bohemian or minority populace they are intimidated by the syntax and diction and they mirror that syntax and diction back to you though it neither represents their language nor their opinions, nor their consciousness. If you ask the question "Is Nixon f . . . up?" as Norman Mailer did when he said, "Where is Johnson's f . . . up?"—if you asked that question at Berkeley during the early sixties and you used that diction you got a joyous, rousing response, "Yes," whereas if you ask if Johnson is handling the war effectively then you get a professional sounding answer saying "Yes."

I was interested in the advertising because as soon as I got into it I realized I was in the middle of the brainwashing technology and I had the chance to study it, and see how dominant political groups and capital groups actually set up a feedback of language which influence the very people they're testing. This has very little effect on my poetry except for teaching me to avoid stereotypes, because all those questions and all the answers were stereotyped.

Louis: When Allen was born I was still teaching. I was living in Newark at that time. I went to high school then I went to Rutgers to get a B.A. and then to Columbia to get an M.A., studying poetry with Eastman and so on. I won a prize at Rutgers my freshman year and then my English professor said why don't you send them out. I began to write in high school when our teacher said we should write an imitation of a Milton poem. I'd never written any poem before and was very reluctant to try it; but it was something way out, not in my métier, but I started one line and before I knew it the whole thing tumbled out, to my surprise; I almost turned around to see if anybody was dictating it. Then I brought it to class and of course the teacher read it. And after that I went to Rutgers. So I sent them out to *The Nation, The Forum, The Republic*, and then printed them.

Allen: And the *New Masses.*

Louis: The *New Masses.* I figured if they were taking them, why can't I continue? So I've been doing that, and now I'm so skilled in making a reasonable facsimile of a poem that I can escape their vigilance and have the poems finally punished in the periodicals.

DO: Punished in the periodicals?

Louis: More or less, yes. In the sense that when you're finished with a poem you're in heat; it seems as if you've transferred everything, but later on it seems that when you read it in cold blood some of the ardor has evaporated; so I use the word ironically or satirically because it's my child and I like it. I have three books: one is out of print called *Attic of the Past*, 1920, then *The Everlasting Minute*, and then about five months ago I had published my third book called *Morning in Spring* published by Morrow and it has an introduction by my son Allen. I've retired from high school after forty years, and now have been teaching at Rutgers evening sessions the last twenty-four years, and now and then I review occasional books for the Book Week of the *Chicago Sun Times*, and I conduct a pun column—I'm a punster—in my mentalpause I write puns in the *Newark Star Ledger.* And then keeping my wife at bay and keeping up with Allen, boy, I keep busy.

Allen: I was thrown out of Columbia . . . I was hanging around with Kerouac and Burroughs; Kerouac had been banned from campus by the dean of Columbia because he was an unwholesome influence on the students, then one day he came and found me in bed with Kerouac, because Kerouac had stayed overnight in my dormitory room. The dean of students was the former athletic coach that Kerouac had known when he quit the football team and started studying Shakespeare, and they immediately assumed the worst. They called Louis into the office.

Louis: About four years ago the poetry society said that as Allen was writing and I was writing, and mine's different because I'm sort of a square and he's avant-garde, they thought let's hear the contrast. So when we gave our first reading together the New York papers said: "In this corner the father, and in this corner the son, the battle of the century." And that proved so popular that ever since we've been receiving invitations. We've been on the Merv Griffin show, and channel thirteen, and we've been to a number of colleges: Berkeley, Boston University, Paterson State; we were even in London Institute of Contemporary Arts. I think this is the fifteenth reading, and the more we read the more invitations we get. They're interested in seeing the father and son together; they think we bridge the generation gap. In a sense we do—I think we transcend it—there's a certain common denominator. We practice peaceful coexistence, I always say; in my father's house they say, there's many mansions, and I say, in the field of poetry there are many types of poems. My father was a humble tobacco store owner, though he was up to snuff, he liked literature.

Allen: He died of cancer from smoking.

Louis: Well, he had a small store where there was no air, only a gas stove, and he smoked to beat the band, a chain smoker, and one thing led to another, so he died of cancer. I used to smoke a lot but I quit, now my struggle is two things: to write a good poem and have a sort of a diet, a mind over platter. Incidentally, I have an older son, who also writes poetry, he's a lawyer.

Allen: My lawyer.

Louis: When a felon needs a friend—and he has a hobby, space law . . . but he's modest, he doesn't want to compete with us. He believes in striking while the irons are hot.

Allen: While Kerouac and I were at Columbia, Burroughs was into exploring Time Square and the lumpden alienated criminal class. It was the time *Junkie* was being experienced. This was '45 to '48 or '49; Burroughs wrote the text of *Junkie* in '50 or '51; Burroughs appears in the Kerouac books, as old Bull Hubbard in *On the Road*, well, that was his comedy. Kerouac was perfect for people like Burroughs, Neal Cassady, people he was confounded by and intrigued by. Towards the end he was shut off from his older friends, due much to his drinking, I think.

Louis: What caused him to drink so much, Allen?

Allen: I think he just wanted to get out of existence. That was the first impression I had upon seeing his coffin.

Louis: And you think, the guy's lucky, his books are selling, and so on, had everything to live for. I can't figure that.

Allen: We all met, we were a small group of friends like you, we met the way you met. I was around Columbia and I ran into a friend who ran into Kerouac's girlfriend, in '44 I guess, and then a year later we heard from another friend about Burroughs, who was a great mind on Shakespeare, actually, he was always running around succinctly quoting Shakespeare. A couple dikes were arguing, I remember, and he said, "'Tis too starved an argument for my sword." So Kerouac and I went to see what Burroughs's soul was like, and it turned out to be very beautiful, melancholy, tender; he was reading Spengler, Yeats's *A Vision*, Blake, Rimbaud, Kafka's *The Castle*.

Louis: He was always chasing Rimbauds. I met Burroughs a long time ago; at that time I had a vague, undefined, floating suspicion, that Burroughs wasn't having such a good effect on Allen.

Allen: Well, we were smoking grass in 1945.

Louis: Then later on we got reconciled.

Allen: When we were beginning to get published, we had known each other over a decade. There was kind of a romance to the megalopolis in those days, walking under bridges reciting Hart Crane, listening to *The Warsaw Concerto* and *Rhapsody in Blue*, a kind of nostalgic melancholy about Manhattan. It's gone down the drain, at least for me, with all the horror, and the realization that New York is uninhabitable finally, the end of the line. I've been on a farm for the last few years. In a sense there is a continuation between the practice of Gertrude Stein, and William Carlos Williams and Burroughs, and my practice and Williams and Pound, and Kerouac is a self-originating genius who learned a great deal from Wolfe and Joyce. And Pound. The tradition of Einsteinian relativistic investigation into the measure of the art work, i.e., the language itself, the means, the matter of the art work, the language; investigation of the consciousness of the artist or the man which goes back to Gertrude Stein studying with William James at Harvard when James was investigating consciousness, religious experiences, and peyote back in the gay nineties.

DO: It seems that when Kerouac was talking about the boppers, that was an extension of the same tradition, in musical terms. Do you keep up with that now?

Allen: Yeah, I just put out a record, with Don Cherry and Elvin Jones; "Songs of Innocence and Experience," the poems of William Blake. I know them on account of a longtime contact with LeRoi Jones during the late fifties and early sixties. I used to go to parties with Ornette Coleman, Kerouac listened to everything he could get all the way up until the end. He used to go to Minton's and hear Parker and Gillespie. Contacts are very heavy in very weird ways; when Leary was at Harvard, I delivered psilocybin mushrooms to Thelonious Monk for Leary in the early sixties when it was all academically proper. And Leary had Dizzy Gillespie and his entire band up to Newton Center where he was doing his experiments. Burroughs and Leary know each other from before—Burroughs went up and stayed with Leary at Harvard; Burroughs, was one of the first people Leary checked up on. Leary's project you see was to check out not only businessmen and scientists and divinity students, but also artists, and he contacted a great number of people in the esthetic world, like Robert Lowell. Everybody has inspiration, everybody experiences it, and generally they push it down to the bottom of their consciousness. What we were into in '45 Kerouac and Burroughs, was the conscious attempt at development of awareness. At that time the war was over, there was a closed consciousness, and we felt that there was the assumption that material consumption was endless, that the nation was the American empire, that was *Time* Magazine; that this was the best of all possible worlds; even by 1959 *Life* magazine talking about us asked, "What's the matter with the great Casaba melon of American Society that these people don't want it?"

Everybody was thinking that it was like some great edible Casaba melon, that we were going to get more and more of, and it was never going to end. Finally we've come to the end of material consumption, because the sky is being destroyed over our heads.

DO: There is an understanding now, even in *Time* magazine, that things are a little bit different now than they were then, don't you think?
Allen: No, just read this week's *Time* magazine. Just as they had this venomous attack on Rachel Carson when she first published *Silent Spring*, which was probably before your time, they called her some kind of dirty c— for bringing up this problem—of pollution. Actually what they called her was some sort of hysterical, feminine, wobbly minded creep. So this new article by the Yale professor that was in the *New Yorker* magazine talking about the new consciousness as being a political solution, *Time* had led a vicious attack this week. It's the same people. It's the same business as usual, old consciousness conservatives that don't see that there really is a direct threat to the planet. They're all over the editorial pages of the *New York Times*, and they're all over *Time* magazine. The Pentagon spends $190,000,000 a year on public relations and the feedback to the public from defense contracts is another three hundred million through McDonald, Douglas, Jones, and the defense contractors. These are figures I got last week from Fitzgerald, who was a Pentagon cost accountant. So the total brainwash funding yearly is five hundred million dollars for the Military Industrial complex.

DO: If there's so much, is it because they have to work harder now?
Allen: No, it's because with all this cash flowing toward military destruction, seventy-five billion a year, at least half a billion flows out to convince the public that it's flowing in the right direction. So, the middle class, business as usual mentality, is not aware of the urgency and gravity of the earth

problem, the ecological problem. Stronger than them are the opinion makers, the molders of opinion in the P.R. business, who sell presidents. As the book says, the buying and selling of the president. They get a half a billion dollars to defend the present system of destructive industrial consumption mainly all military.

We were looking out of the plane coming from New York. There was this great blackish cloud hanging over New York for about thirty or forty miles, then the air got blue again, then slightly grey again over Syracuse. I was told that there are no fish left in Lake Onondaga. There are some in the Finger Lakes and Otsego, but not in Onondaga, which is one of the main Indian Lakes. The *New York Times* editorial about three weeks ago said that by the year 2000 the oceans will be in the condition of Lake Erie—dead. That was their conclusion in the editorial on the basis of all the scientific evidence they had.

Louis: Don't you think that there are alarms being raised now so that some measures will be taken?

Allen: Alarms raised? I don't think measures can be taken fast enough to deal with it.

Louis: Maybe as time goes on there will be more and more alarms raised so that the government and the other powers that be might be forced to take energetic and radical measures.

Allen: We have a cousin who works in New York in the city government, and he's working with garbage disposal. He said that out of fourteen thousand tons of daily garbage, something like six thousand were left on the street every day. Then I asked him if there was any plan in City Hall, on paper even, for garbage recycling—for real modern twentieth-century recycling—and he said on paper it doesn't even exist. On paper, such a plan doesn't even exist. Regarding industrial pollution, there doesn't exist on paper an inventory of pollution sources in America.

Louis: So it's still the best of times and the worst of times. There was a commission set up to study the Passaic River, and they came up with a diatribe against the authorities, so now people are beginning to be active in it, and pressure the city governments and state authorities to do something. When more pressure is applied, and more alarms are being raised, I think eventually in the nick of time, we'll be saved.

Allen: You know what the first public notice of the pollution of this was? Historically? In Williams' poem called "The Wanderer" which was in the Conrad Aiken anthology, in which he went down to the river bank and prayed to the goddess of the Passaic and asked her to bless him as the poet of the Passaic and the last line of the poem was "and the filthy Passaic consented." 1924. We must stop the population growth—keep it as zero, or else I don't think we can make much headway. The end of the consumption fetish hasn't begun to penetrate yet . . . penetrate the financial pages of the *NY Times, Forbes, U.S. News, and World Report,* the Chamber of Commerce, the National Association of Manufacturers, the housewife. I wonder if it's even filtered down to the college students, the idea of the end of the growth economy, the end of the upward spiraling economy that's absolutely necessary.

Louis: What about when the youth grows up, won't they have a little more enlightened viewpoint? Not old people like me who are almost gone, but the young people are more active and maybe if they get into positions of power, maybe they'll be able to do something.

DO: So many of them don't even want to work inside of the current system . . .

Louis: Maybe there'll be certain poets like Allen who'll prod them.

Allen: It'll take a lot more than me. The simplest way to think about it is that you dig New York has a power crisis now, or they had in the summer, and they're expecting it all the time. Now the specific moment of crisis is when it gets very hot and people turn on their air conditioners. So, because of the air conditioners, they're proposing to build atomic and other power sources along the Hudson and Long Island even though everyone knows that the atomic power sources will provide thermal pollution of the waters and also non-disposable radioactive waste. So, the obvious solution would be to turn off all the air conditioners—to end air conditioning in America as being a honky luxury that separates us from our environment and protects us in a sick way. But no one has proposed even a reduction of the air conditioners. All the propositions have to do with a growth rate in power, when the obvious conclusion is that we have to cut consumption not increase production where production is of uncertain feedback. Which means a reduction of the standard of living of the middle class in America, and the middle class I don't think will accept that because they're like a bunch of junkies basically who are addicted to air conditioners, addicted to gasoline, addicted to electricity.

DO: That's what Burroughs was getting at in *Naked Lunch.*

Allen: Yeah, that the heroin addiction was a parable of the addiction of the entire country to its growth economy which finally will burn down its veins. I had never formulated it as clearly as this year, but it seems to be more and more the analogy. If you say cut down the standard of living, that's shocking to a lot of people.

DO: But the "standard of living" you're talking about is keeping us alienated from our environment.

Allen: Luxuries. Luxuries which separate and alienate us from our environment, like individual automobiles which plaster over the landscape.

DO: If you cut down the standard of living now, what would you have left?

Allen: A lot more alert people.

Louis: Science and poetry. Science is power . . . poetry and literature are more like goals. Science is the means, and poetry and literature are the ends, giving man greater awareness, deeper insight, and richer delight in life.

Allen: The beat era was involved with an expansion of consciousness. Drugs were one instrument among many towards that.

DO: Do you think there is a danger in the overuse of drugs?

Allen: About the same as in an overuse of television.

Louis: When we were in Florida, I said to Allen to set a good example and not preach the use of drugs with the young people. I don't really see why someone should be such an emphatic expositor of the use of drugs. I think you can get high on words, or on literature, or on imagination. Marijuana is not very dangerous, but I tell Allen, if it's against the law, why tangle with the law? If we should abolish the law against marijuana, do that. Don't tell the young people that they should use drugs. I personally think that the use of some of them, speed for example, it's like embezzling their own nature. They don't know where they are. Maybe for Allen, who's a specialist among those who explore states of awareness, it might be all right. But for the average kid, I think it's a bad thing. One time Allen thought he was seeing reality; he thought that drugs were making him see the ultimate vision of reality, beyond the bounds of the senses. I told him he was merely deranging the senses. He thought it was new, he thought it was reality but it was just a different relationship.

Allen: I've got one thing to say about drugs—very simple. Their function is as counter or anti-brainwash. Deconditioning. They're one of many different methods of deconditioning. For maximum usefulness in deconditioning it's best to combine them with mediation-yoga.

Louis: Poetry really is an exploration of consciousness. If you ask poets what they're gonna write, they answer how do I know until I write it? In other words their writing is a means of exploring themselves, and finding themselves on paper. There's a fellow called Bruner who says that literature and poetry are both ways of knowing, because when you make comparisons or use figures of speech, you discover what most people are not aware of—the similarities and dissimilarities; you're widening the area of consciousness.

Allen: The best poetry is psychedelic, with its actual and potential effect on the body. What I suggest for anyone using drugs or politics is one hour of sitting every day, specifically, flatly, pragmatically, a way of balancing out that sort of thought and providing a center for experimentation, so that if there is any TV-like overuse, there's a place to go to clean the mind. Anybody who's had any experience with mushrooms or acid knows there's a total amplification of sensory data that comes in, an entire mandala appears of different sensory input, detail, during normal consciousness most of us are not aware of all that, of the ticking of the radiator during the conversation; we're filtering out the ticking as Leary used to say. We're conscious of everything at once, the highway noise, our own breathing, all the little motions and eye blinks and jaw chews simultaneously; the appearance of reality changes entirely, there is more detail in consciousness than is usually held by the mind.

Dylan reflects the tradition we were speaking of before, in the search for a politically divine consciousness, originally with "Blowin' in the Wind." Dylan's changed as we all have, as America has, he's changed; he's got five kids in his house; he's no longer standing at the door, wearing the clothes he once wore. I heard "Self-Portrait" and I like that, there's a lot of nice stuff in that. His poetry's become more condensed, that's what he was seeking about "John Wesley Harding" time. He told me his earlier words have a lot of holes in them, and he was looking for words in which every line advanced the story. When I asked him what he was doing like that over the phone he recited the one about the courthouse, "Drifters Escape," which, when you think of it, is like a Scotch border ballad, in which every line goes forward until the story's told. Dylan's attention is focused on minute particulars, like Blake said to do. I see him becoming less the poet, he's giving himself more to the musicianship lately. I listen to jazz musicians; I listen to the Byrds a lot, I used to sing Hare Krishna with them . . . that was when Crosby was with them. I spent a lot of time at McGuinn's house in '65. The Byrds are a rock group from the west coast, Dad, they sang a lot of Dylan songs to begin with.

At present, since '67, I'm interested in eliminating words, in condensation. Because I read my poetry in England to a poet I admire a lot, Basil Bunting, an old friend of Pound's, and he told me "Plenty energy, good poetry, too many words." Then I began condensing. "Kaddish" and "Howl" are less condensed; "Planet News" is more condensed. Williams told me, "If you don't got nothing more to say, just cut it off and put a couple of dots in the middle of the sentence, just to keep the active presentation of fact."

Louis: Don't you want to end it with some air of, say, conclusion.

Allen: The world is coming to an end.

Louis: Art or literature is supposed to impose a pattern on the welter of everyday life, so a poem isn't really life, it's sort of examining it, and picking out the most significant parts, so you can understand it better. That's what literature should do. If you just start a poem, or just end a poem anywhere, it's incomplete, I would say.

Allen: We don't know what a new art is yet for our modern consciousness, and anything that is active in presentation and seems to be real, keep, but when it begins slackening off into generalization or editorializing on the subject matter, or ending to have an ending, cut that off. Keep the fragments of the mind if you can't get the whole mind . . . Williams was influenced by Celine just as Kerouac was, as I have been, as Burroughs is, by the way. When I sent Williams "The Empty Mirror" manuscript, there was one long poem about Paterson, and he made a mark on the poem, in the middle of the paper, that he thought was really interesting, and the rest he thought was a beginning, and an end, and he thought it wasn't interesting. He said why don't you cut the rest out, keep to this, keep to the gist. If you have a fragment of the active, be satisfied with that, put that down.

The greatest technician that I knew was Kerouac. Every session of writing was a complete integral unit. If in the middle of the night he remembered something, he would begin another section marked off by a star to indicate a new, fresh beginning—it might be just a line, or a word, or a page, but instead of trying to go over the last, he would start, and go on, he would add on. Long and short sections, and each one is a day's work, in the *Dharma Bums*, or any of the later works.

DO: Do you do much rewriting, Louis?

Louis: Some, yes; but some of my best poems just jump out. My forte is the lyric, the expansion of an exclamation; Allen writes in long, looping lines, free verse; mine as a rule is more regular, traditional meter—my mental cast, my psychic outlook . . .

Allen: He writes like Dylan. He has a poem called "Terse." When verse is terse/ its zest is best."

Louis: Here are four lines, called "Fetters." Only fetters, is liberty/without its banks, can a river be?

Allen: He's a bondage freak.

An Interview with Allen Ginsberg

Harry J. Cargas / 1974

Nimrod, 19, Issue 1, Fall/Winter 1974, 24–29. Reprinted with permission.

Q: Poetry is rhythmic articulation of feeling—a phrase I've been arriving at for the last two years. Rhythmic and perhaps melodic articulation. But in any case, for spoken or nonmusical poetry, rhythmic articulation.

Is there an element of prophecy related to poetry?

Allen Ginsberg: Well, the articulation becomes most rhythmic when the body and mind are most elevated and the body and mind are most elevated when the inspiration, or breathing, and expiration, are long and open as in exalted states of body-mind consciousness. And at those moments the mind is very clear and mortal motives are seen and the voice often comes directly from the heart area of the body. And so there's likely to be an accuracy of speech that could be considered prophecy since the accuracy generally penetrates past, present, and future in its evaluation of emotional states, and the consequences of emotional states; actions and consequences of actions.

Q: Is a poet then different from other people?

G: Yes, in that his specialty is the rhythmic articulation of feeling during exalted or inspired states of consciousness. Other people have the specialty of perhaps being able to run faster during an inspired state of body-mind consciousness. Or cut open human bodies and pluck out defective kidneys or dance; with the poetic specialties articulating language.

Q: Is the poet's product, poetry, for everyone?

G: The more inspired he is, the more likely his language will penetrate through the fogs of imprecise language into other people's consciousness, directly or indirectly, and affect their breathing and their apprehensions.

Q: What do we do with translations, then? Is the translator a whole new artist?
G: I'm describing ideal, abstract poetry in response to an ideal, abstract question. You're in a sense changing the subject to translators and translations. One language to another, you mean?

Q: Yes.
G: Well, the guru is equal to the *om* of the seeker. The translation is as inspired as the translator, and the translator is as inspired as . . . he is. I don't know. Ezra Pound made like an intellectual and moral and spiritual yoga of translation. Put it to uses that other translators hadn't conceived: made it a part of his studies of rhythm, his studies of music, his studies of intellectual virtues and used it to correct his practice of English. There are very few translators whose purpose is so universal or so catholic.

Q: Do you see development in contemporary poetry?
G: There is a very definite sequence of logical developments throughout the whole twentieth century in poetics, starting with the silent poem between the eye and the mind which was not vocalized, a by-product of mechanical reproduction and printing and mass scale of books. And people having their own books and sitting at home by radios and firesides reading. So there was a late nineteenth-century development of non-vocalized poetry: with Yeats, Pound, Williams, Marianne Moore, Eliot, and the development of the spoken poetry sometimes tuned poetry with Yeats or chanted poetry with Pound. Or a completely spoken American East poetry vocalized with Williams. Then, as Pound pointed out, the nomenclature for measuring the lines of English poetry was taken from the classical poetic division of the line into feet. And the word feet came originally because the lines of poetry were danced as in the choruses of Greek plays. So Pound returned the body to poetry in the sense of poetry being spoken by a living body rather than just read, a voice aloud, on his way to pushing poetry back to dance. After a period of sleepiness in which the lessons of Pound and Williams weren't being picked up, mainly because of the war preoccupation of the academy, and a tendency toward satanic abstraction, the post-war poets continued the tradition of Pound. The post-World War II poets continued Pound's tradition of vocalizing poetry and an outgrowth of our efforts was the emergence of singing minstrels like Bob Dylan, who returned poetry to the condition of song. When it became song again, it renewed its hold on the general populace so that language was attended to by large masses of younger people who were sensitized to music, and formal music sensitized

them, or formal music made language sensitive matter. So they began listening to texts with the same precision that scholars had used to listen to Eliot texts, with footnotes and interpretations, so at this stage, the most advanced poetry in the American language is alive with music. And then in my own case, in the case of black brothers among poets, and some white minstrels, poetry's even gone forward and backward simultaneously to turn to the bardic practice of chanted, sometimes rhymed improvisation. Undoubtedly before the end of the century it will take on all of its ancient limbs or awaken all of its ancient limbs and do bardic, shamanistic, oral transmission including, perhaps, dancing. The nearest hint of that is the behavior of Mick Jagger, who sings language that he composes and dances at the same time.

Q: There are also people dancing the liturgy now in Christian churches.
G: And the body is returned to the liturgy.

Q: How about the notion of the political dimension of poetry?
G: Well, that's been traditional in the high, academic poetry, as Shelley, Blake, and Whitman proposed through their poems. That continues in this American apocalypse time in Robert Duncan's "Passages," in my own poem "America," in Burroughs' prose poetry books describing poetically the characteristics of our advanced police state: in poets that you're concerned with, the Berrigan brothers, who have actually gone to jail on the basis of poetic ideas.

Q: To switch to you personally, why do you write poetry?
G: Because I have permission to do so from my father and from William Blake and from Kerouac. Or, in the right order, my father, Kerouac, and Blake. Encouragement to do so from them. My father, having been a poet, Kerouac, having been a friend, and Blake having been an invisible guru.

Q: I want to get briefly into the question of poetry that's written under the influence of . . .
G: That's an old tradition: among Sufi poets and in India among some divinely inspired, intoxicated, god-intoxicated poets. The use of cannabis for intoxication or as an aid to that intoxication is very ancient. I'm interested in it as I'm interested in restoring certain archaic modern forms like music and chanting and speech. I have explored the drugs that were used by American Indians, Mexican and Peruvian Indians or Amazon Indians, as well as the herbs smoked by the Oriental Indians and Arabs, who were

poetizers. I've written poetry on all different drugs and without all different drugs. I've written poetry on the basis of meditation, on the basis of no meditation, on the basis of actual regular day mind, and also on the basis of LSD (for "Wales Visitation"), peyote (for Part II of "Howl")—but the bulk of my published work is not on any drugs at all. But some of the best work was done on drugs: some of "Kaddish," some of "Howl." So my conclusion is that you can't really make a rule, but that drugs and herbs are not incompatible with strong poetry, as many drunken novelists and poets all the way back to Anacreon attest.

Q: Given your wide range, are you being understood? Is your work being understood?

G: By many people. No poet is completely understood by everybody in his own time, generally. Except Homer, theoretically. Or unless it's a small group of people, a tribal group, or in a bardic situation. But given the giant overpopulation on the planet and the giant interconnected electronic network in my own nation and time, I'm pretty clearly understood by a large group of people, a large minority of people, partly because I've survived so long.

Q: Do you have a work schedule?

G: No work schedule at all. More and more random. I write at random. I carry a notebook all the time. Put a notebook out before I go to sleep, put a pen out, and I always have my implements ready. I just scribble little notations whenever I have a thought that's clear and strong enough to be writeable down. And after a while you get to a certain tact, or granny wisdom, as to what might be interesting to read later. I don't write by any regular hour schedule, though I do generally meditate on schedule when I get up in the morning when I have time. Today is the first day in about a month that I didn't first sit an hour.

Q: Are you the last person in the world to be using a fountain pen as you write things down?

G: What I heard is that some of the "magic marker" inks have a certain acid in them so that the "magic marker" ink eats through the paper in ten years. I have papers in my collection like letters from Burroughs or scribblings of my own that are twenty, twenty-five years old. So I'm old enough to measure the dangers of messing around with inferior robotic equipment. So I've got an Esterbrook, I think it is, pen for $2.50 from an old Jewish candy store on the Lower East Side, a stock of them 'cause I don't think they're still being made, and a bunch of nibs, and this year went back or about two years ago went back to the regular ink pen. I find it very convenient. It's more convenient than ball points. The ball points are hard to write with on all different kinds of surfaces.

Q: Do you read much poetry?

G: I read a lot. I get an enormous amount of contemporary writing in the mail. There are all sorts of books mimeographed and printed and typewritten and fragments sent to me on toilet paper. I read all of it when I can. I read Blake, I read Shakespeare, Pound, and a lot of fragmentary other poets on and off. I read a little poetry every day. As a poet, I have been given the freedom of live language, dancing like fire on my tongue.

Allen Ginsberg

**Lauren Jones, Barbara Weinberg, and David Fenton /
1974**

Ann Arbor Sun, May 17–31, 1974, 14, 22.

It's not every day that Allen Ginsberg comes to town. Yet it seems that he bestows his presence upon us here just often enough to make himself a true and trusted friend, rather than a welcomed visitor. He brings with him his poetics, his visions, his incredible knowledge, and an undying interest in everything about him.

This spring he came to town under the auspices of the Gay Liberation Front. He appeared "in concert" at Hill Auditorium on the evening of April 11. Along with his fellow traveler Bhagavan Das. An American who sings in traditional Hindu style, Ginsberg conducted a calm evening of chanting, singing, reading, and breathing.

The SUN and other local media-people were invited to attend a news conference-interview with Allen at the home of one of the organizers of the conference. We spent an enlightening, joyous afternoon talking with him. Starting from a description and demonstration of his present form of meditating he ran through a tremendous number of interesting and important questions and ideas: What follows is a transcript of some of our conversation.

SUN: What sort of meditation do you do?
Allen Ginsberg: A very simple form. First you need a pillow to get your ass up so you can get a three-point landing, or any way you can do it so your back can be straight. Then ears are aligned with shoulders, the small of the back in, belly out, belt loosened if you have a pot belly like I do, just to make sure you relax the belly. Back of your head supporting Heaven, hands in peaceful posture, peaceful mind—it is a traditional Sete-Zen posture.

SUN: Do you say a mantra?

AG: Instead of a mantra, something similar. The point of the mantra is to focus attention and to interrupt the thought forms, the mechanical flow of thoughts. The main activity in my meditation is paying attention to the breath leaving the nostrils and dissolving in space, so that as mind wanders into discursive thought, thought forms, fantasies, or sleepinesses, attention is switched back over to the breath coming out of the nostril dissolving into space. Paying attention to the slight touch of the air leaving the nostril, and mindfulness of the space into which the breath dissolves, so mixing breath with space, real space, mixing the mind with the breath, and so mixing mind with space. Not paying attention to anything that goes on inside, that is not tripping, not getting high, and not looking for a vision, but accepting space as the place where you actually are. It is a basic Buddhist exercise called mindfulness and a sort of atheistic form—it doesn't require superstition and it is just sort of an elemental observation of mind forms. In the process of sitting a long time you become familiar with all the different thoughts that arise in profile and also have the experience of cutting through them and switching back to breath.

SUN: From "Howl" and "Kaddish" to Kerouac, and Chicago to OM, and now breath—how did you get from there to here?

AG: Well, I'm forty-eight years old—I've survived. But to begin with the basis of my poetics always was a sort of visionary thing beginning with a breakthrough in 1948 when I had a hallucination of hearing Blake's voice and thought I saw some sort of eternal space. Then about 1950 Neal Cassady, a friend and lover, got into Edgar Cayce, a weird spiritualist trip that involved a lot of reincarnation theory. Kerouac thought Neal had gone crazy and decided to check out the sources of reincarnation and spiritual-ism that Casey was proposing and went back and read a lot of Buddhist Works. So Kerouac went through a sort of Buddhist phase which was very beautiful and very productive, based on the one Buddhist tenet, the first noble truth which is existence is suffering—the idea dominated Kerouac's writing from *Big Sur* until he drank himself to death.

Then by 1955 the San Francisco poetry scene was heavily loaded with Buddhist meditation—people were going around the mountains and prac-ticing yoga and meditation and fucking like Tibetan tantrists. In 1962 I was in India with Peter Orlovsky and picked up on some Hindu teaching and the Hare Krishna mantra and brought that back and began chanting about

1963. My poetry anyway is basically based on a long breath and long lines, so I found the theory of mantra to be really interesting in relation to my own poetic practice as exercises in awareness of breath and uses of breath. That trip I also began branching out and doing some sitting in Zen monasteries with Gary Snyder in Kyoto.

I ran into an interesting Hindu in '70 who gave me a good mantra so I started doing some kundalini sitting, and in '71 I ran into a Tibetan lama. He has had a lot of experience in hip culture, so he knows that whole scene, and also talks hip talk. He took off his robes and started drinking scotch and dropping acid to see what that was like, and he concluded that what was wrong with the American scene is that everyone was trying to trip all the time, but that the basic nature of mind-consciousness was no tripping and that the best way to arrive at a grounded state where there is no tripping at all—which is no projection of fantasy on the outside at all—was just basic sitting practice. So he began teaching the potential of the breath. I ran into him.

So what was at first considered to be beatnik bullshit about Buddhism or dilettantism twenty years ago had developed into a very firm, very strong practice for a lot of people. Sitting was always a part of the whole beatnik heritage, so everyone was mocking it, saying, well, what a bunch of goof-offs, and now we're sitting all the time and everybody else is running with ulcers.

SUN: Well, there is now a very large spiritual movement encompassing young people and I wonder how you react to that?

AG: Well, the impulse is legitimate, so the problem is finding a sensible practice, like the revolutionary impulse of the sixties was typically legitimate, but the problem was to find a proper practice. I'm more interested in getting into something that is useful than in something that is not useful. I think the whole movement toward inwardness, introspection, meditation, is absolutely necessary and useful, socially. I don't see a conflict between political activity and meditative activity because the prospect is of clarification of one's own awareness, which, as in the case of jiu-jitsu, necessarily precedes action, so that you don't make a hysterical move, and hit the air instead of the nose. It's basic common sense, you don't act out of blind freakout, so that if people want to take action, they know what they are doing and can get it together. Like way back in '68 in Chicago I was using the mantra OM as a chant to try and cool the scene in the midst of a lot of rapid hysteria on either side. There were enough people who had the realization that some really calm center was necessary and would even cool the tear gas scene, which it did occasionally.

SUN: Speaking of Chicago, how do you find the people who organized that doing now?

AG: I went to Chicago and talked to Dellinger during the recent conspiracy-contempt trials, and one thing is that a lot of people who were carrying a heavy load during the sixties have had like physical damage from the action and the strain of time. John Sinclair has gone through such a heavy conflict with the entire apparatus of the police-state and beat them, finally. His wire-tapping case was actually the first court judgement to limit Nixon and the plumber's power. John won the decision that the government did not have the right to tap, and that was a crucial decision in the development of Watergate. But now Sinclair has been warned that he needs to take it easy, and Dellinger has had a whole bunch of operations on his gall bladder. Others have decided that they had better do some introspection like Rennie and Jerry. Ed Sanders has gotten more and more involved in literary work, putting his poetry together, but also into meticulously detailed research into police state structure and technologies.

SUN: You were involved with him in that whole thing about the CIA importing heroin from Indochina, right?

AG: That was more my specialty. It resulted in a very good book, *The Politics of Heroin in Southeast Asia* by Alfred McCoy, and also resulted in a spread of knowledge of that situation to the public, so it was somewhat successful, although it has not come to any court or congressional activity.

From the point of view of local journalism there is an interesting Watergate-connected business in that most of the plumbers unit were also narcs, interchangeably. Egil Krogh was head of the White House Cabinet Committee on International Narcotics Control (WHCCINC), and also head of Operation Intercept. G. Gordon Liddy was the original prosecutor of Timothy Leary and led a series of Watergate-like warrantless raids on Leary's Millbrook *ashram*. Hunt was White House specialist in Corsican and Syrian narcotics connections. Corsican smugglers in small planes (as reported by *Life* in the early sixties) ran the opiates from Indochina to Marseilles. After World War II American intelligence groups, in order to win allies against the commies, had worked with the gangster Corsicans to take over the Marseilles docks, and so created a situation for international smuggling there. The expert in all of this was Hunt. Barker was Batista's narcotics advisor at a time when Battista was taking a rake-off from Meyer Lansky for the drug traffic through Cuba. Barker, McCord, and the others were all involved with a Cuban refugee group which was involved with taking over the heroin traffic in the east coast according to the Narcotics Bureau.

Seymour Hersh of the *NY Times* surfaced a hitherto secret report from the CIA saying that our allies were not cooperating with us in the attempt to stop heroin traffic. The next day Egil Krogh, as head of WHCCINC, denounced that report and said there was no truth to it, yet he had ordered it up. So WHCCINC was busy attempting to denounce, deny, or suppress the story about US government involvement in opiate trafficking, and that, plus the persecution of Leary and trying to get him kidnapped from Afghanistan, and Operation Intercept were apparently the major activities of this cabinet committee on international narcotics control.

Another activity was going around interrogating people to find out if they could get anything dirty on Ellsberg with relation to narcotics. That was one of the things they were stealing from the psychiatrist, to see if Ellsberg had dropped acid.

SUN: Of course, most people would totally disbelieve that the US government has a strategy to bring in heroin and stop marijuana.

AG: Well, when McCoy's book came out, the CIA tried to stop it. Cord Meyer Jr. tried to stop it. He was the CIA man who had also organized the subversion of the National Student's association years before and had been the big payoff man who organized covers for cultural freedom and *Counter* magazine, a CIA-front intellectual magazine—interferences in domestic intelligence and intellectual life. Which means that the CIA all along has been involved with interfering in American domestic politics and discussion, just like they are to stop Marchetti's book on the history of the CIA's illegal practices now.

SUN: I thought they succeded in stopping Marchetti's book?

AG: No, the book's coming out—with forty-four blank spaces the CIA won't let them print, but everybody will know that the forty-four are by gossip, and Jack Anderson will probably have them.

SUN: But the other deep question is did they desire to have a planned effect on the US population through the manipulation of drug traffic?

AG: Simultaneous with Operation Intercept there was this tremendous flood of pure heroin into New York City, while they were busy just trying to stop the grass.

But also, since there were attempts on all levels of police bureaucracy to isolate, identify, infiltrate and disrupt left-wing and anti-war movements, to what extent was the local drug scene infiltrated by cops or intelligence of some sort, and sort of corrupted from a flower-power acid grass scene to a downer, Quaalude, junk and speed scene? There is a great deal of knowledge now that most narcotics cops were also involved in peddling and have a working relationship with organized crime, as police busts across the country have proved. And we also know that the Narcotics Bureau and Army Intelligence were always conferring with each other on the dope counterculture—the threat of it and the threat of underground newspapers. And we know that narcotics always was an instrument of the police bureaucracy for repression of political activity.

SUN: What does an individual who is aware of this do? How does he try and stand up against the government or country that is based on this?

AG: For one thing, go around and do actual research on information. I did a lot of research, and helped conceive McCoy's book, contributed to it. One thing I did was sneak through the files of *Time/Life* in '71 and xeroxed everything I could find. So general infiltration and research, and of course, mass education. A poet can contribute poetry also. What the poet does is write the truth. I thought it was a really important part in the demythologization of the police bureaucracy to show that they were involved in dope pushing.

The police bureaucracy is really so huge that nobody knows its extent or its plans or its penetration. So, what to do? Propaganda in a general consciousness is necessary so that people understand how easy it is, and what a threat it is. For political change techniques probably the only effective way is to have a totally transparent head, you know, so that every gesture that you make is public and open. That purifies the motives in a way by political necessity; you can't have secret paranoic cells organizing aggressive violence.

SUN: Like the SLA?

AG: The SLA gestures tend to be supportive of police bureaucracy groups. The traditional tactic of the police was to send in agent provocateurs to provoke crazy street actions. Like Fred Hampton's chief of security was an FBI agent. He was the loudest mouthed violent talker and the one bringing guns and making sure that everybody had the right kind of gun, he knew which guns they had. Turns out that he brought guns that day to Hampton's house, and also brought some downers and knocked Hampton out so that Hampton was downed, dead asleep in his bed when the police burst in and started shooting.

SUN: Then it seems that you are implying that the actions that are most effective at this time are mass-based, mostly legal actions, public and open?

AG: The actions that are most effective are the actions that are not manipulative. Because the purpose of the police groups is to manipulate and create distrust and paranoia, open non-manipulative actions by people with transparent heads are necessary to create trust again. The left went into a long period of manipulative hysteria or fear and paranoia, and the police agencies took advantage of the situation and made it impossible to have mass meetings. Everybody is scared of it; nobody wants to call one for fear they'll call a confrontation with the police and get people shot down like at Kent State.

I think that basically it would be a good idea for everybody to have knowledge that the situation is hopeless to begin with, and until people stop tripping and actually realize the extent of the situation and the vastness of the police bureaucracy—until then I don't think people can begin to take clear action to try and deal with the situation as it is. The Buddhist suggestion is that the first noble truth is that existence is pain, existence is hopeless—that's like a very sensible attitude from which to take whatever clear straightforward action can be taken to relieve pain and suffering. Until you hit the bottom you can't really begin to act compassionately. Until you realize the full extent of the difficulty you can't measure it or take steps to alter it at all.

Like late sixties people were assuming that the entire American public would want dope, rock and roll, and fucking in the streets, which actually was a sort of charming mantra, or poetic imagination, as an ideal thing. It was the Fugs and Ed Sanders who came up with that and everybody blamed it on Sinclair. Why does the Gay Lib group attack Sinclair for that phrase—the context is obviously such a cheerful thing?

SUN: It was the emergence of a naïve, but future-looking movement.

AG: I don't think it was so naïve, and if not future-looking, at least a platonic ideal to measure our present degradation, or to measure the hardness of the streets. The gay lib group thought that the word fucking was sexist, but I don't. We went over to Sinclair's last night with Harry Kevorkian and Stephen Miller who had never met John, but who had all sorts of ideas about John's machismo. It turned out that John was sitting there in a completely gentle awareness of his own physical doom: he apparently has a problem arising, a very painful back problem. It has deepened him enormously. He always was very sensitive, but now his sensitivity is clear and near the surface. He is having to reappraise his entire world view and his lifestyle. I don't think he regrets all that activity he did because it was a major contribution to whatever success the movement had in the late sixties. The reason John actually got in trouble was that he was organizing in Detroit the first

communal mixing of black and white artists on a large scale that was having international reverberations with black and white musicians and poets.
I was involved with his Detroit Artist's Workshop; I used to come and do
benefits. John published a piece of mine in the Artist's Workshop Series.

SUN: It's a history that a great many people are not aware of.
AG: Yeah, well he did pretty good. Ten years of it—it all started back in
Detroit. It's amazing—I wonder to what extent the gay community here is
aware of what it involved. John has a tremendous historical memory and
experience with both police bureaucracy and the law, on the national level,
and local organizing. So they have great fundamentals and obviously should
be included in any kind of community organization, in terms of local politics. They sort of led the way to try and organize locally, way back early.

Allen Ginsberg: Interview

Michael Andre / 1975

Unmuzzled Ox, Vol 2, No. 2, 1975, 14–25. Reprinted with permission.

OX: I was wondering how you felt your method of composition differed from "projective verse" [the verse-theory of Charles Olson]?

Allen Ginsberg: Well, I don't think it differs particularly. . . . On the other hand, you'd have to say, is projective verse anything other than "spontaneous bop prosody"? If you want to subsume it under a literary category, then sure, I like that phrase . . . What is projective verse? I've read the essay a number of times and it's very technical but it was intended mainly to impress college professors with an excusable terminology for why people could write as freely as they wanted. . . . That's what Olson—

OX: Are you suggesting—

AG: Did you hear that? That's what Olson *once said* the intention of the essay was. Not to prescribe rules for writing but to describe a *fait-accompli* in academic terminology so that professors would have less resistance. And also, maybe, to define a method for people who weren't sure, to clarify what was going on. As far as I understand what was going on, it's simply just follow the zig-zag of your mind while writing. If you're working on a typewriter, the typewriter imposes a few rules like a margin or no margin, and a few extra slash bars, and spaces, so that you can play on the typewriter like an instrument while writing. . . .

OX: Just yesterday I was reading an essay by [Erwin Strauss], a phenomenologist—I guess—who had taught at Black Mountain and used some of the same phrases as Olson—"the human world"—

AG: "The human universe"?

OX: Right—the essayist used "world."

AG: I haven't read Olson's essays in the *Human Universe*. What I've looked at I approve of. . . .

OX: Does "phenomenology" mean anything to you? Would you characterize yourself that way?

AG: The word is interesting. Under yoga or LSD or paying attention to surroundings, I wind up saying, "I'm studying the actual phenomenology of mind consciousness." But as a body of texts, as a body of philosophical texts, I haven't read any of them. Why does this interest you?

OX: Just that over the past few days I've become curious about the relation of philosophy to your work. In an old copy of *Tri-Quarterly* I happened upon last week, a Rumanian named Cioran was criticizing Westerners interested in Eastern philosophy as necessarily inconsistent. Do you feel that you are inconsistent? Are there certain aspects of Eastern thought, such as reincarnation, in which you don't believe?

AG: My interest in yoga isn't an interest in philosophy so much as a physiological practice, that's one thing. There are some philosophical attendants to that. I don't particularly believe in reincarnation—I'm not interested in it anyway—I'm interested in other matters. But I wouldn't put reincarnation out; it's just not my concern. I don't know why Cioran makes a statement that there is something inconsistent with being interested in Oriental philosophy or Oriental methods, particularly in the twentieth century. What philosophies would be more consistent to [a] strange American esoteric? Aryan philosophy? Or Rumanian? Or Russian? It sounds like a generalization of a vague order. . . . If there were some specific arguments—. . . it's just a big statement, and I just answer, "No, I disagree." Period. Okay?. . . .

OX: He claims in the course of this essay that the chief Western urge was towards being and suffering and being-in-suffering—

AG: What? Utter bullshit. I mean, to begin with the phrase "the chief Western urge" and then end the sentence with "being-in-suffering" makes you sound like some horrible German talking asshole. I mean, something out of Burroughs. Or Hitler.

To resolve the problem, or get it back to order: underneath the academic or public traditions of the West, there's always been the esoteric private hermetic stream. Go back through the great Western poets—Whitman, Emerson, Shelley, Coleridge, Blake—back through Boehme, all the way back to Pythagoras who said, "Everything we see when awake is death; and when asleep, dream." This Gnostic transmission begins very early and, though I am not a scholar, I've read in scholarly books that it proceeds originally out of the same middle Eastern consciousness that also travelled into the Orient, and brought ideas of the Sun God . . . to India, and served as the foundation of the Vedas. So that Eastern metaphysics which involves multiplicity of consciousness and multiple universes and simultaneous universes and alteration in mind consciousness in yoga has its Western traditional school of thought up to Basilides. The Great Void—Sunyata—of the Buddhists has its Western equivalent in the Abyss of Light. So that the basic conceptions of thought are parallel, as basic conceptions, in the more sophisticated realms of Western thought. So the whole argument about the Orient being alien to us is in essence silly—and not interesting—because it assumes that Western thought is all hard Jehovah Christ the Church liberal humanism but forgets the more interesting thought. Shakespeare's "our little life is rounded by a sleep" and "we are such things as dreams are made of" is, precisely, the same statement about the nature of suchness, the nature of existence, as the Prajnaparamita Sutra, the "highest perfect wisdom" Buddhist sutra. Is that making sense?

(*The talk moves to Robert Creeley*)

AG: I think Creeley realized I suffered from a feeling of being put down for some sort of vulgarian, and so he brought all his fine brain at one point to support me. That did me a lot of good because it also gave me permission, you know, to go and run around in my own mind.

That's an interesting aspect about the whole community of letters, that's emerged over the last twenty years. There's a comradeship and natural telepathic friendliness and mutual encouragement based on a desire to change the nation as much as on, or more than on—mutual back-scratching. A realization that we want to move forward, we want to locate ourselves, and, if we can, maybe also find a place for America.

OX: James Wright in his interview in *Unmuzzled Ox* said you brought writing a sense of community.
AG: I've wanted to actually, consciously wanted to. . . . It's a notion . . . from the forties and fifties—except it had to be based on more than being geniuses together. *Being Geniuses Together* is the title of a book by Robert MacAlmon about the great circle of D. H. Lawrence and Hart Crane and so

on—a very good book, by the way, filled with gossip—if you want to know who was sleeping with whom, who fell out of their bed and almost expired. Recently reissued with some prefatory addenda by Kay Boyle. Finest book on the subject I know.

But what I'm saying is—for our own times—the prophecy and the desire was to have a community of bards whose perception might alter the consciousness of the nation as Gertrude Stein's did, as Whitman's did. And now even more urgently needed because of the extremely bad karma in the country at large, as it becomes, contrary to Whitman's instructions, more and more materialistic, more and more involved with conspicuous consumption to the point where America with six percent of the world's population today produces seventy percent of the world's waste garbage. So that's a very heavy karma for an American poet to deal with if he's a member of a polis called America—which at one time was a very interesting conception for a poet—it was Whitman's, it was Crane's, it was Pound's. . . . So to the extent that anyone gets enraptured or entrapped into that particular elitist role or necessary humble service—whichever way you want to put it—you're stuck with America.

(*The conversation moves from America to poetic improvisation*)

AG: I was talking with Chogyam Trungpa, Lama, about a year ago last summer in San Francisco. I noticed how he was travelling around giving lectures on Buddhism and I said, "Don't you get tired of it. I find I'm tired runnin' around reading my poems." And he said, "Ah, that's because you don't like your poetry." And I said, "What?! What do you know about my great poetry anyhoo?" And he said, "Ah, you don't like poetry otherwise you'd enjoy doing it. The trouble is you're always reading it out of a book there, out of a text, you're always doing the same thing, what's the matter with you, why don't you go up on the stage and improvise, improvise like a great poet? Like Milarepa? He used to improvise. Why do you have to read something on a page?" He also said, "I don't like your beard. I want to see what you look like." And I said, "Why don't you stop drinking, mister?" And he said, "Ah c'mon, let's see what you look like under that mask." So I went into the bathroom and cut off my beard.

OX: That's why you did it?
AG: That's the way I did it. Why? Then we went immediately to a lecture he had and at the end he asked me to sing something, so I improvised a little

singing—moon, June, spoon; beard, weird, tear—something monochordal—a ditty which wasn't very good. And he said, "You're not singing from your heart. You're just too smart." But the next night I had to give a reading for another Tibetan lama and I didn't feel any poetry I had written was appropriate, so I just went from chanting using a few chords on the harmonium to a long sort of almost poetical monologue bittersweet chant—"How sweet to be in America surrounded by petrochemical leprosy," and that led to a twenty minute improvisation about safety in the city, bombs, China, how we were enjoying the Viet prosperity. From then on every time I gave a reading I tried to do some improvisatory work. Then I learned the three chords of the blues, so that gave me a form I could work with, using as a model "James Alley Blues," a twelve-bar blues by 1920s musician Richard Rabbit Brown.

OX: This might be a jump. You are one of the few poets who are still willing to candidly attack other poets.
AG: I don't think I've ever attacked anybody.

OX: What about your controversy in the *New York Times* with Richard Howard?
AG: If you notice in that I didn't spend much time putting down Howard; I spent most of my time proposing and protesting the virtues of Gregory Corso. That's one thing I learned a long time back from Mark Van Doren. I noticed he never criticized anyone, so I asked him, "How come you don't write about things you don't like?" And he answered, "Why in heaven's name would I write about something I'm not interested in? Why waste time?" I always recalled that remark in the fifties and sixties when there were a great many attacks on Kerouac's work and on my work. For the most part I never replied in public, and avoided as much as possible direct personal attacks. I made a few generalizations which seemed angry—like academics "wouldn't know real poetry if it came up and buggered them in broad daylight"—those are apothegms of a mock heroic nature.

When I first sent Williams [my] poems, he said, particularly regarding one poem called "Paterson," that the center was all right, but the beginning and end were weak, so why not just, like painters, paint out that area, and only preserve what is active? If you want to present the method of the mind, present what is active, even if it's only fragments—a fragment that has punch is of more interest than endless reams of denunciations of bad poetry. As part of the economy of means, it's not worth attacking inferiors. That's why I keep wondering why D—doesn't stop attacking me—he contributes to the energy of my nature. Poor old D—, he's done me many a service. He mentioned my name in *Life* magazine. Attacking a poet only interests people; that's what happened to me, that's what's happening sometimes to Berrigan and Padgett.

OX: Talking some months ago, you asked me what kind of question I was going to ask you, and I said I was going to ask you what you thought of Maynard Krebs, and you said you'd never heard of Maynard Krebs. And that not only fascinated me, it fascinated everyone my age I told that to—
AG: Who's Maynard Krebs? Who, who?

OX: Who is Maynard Krebs? Maynard Krebs was a TV character, who was loosely based on your character, he was on television for five years, and every kid I know grew up thinking Maynard Krebs was what a beatnik was. It fascinated me—
AG: I literally never heard of Maynard Krebs. What was the name of the program?

OX: *The Many Loves of Dobie Gillis.*
AG: One thing, I don't have a television. I've been on television a lot but I have so little access to television that I've rarely seen myself on it. . . . The main interest in looking at television for me was to check on what is being fed the populace; what is the party line?. . . . That's different from trying to read Shakespeare to see what the heart line is. . . . I rarely look at television for the same reason I rarely read the masses of literary criticism that come out, or advertisements; it's not that interesting. I just get bored. It's like I don't take junk. I used to take junk on and off but I found my own natural healthy metabolism began rebelling against the somnolence of junk as well as against the secondhand nature of the experience of junk . . .

OX: An awareness of media puts you in a different class from most other poets. Comparing your "Wichita Vortex Sutra" to other political poems, the reason it seems so much stronger was because the other poets act as if they had first hand awareness of Johnson, or, say, McNamara, whereas you realized we were getting it through media, and you were able to talk about politics the way it's really experienced.
AG: My basic method was transcription of data of my consciousness. . . . Since the data of my consciousness included radio and newspaper, then that was part of my primary data . . . [But] I don't agree with a generalization I first

saw in Rexroth that the Beat Generation is a creation of the media. . . . That was always sort of a media way of putting us down. . . . Our breakthrough to public consciousness was at the Six Gallery Reading in San Francisco, and that was just an old-fashioned poetry reading. As Shakespeare said, "One touch of nature makes the whole world kin. . . ." Our ethos was explanation of our own nature—not necessarily exploitation of the media, use or abuse of the media. It then fell into place that, once we knew our own nature and were grounded in our own nature, we could communicate not only to our own nature but to our fellow nature. We didn't have to be excited in front of the media; we could be sincere in front of the media. And sincerity in front of the media was not a virtue widely advertised in 1955. It wasn't manipulation by the media; it was a refusal to be manipulated by the media. It's very easy to "use" the media and the way you use it is, just be absolutely sincere under all conditions. . . . Speak from the heart in every circumstance, even if it is clear that nobody but you will be listening. . . . That means in poetry and in television and someday your maiden aunt in Idaho will slap her knee and say, "For the love of God, Ginsberg's making sense."

OX: You've written a lot about your mother's illness.
AG: I wrote one poem.

OX: And the play.
AG: It came from the poem.

OX: Is there some psychiatric analysis of the illness you accept?
AG: I never heard one really formulated; it was very vague as I remember it; dementia praecox was the term for schizophrenia. But I don't believe any of the professional people involved ever made any analysis longer than three sentences, really. So there's none for me to accept or reject. So I just see it in experiential terms, what my relationship to her was, and what her relationship to her father was, and what the contact was. Actually the dominant conception that I have at this point is that her so-called madness was, as Ronny Laing pointed out in relation to psychotic experience, a somewhat distorted but genuine message of social difficulties in the neighboring society as well as her own position in society. Her madness was as it were a sort of Aesopian language in which to break through the limited consciousness of Paterson, 1935–1945, and talk about world consciousness and planetary consciousness and planetary robot hysteria, and Armageddon and Apocalypse. In other words, she's saying if the radio is talking to her

or if she hears wires in her head from the ceiling, they go back to Roosevelt and the potentates and powers and Hitlers of the world. It's a metaphorical but almost a literal way of describing what the actual circumstance was in America then and now. If anybody wants to say, my house is filled with wires leading back to the White House, it's quite true. Because you pick up a copy of *Time* magazine and you see that they're writing a big thing on the world dope problem and they're ignoring, completely ignoring, the CIA role in the very week that Al McCoy's book, *The Politics of Heroin in Southeast Asia*, appears. It means that *Time* magazine which is in my house is, in some way, an agent of the CIA. You turn on the radio and you won't hear any pertinent news about what's actually happening. You open the *Times* and they're talking about the "enemy," as if I had an enemy in Vietnam, or as if anyone had an enemy there. Turn on the television, and turn on the Republican Convention, you didn't actually get what was going on in Miami because, as *Time* magazine pointed out in a slip of consciousness, because television has been accused of being an *agent provocateur*, they played down any street action including the mass arrests, month-long fasting and tear gassing—which were just as interesting this year as in Chicago had they been played up. So all the wires in the room do lead back to the CIA and the White House and the Authoritarian Powers That Be—if you want to interpret it so. In a sense my mother's illness was only a metaphor for a statement of fact and an attempt to break through that network. Very often in such situations you might get your wires crossed, you might get your facts messed up, you might mistake one set of persecutors for another, you might get things balled up a little; but the basic thrust of her breakthrough of consciousness was legitimate, I think. The point finally is, my mother, politically speaking, is no more mad than I. K.—or, say, Max Lerner. My mother died in '56, the war had been going on three years already in Indochina, so let us say Cardinal Spellman, agent Edward Lansdale and the CIA were all conspiring to thwart Ho Chi Minh, and put in their own paranoiac Christian government in Vietnam. They were considered hard-headed realists and my mother was considered mad, but between my mother and that gang of murderous psychotics, who was mad? Who was sane? Who really had a grasp of reality? Their madness was perhaps more subtle so they could inflict their vast mad trip on everyone. They were just as disoriented as my mother and they did more harm than she did. . . .

OX: There was a poem in *Empty Mirror*, "The Terms in Which I Think of Reality"—are they still the terms in which you think of reality?

AG: Somewhat. It was really an attempt of define local particulars. I wrote it in the madhouse. At the time, I had had a visionary experience and I realized the only way I was going to articulate it was detail by detail, concrete example by concrete example, particular by particular, to make a larger pattern and an interconnected consciousness. The vision was of that—the world was an interconnected consciousness, one single being interconnected, a vision of Indra's net, so to speak—a Buddhist Hindu metaphor.

The terms were: "The world is a mountain of shit, and if it's going to be moved at all, it's going to be moved by handfuls."

Interview with Allen Ginsberg

Alan Twigg / 1978

Georgia Straight, Vol. 12, Issue 575, December 1–8, 1978. Reprinted with permission.

Allen Ginsberg is The Great Fraternalist.

Descendent of Milton, Blake and Whitman. . . . Lover, Best Man, then Pallbearer of Kerouac. . . . Pallbearer of Olson. . . . Confidante of William S. Burroughs . . . Rider on Ken Kesey's Magic Bus. . . . Deliverer of Sergeant Pepper's Lonely Hearts Club Band to eighty-two year old Ezra Pound in Italy. . . . music maker with Dylan and Lennon. . . . Elected King of the May in Prague, then expelled from Czechoslovakia . . . Expelled from Cuba for criticizing Castro's anti-gay policies . . . Teacher at Jack Kerouac's School of Disembodied Poetics . . . Fund raiser for *Georgia Straight* on numerous occasions . . . Leader of anti-Vietnam War initiatives . . . Lover of Men . . . Leader of anti-Nuclear Madness initiatives . . . Lover of Man. The following interview was recorded in Vancouver, November 25, 1978.

Alan Twigg: It seems Ronald McDonald has a firm grip on the consciousness of North America these days. And it's getting worse.
Allen Ginsberg: That's what (William) Burroughs says: You take a bad situation and it only gets worse and worse. But on the other hand, I don't see any cause to be totally depressed about it. It's just a lot of illusions. It's better to acknowledge them and make use of them. To work with it. Instead of resisting or being optimistic or pessimistic, why not just accept the mind as it presents itself?

Twigg: Like in the title poem to *Mind Breaths*?
Ginsberg: Yeah. Most of the poems in that book were written as by-products of simply sitting. The mind is consciousness; the breath is the vocalization of that consciousness. The title poem was written in '73 when I was

sitting ten hours a day for weeks at a time in Teton Village (Colorado) with a whole group of Tibetan-style meditators. It was a set of thought forms which I reproduced as a mind trip . . . imagining my breath going all around the world, passing through places I'd been to, coming over my father's head in Paterson, New Jersey and back into the meditation room.

Twigg: As you get deeper into meditation, are your feelings about the political influences of art changing?

Ginsberg: No. I don't think art has anything to do with politics in its motive. The art that I practice is just intended to record my mind which might include politics. So there's gay material, or political material, or meditative material or autobiographical material, or spontaneous funk material. Whatever comes up. Politics just naturally comes up when you're living in the industrial revolution-degeneration of the United States.

Twigg: How would you approach writing a "Howl" for 1978?

Ginsberg: As a matter of fact, I started writing another little "Howl" last night. I've been ill with Bell's palsy and herpes and that depression has given a lot of insight. I realized I was suffering and everybody else was. Today there's an enormous amount of unrelieved suffering. There's inflation, deprivation of private relations . . . constant frustrations of machinery . . . the constant threat of plutonium poisoning. But you can work with that depression. You can work with that hopelessness. It can all lead to compassion.

Twigg: The way you talk, I get the impression you're becoming more of a teacher than a poet. Does that instructive role ever get in the way of your writing?

Ginsberg: Naw. That kind of material is too transitory and it isn't intense enough. If I've had a transition at all, it's been more into music.

Twigg: What happened to those songs you recorded with Dylan?

Ginsberg: I have them at home. I did another album in 1975 with David Mansfield who's with Dylan's orchestra now. But Columbia records wouldn't put it out because it was too dirty. Also it had *CIA Dope Calypso* on it. Carl Bernstein, in the *Rolling Stone* article on CIA penetration into the media, pointed out that William Paley, the head of CBS, had CIA associations. So the merchandizing people said they were afraid to play the record for Paley, lest they lose their jobs.

Twigg: How long have you known Dylan?

Ginsberg: Since 1963. He's the greatest orator I've ever heard. Like Milton or Blake. I saw his new tour in Buffalo and I was astounded.

Twigg: And John Lennon? Do you still see him much?

Ginsberg: Yeah. I spoke to Yoko Ono about two weeks ago. They've been living in Japan. I've known him (Lennon) since '65. Dylan introduced us in London during the *Don't Look Back* period. Then about 1975 I saw him in New York and we were jamming together. He said he'd been lying around in bed with his earphones on, listening to the radio. He'd heard this guy reciting a poem and he thought it sounded like Dylan. Then they announced it was me reading "Howl". . . . He told me he always wondered what I did. So this recognition was charming because he had been so open and listening to me even though he hadn't known who I was.

Twigg: Do you see the current punk trend as an evolution out of the beatnik/hippie things?

Ginsberg: Yeah. I see punk as more or less a kind of "kabuki" (Japanese semi-illusionist theatre). That is, I don't think the punk people are as obsessed with their images as the press would say. There's a certain distance and art form involved in displaying punk aggression. There's a sort of playfulness in their S & M. It's healthy to acknowledge that area and the hopelessness. Like the Sex Pistols saying, "No future for me, no future for you."

Twigg: Are there punk artists you know or feel are important?

Ginsberg: Elvis Costello. And in the apartment I live in, there's Richard Hell who runs *The Voidoids,* a big punk band in New York. And Denise Mercedes—who's Peter Orlovsky's girlfriend—she lives with me. She has a heavy metal rock band of half girls and half boys called *The Simulators.*

There's a sort of funny cultural interchange happening now. We just had this big poetry benefit for the St. Mark's Poetry Project. One night Patti Smith played. On the other three nights we had myself, Richard Hell, and Elvis Costello. Plus there was Andrei Voznesensky, Ted Berrigan, Anne Waldman, and John Giorno. Coming up there's a big Burroughs festival in New York at the end of the month. One evening we'll have me and John Cage, Merce Cunningham, Ed Sanders, and Anne Waldman. Another evening we'll have Burroughs, Keith Richards, Patti Smith and Philip Glass, Brion Gysin and John Giorno. And there's an afternoon conference with

Susan Sontag, Timothy Leary, and Robert Anton Wilson. Plus a lot of punk bands and plays.

Twigg: How's Burroughs holding up these days?

Ginsberg: He's at his peak. He's just finished his magnum opus of the seventies, a novel called *Cities of the Red Night.* It's about five hundred pages with a regular plot people can follow. It's taken him five years to do.

Twigg: You once said that when Burroughs kicked his habit, he kicked his identity habit. You wanna explain that?

Ginsberg: Yeah, most people have an identity habit they have to relate to. We all have a fixed sense of who we are which constantly gets interrupted by broken legs or divorces or car crashes or orgasms (laughter). Extremes of pain or pleasure make you break through and realize you're not as solidified as permanent as you might have thought.

Twigg: What do you think of Burroughs' idea that sex is a form of junk, the consumption of which is encouraged by the state to keep people enslaved to their bodies?

Ginsberg: Right. That's a real interesting theory. It fits into Buddhist theory in that any attachment where there's grasping is an addiction. It's a question of how you relate to passion. Sexuality where there's no attachment is a lot more liberated and liberating. Blake said, "He who binds to himself a joy, does the winged quality destroy. He who kisses the joy that flies, lives in eternity's sunrise."

You can learn that from meditation practice, watching passions rise and dissipate. Recognizing that thought forms are discontinuous. Watching the gaps in between. The ego is not solid. It breaks all the time. Like in a movie where there are film frames and then there are gaps in between those frames. Some people think it's continuous and they try to get into the moving.

Twigg: Do you differentiate between Western thought and Eastern thought?

Ginsberg: No. Oriental wisdom is simply universal psychology. The key idea is that ego or thought is discontinuous. That's implicit is some Western thought, too. Pythagoras said, "Everything we look upon when awake is death." That means everything we look upon when awake is dying, is changing, is transitory. And Heraclitus said, "You can't step in the same river twice."

This all comes from the Prajnaparamita sutra presumably authored by Nagarjuna in the second century, A.D. It says form is emptiness, emptiness is form. Things are real; but because of transitoriness, at the same time, they're empty. If you get stuck on the real side, you're stuck. If you get stuck on the empty side, you're stuck.

Twigg: So you have to be able always to go back and forth?
Ginsberg: As we naturally do. If you're walking down the street and you fart, your thought disappears. Then off you go on another daydream and you stumble and your thought disappears again. I first heard this from Kerouac in 1953. Your thought is discontinuous.

Twigg: Jack Kerouac seems to be getting more popular again.
Ginsberg: Yes, everybody thought he had declined but now everything is in print so people can see the extent of what he did in the fifties and the sixties. Now they're making movies about him. He's become somewhat mythologized.

Twigg: Somebody once said that Kerouac was America's singer, and when his America died he had to die with it.
Ginsberg: That's from a great poem by Gregory Corso called "Elegiac Feelings American." It's what happens to a nation's singer when the nation fails him.

Twigg: How did it fail him?
Ginsberg: By a solidification of paranoic egotism. There was an attempt to project an American century, a CIA-Henry Luce vision of military and industrial dominance over the world, to penetrate the very ices of the North Pole with their DDT, to leave no part of the world untouched by their satanic industrialization.

Twigg: Do you think that kind of CIA repression has eased since the sixties?
Ginsberg: Probably under Carter there has been some improvement. Since the Freedom of Information Act, and since some of the FBI people have been indicted around '75 or '76, the wings have been clipped. But a lot of these goons from FBI and CIA and Army intelligence have moved over to private intelligence agencies. Or private industries like Rockwell and ITT have hired them. So I think we're going to have somewhat the same situation again with the same tactics in the disputes ahead over nuclear energy.

This week, as a matter of fact, there's a big trial in Jefferson County relating to the Rocky Falls Rockwell Corporation plutonium bomb trigger plant. I was arrested there a couple of times this summer with Daniel Ellsberg,

Peter Orlovsky, Anne Waldman, and a hundred others. Our argument there is that Colorado has this law which says you can commit a misdemeanor to prevent a larger catastrophe. We were alerting the public to the dangers of plutonium.

Twigg: So energy is the new frontier to replace the Vietnam War?
Ginsberg: Yes. It's going to be the big psychological battle of the coming decade. The security men from Rockwell Corporation are already out taking everyone's pictures. The counter-intelligence, dirty tricks activity will shift to the nuclear protests. As with Karen Silkwood.

Twigg: How much do you think counter-intelligence was responsible for the dissipation of the counterculture? Or was it mostly economics?
Ginsberg: All sorts of things contributed. But in the mass subconscious, I would say the trauma inflicted by counter-intelligence, dirty tricks, and illegalities by the government is much more vast than anybody realizes. It dismayed and disrupted the formation of a permanent phalanx of radical thinkers and activists. The split between blacks and whites in the sixties was cultivated by the FBI. They churned out a tremendous amount of propaganda and secret letters to make trouble between blacks and whites.

Twigg: Do you have any sympathies with groups that advocate aggression?
Ginsberg: Naw. They just create more problems. The whole problem is aggression to begin with. Military aggression, capitalist aggression, industrial aggression. Ultimately it's ego solidification, defense of territory. It's everybody coming on paranoid. "Give us the weapons we need to defend ourselves." That's the mantra of the people who make plutonium.

Twigg: Have you learned to control that solidification of ego in yourself?
Ginsberg: Not always. A good example is that once I got really outraged and pissed off with Tom Forcade in a long interview with the *Georgia Straight.* I denounced him and said maybe he was a cop. It was really unjust for me to lay it on him so heavy. He was actually influenced by secret agents in Miami in 1972. Now I just heard he committed suicide, two days ago. My own aggression made me jump the gun on him.

Twigg: Something in *Mind Breaths* that struck me was when you said it's become a lot easier to get love when you learn not to go after it.

Ginsberg: Right. That's the by-product of a meditative mind. Gary Snyder's favorite image on this is Indian hunting. The way the American Indian hunted was by sitting in one place and becoming part of the landscape. Rather than run around in a hysterical frenzy and frighten the animals away, the animals simply came to them. The anxiety to get laid, as any kid knows, interposes a self-consciousness and a frigidity and an awkwardness. That prevents a natural flow of erotic energy. Again there's Blake's line, "He who binds himself a joy, does the winged life destroy. He who kisses the joy that flies, lives in eternity's sunrise."

Twigg: As you get older, you seem to believe more strongly in purely platonic love.

Ginsberg: As you get older, you're willing to settle for what you can get (laughter)! Like if somebody doesn't want to suck your cock, you can play music with him.

Twigg: You mean your music is like a sort of spiritual "carezza"?

Ginsberg: Sure. With that little element of eros. Sometimes you find among musicians a tremendous erotic or sentimental and emotional relationship. The discourse and community and playfulness makes for an ecstatic intimacy in music. If it works, it's blissful.

Twigg: You've said the gay movement will have to come to terms sooner or later with the limitations of sex. Do you mean people shouldn't define themselves in terms of their sexuality?

Ginsberg: To the extent they define themselves in terms of genital sexuality. Like about a week ago I was trying to jack off. I couldn't come for the first time in my life. For a whole hour! "Wow!" I said to myself. "This is interesting."

It reminded me of a scene that made Kerouac shudder. Back in 1954, he was in the merchant marine staying at the Mills Hotel on MacDougall Street. It was a flophouse and there was an old guy across the atrium. He was old, old, old. But he was jacking off for hours and hours. The hopelessness of it made Kerouac shudder. But I find it pretty interesting to think you can keep an erotic fantasy going so long.

Twigg: Have you returned to Kent State recently?

Ginsberg: No, but I've been in touch with Kent State people. They've come up with a document to Ehrlichman about it. (He reads the White House memo advocating a stonewall on any Kent State investigation). Kent State made everyone scared to get together for their constitutionally protected right of mass assembly. You could get killed. Nobody wanted to lead a bunch of kids to that. Certainly not David Dellinger or myself.

So the Kent State killings were like the body blows to people having trustful, free associations. Until that stuff is raised up from the subconscious and clarified, there's going to be this hangover of fear. That's why I want to do this book with Ed Sanders tentatively titled *Smoking Typewriters*. It's a compilation of memos and orders from the FBI.

The sixties generation never knew how extensive the surveillance was. The seventies people didn't know the whole scene. So by the eighties, nobody will know what happened at all. Everyone will think the sixties was just a lot of people shitting on themselves in the street.

Allen Ginsberg: An Interview

Connie Goldman / 1982

Nit and Wit, Vol 4, Issue 6, November/December 1982, 54–55. Reprinted with permission.

No *hope communism, no hope*
 capitalism, yeah!
Everybody's lying on both sides,
 n'yeah, n'yeah, n'yeah!
The bloody iron curtain of
 American military power
Is a mirror image of Russia's
 red Babel tower.

Allen Ginsberg, once enfant terrible of the poetry world, recently celebrated his fifty-sixth birthday. But before you start thinking of this as a requiem, be advised that Ginsberg has a new record coming out on which his poems have been set to music. He also has a new book, *Plutonium Ode and Other Poems—1977–1980,* which has gotten good reviews.

Ginsberg remains a protestor, always speaking up for, or against, *something.* As you might expect, as many people have said unprintable things about him as feel that he's very important. When we talked, I asked Allen Ginsberg to describe himself.

Ginsberg: A poet, a musician, Jewish, balding, homosexual, meditator, loud-mouth, contradictory, ordinary mind, imitative, intelligent in picking up hints and perspectives from other minds, dependent on many other people for my intelligence, respectful of the elders, respectful of teachers, solitary, often lonesome and often overworked.

Connie Goldman: You write because you have something you say and something you want to say, and your form is writing—or singing and performing—but you know people are going to read it or hear it. What would you like from us who hear it, read it?

Allen Ginsberg: Gee—I'd like people to weep (laughs). To weep, as I have wept reading Hart Crane in certain passages. My ideal is, that if somebody read all of my poetry from beginning to end, it would so affect all of his sensibility that he would thenceforth be constantly aware of being on a mortal planet. He would be infinitely gentle with his friends. He would stay open and have a slight bohemian revolutionary humor about everything. He wouldn't indulge in put-down things—oh, endless intelligent things in every direction. So, I would expect everybody to get hip (laughter)! In the sense of a gentling of the soul—the spirit. Recognition of the blank emptiness of the soul. Maybe disintoxication from the notion of God, and opening of the mind to the vastness of its own nature.

Goldman: Do you think that the new vocabulary might help a new kind of understanding? Might we get bogged down, if we try to look at new things with old words?

Ginsberg: Yeah, it's very difficult, but a new vocabulary rises from the street, and has in punk. Actually punk and new wave have provided somewhat of a new vocabulary. Not enough for matters of state, perhaps, though I think if statesmen understood the punk music, the new wave music, I think they'd be a lot better off in terms of their attitude toward other people and other nations.

Goldman: Explain that a little more for me.

Ginsberg: Sort of like—attitudes of disgust with a whole military game, and disgust with the fact that the younger generation is faced with destruction and no growth—which seems to be the universal insight of both middle class and punk, and upper class boys and girls nowadays in schools. That they don't know how long the society will last, or with the world—that they're ready for it to blow up any minute. That they can't really make a career choice on the basis of this, or family planning on this basis. There's quite an openly stated notion that the entire nature of civilization and family and home and house and service of the earth is quite insubstantial these days, because you never know when there will be a nuclear war and everybody will get blasted out. And mostly, young people I've talked to do take this into account quite clearly, as we used to take into account depression, war.

(Ginsberg recites)

I roar your lion roar with mortal
mouth
One microgram inspired to one lung
Ten pounds of heavy metal dust that
drifts slow motion over gray Alps
The breath of the planet.
How long before your radiance
speeds blight and death (inaudible)
beings?
Enter my body, or not, I care, O My
Spirit inside you, unapproachable
weight
Oh, heavy, heavy element awaken
thy vocalize you consciousness to
six worlds,
I chant your absolute vanity
Yea, monster of anger, birthed
in fear,
O, most ignorant matter ever
created, unnatural to Earth
Delusion of metal empires! Destroyer
of lying scientists! Devourer of
covetous generals!
Incinerator of armies and melter of wars!
Judgment of . . .

Oh, I think we're going to blow up the earth. I don't think there's any hope at all. Politically in any direction. I think we've definitely created ourselves a real monstrosity this time, that nobody's going to get out of. And I think we probably all deserve it. I think the officials that we've elected are—be the ones to do it, push the button, actually do the dirty job. But we've created it.

Goldman: But the way you live, you keep writing, you keep saying the things that matter to you, you feel that will be the ultimate reality.
Ginsberg: Well, no. I'm running for the migra-vast audience of cockroaches who'll survive the bomb.

Goldman: Is this a fair generalization: Although things look very grim to someone who sees things as they really are, there are more people who are willing to see that. You're not fighting the naivete of the fifties, when you first started speaking out.

Ginsberg: Yeah. The naivete of being into the world before the bomb, before the possibility of universal destruction, is no longer the same problem that it used to be. One now is not fighting a universal blank squareness which was—how do you describe it? It's like living in the land of the blind where people were totally brainwashed into thinking that my country, right or wrong: America—the greatest country in the world, progress is ordained by God and his universe will go on forever; it's unthinkable that a government and the high people in it should be corrupt to the poor; it's unthinkable that a police state should ever take place—it can't happen here in America.

(*Music*)

> The moral of the song is that the
> world is in a horrible place
> Scientific industry devours the
> human race
> Police in every country armed with
> tear gas and TV
> Secret masters everywhere, Bureau-
> cratize for you and me.
> Terrorists and police together build
> a lower class rage.
> Propaganda murder manipulate the
> upper class stage,
> But you can't tell the difference
> between the turkey and
> the provocator.
> If you're feeling confused, the
> government's in there for sure.
> Aware, aware wherever you are.
> No fear.
> Trust your heart. Don't ride your
> paranoia, dear.
> Breathe together with an
> ordinary mind
> Armed with humor, feed and help
> enlighten, whoa, mankind.

Red Bass Interview: Allen Ginsberg

Jay Murphy and Mary Jane Ryals / 1984

Red Bass, Issue 7, 1984, 28–30. Reprinted with permission.

Allen Ginsberg for over a quarter of a century now has been one of America's most important and innovative poetic geniuses. A wordsmith and scholar of global pertinence, Ginsberg's 1956 long, Hebraic breathed poem "Howl" heralded an entirely new decade of sexual and social experimentation, and a host of new art forms directly or indirectly influenced by Ginsberg and the Beats.

We talked to Ginsberg during his visit September 22, 1983 to Tallahassee. Tired from a day of interviews and a raucous reading he gave in the Union Courtyard at Florida State University of "Birdbrain" and "The Little Fish Devour the Big Fish," the latter backed by teenage punkers Sector 4, Ginsberg had little patience with questions of politics, clearly preferring to speak about the craft of poesy.

In the talk with Red Bass, Ginsberg exhibited much of the erudition and wide-ranging concerns that have made him the major force in the literary arts that he is. Ginsberg has never ceased to be one of the great communicators, one of the prime transmission belts of culture. Whether it be the transmission of the knowledge of Australian aborigines or of fifties Beats seeing Times Square in their sacred vision as one great room, or whether it be the ceremonies of the curandero in South America, Ginsberg brings his diverse experiences of consciousness to bear on the perception of everyday America and the practice of poetics.

Our conversation traveled from the situation in Nicaragua under siege from the US backed contras, to the wisdom of Buddhism, nonviolence, ageism, poetry and what he sees as the firm establishment of the tradition of "Open Form Writing" now in the United States. Ginsberg's continuing concern with the relationship of poetry to music is discussed, as well as the influence of LSD on the anti-war movement of the sixties. Especially relevant are his comments on the function of poesy.—Jay Murphy

Jay Murphy: When did you go to Nicaragua?
Allen Ginsberg: February of 1982.

JM: I was wondering what your impressions were of that country?
AG: One thing is that it's a big country. You've got to realize that there's quite a lot of beautiful land and a lot of the people farm the land. I think that a quarter or a half of it was owned by the Somozas until the revolution. It's quite extensive and idyllic and along the shores of Lake Nicaragua to the south, that's a huge lake, one of the biggest in the area—where they have freshwater sharks. Anyway, it's sort of like an Everglades situation in some parts with these islands and channels, households on the islands and cantinas on these tiny pieces of land. It would be great to retire to Nicaragua, like Puerto Rico and Mexico, if it weren't such a messy political situation.

And the town is devastated—Managua. The whole town was bombed out. The other part is earthquaked out.

The political thing that everyone is interested in is whether they're Marxist-Leninist dictators or not. And they're not. They've abolished the death penalty. The leaders I've talked to, including Ortega and the Minister of Culture, poet Ernesto Cardenal, said that they were trying to avoid getting tied to the Cuban-Russian model and economic dependency. But they're forced to rely upon them as allies because the United States, not understanding that they wanted to keep a kind of neutral role—not neutral, it was an open role—were pushing them into an alliance, into a military alliance by attacking them.

So I have this song, "Hypocrisy is the key to self-fulfilling prophecy," meaning the neurotic hypocrisy of projecting a rigid Marxist, Cuban-style model on them and acting as if they were already, is like a self-fulfilling prophecy, pushing the Nicaraguans into an untenable position. Alternatively, maybe that's just intentional, that the right wing here in America wants to prove that nobody can have an independent government and full self-determination as a nation.

JM: With economic and political rights.
AG: So that they're making the conditions of war impossible. And the CIA is probably infiltrating La Prensa, one of the newspapers there and then accuse them of trying to censor it, as they did the El Mercurio in Chile.

So it's a mess, and it's a US paranoid mess, I would say. It's just a shame that they can't be allowed to conduct their revolution and have their literacy campaign and write their history "with ink, not blood."

JM: I was wondering how you saw the more open revolutionary process there reflected in its poetry and culture.

AG: Yeah, I've been in Cuba and Russia and I couldn't give a poetry reading, and there in Nicaragua I did give a poetry reading.

I was kicked out of Cuba in 1965, so I have some experience with the police bureaucracies in socialist countries. Here in Tallahassee I sang a song and I read the poem "Birdbrain" which is a parody-attack criticism on communism and Stalinism. There was no problem doing that in Nicaragua.

In Nicaragua there is also the idea of open poetry readings, which is supported by the newspapers, and the situation is so tight in Russia, in Czechoslovakia or Cuba, that it didn't get a chance.

JM: Since you are a poet who deals a lot with the media, how do you see the media's role in reporting what's going on in Central America?

AG: Well, I had a question and answer meeting with most of the reporters reporting on Latin America in Mexico about two years ago. Beth Nessen of *Newsweek*, Ron Zamora from UPI, a fellow from NBC, Dickey from the *Washington Post*, so these were high level newspeople who were in charge of covering Central America.

So first of all, they said there was a lack of personnel to cover it. They said they had to cover everything from Panama to Cuba. There was only one person to cover all the news all over the area, all the different wars.

Second, they had to compete, they had to restrain themselves. They had to be judicious in selecting what they thought was important and what they thought would play in the headlines. They said one murdered baby is no news. They said they had to have a big massacre. There was some difference between what they reported and how it was played in the papers.

They said that the Americans could not win in Central America, the Salvador war, without sending in American troops. They said it was a popular war in which the majority of the population was on the side of the left and the church or the church of the left.

They said that the elections in Salvador have been a fraud because none of the left was allowed to run for fear of death squads. Thy said that the death squads were responsible for eighty percent of the killings in Salvador. At this point it's forty thousand people murdered by death squads, including the centrist candidates, or the non-Marxist centrist people.

So they saw the American intervention as a big mistake and the accusation of the revolution in Salvador as being an externally fomented Soviet plot as not being correct.

While I was there they were building up militarily [in Nicaragua]because there were these giant headlines in the papers, in *Time* magazine, the American papers, the Miami papers that the CIA and State department were accusing them of smuggling dope, or accusing them of smuggling guns or fomenting revolution in Salvador. Particularly of building up an army to invade Central America.

At the same time they were being forced to arm to defend themselves from American invasion, which US papers were announcing; at the time General Haig was in the headlines saying he was not ruling out armed intervention. There were stories in the *Times* about Somosista soldiers training at Fort Bragg.

Time magazine arrived at the Hotel Continental in Managua accusing the Nicaraguans of building up to invade Central America rather than accounting their build up as a defensive measure. So, it's a Tower of Babel being built by the media here, I would say, a schizophrenia.

There is an example several days ago in the *Miami Herald*. This particular instance was on the 21st of September when the front page headline was "Island Base Called Evidence of Sandinista Gun-Running," so it's as if it were a proof of something, but their own story by Sam Dillon said the opposite when it finally got around to the story.

It said: "US officials had persistently refused to provide evidence of the Nicaragua to El Salvador arms flow. The arms trafficking operations described by the residents," which is the subject of this giant headline on the front page, "the arms trafficking operations described by the residents appears to show more of the trappings of a tropical rum running ring of dugout canoes and back-water buccaneers than a military movement of major geo-political significance."

So the entire administration and media campaign against the Nicaraguans, based on the contention that they're originating and directing the revolution in El Salvador, is based on no evidence at all or flimsy evidence, which is the dominant theme.

At the same time, the United States hypocritically is doing precisely that: arming and supplying guns and materials and bases for intervention into Nicaragua. So it's a case of lying, and then accusing them of what we're doing. There's something really immoral about that— like it's a hypocritical hype.

And the media, though it has evidence of that, is not pointing it out in that rough way that they would point out the weakness of a Carter administration speech. Everybody was laying a trip on Carter that he was confused and confusing on his foreign policy, whereas the Reagan foreign policy is ten times more confusing, inconsistent, and irrational and nobody's laying a trip on him. So they're letting actor Reagan get away with an awful lot.

Now it's amounting to mass murder and now all the Americans are good Germans, so to speak. Sitting there and taking it, accepting the Big Lie. There's something very obnoxious about it and it bodes ill for the health, the mental health of America, whether we can even survive at this point.

JM: What is your outlook for the eighties since you were a leader of the peace movement in the sixties?

AG: I wasn't leading a peace movement, I was participating in it like everyone else was. It was a national thing. By 1968 a majority of the American people felt that the war in Indochina had always been a mistake.

It was a minority that was conducting the war. And it is a minority now because most people don't want an intervention in Central America. So it's a minority of aggressive jerks who are pushing everybody else around and the reason is that they got $230 billion in appropriations for the military.

So there are a lot of people who are very well-armed and well-paid to suck off the majority. Suck all the energy out of the majority and push everybody around, and in a sense everyone is scared to oppose them because they've got guns so when you have a peace march, you never quite know whether you're going to have another situation like Kent State where people got shot. If you were president you would never know that if you stopped the war you would be shot.

It's a dangerous situation when we've had so many butchers in Central America; we know how to make butchers, and doing it here may not be beyond the possibility or imagination. It may have happened already with Kennedy. Like stringers in the CIA and stringers in the Mafia out of Tampa getting together, angry at Kennedy that they didn't get their turf back in Cuba, bumping him off.

JM: So how do you think we can counter that? How effective do you think the peace movement is?

AG: I have no idea. I don't know any more than anyone else does.

One thing people can be encouraged to do is to open up their mouths and say what they think. Cause everybody's a little inhibited saying, "Oh, maybe we'll have a repeat of Vietnam when the Vietnamese came out bad, bad, bad." Or maybe they're secretly right and unconsciously scared that they're going to impose a Marxist style dictatorship. So everyone is a little hesitant to assert themselves except the loudmouths with aggression and guns, they don't hesitate to assert themselves violently. But we the people who want to be nonviolent are a little timid because no one knows whether they are one hundred percent right or not.

So it's sort of like William Butler Yeats' poem "The Second Coming": "The best lack all conviction while the worst are filled with a passionate intensity." So you get this passionate intensity in the Young Republicans, the Moral Majority, the poisonous military and loudmouth actors like Reagan, shooting their mouths off, being supplied with money from Coors and breaking the Constitution and breaking laws and then yakking about morality and law and order. It's like total immorality in public. People come to be numb, sort of.

But I thought you were a literary magazine.

JM: We're political too.

AG: Well, I'm not that political. I'm not that interested in politics. Politics is just a byproduct of the general neurosis which is much more interesting. Politics is a byproduct, a chip off the giant block of consciousness, the whole of consciousness.

JM: Do you think that poetry can be effective in curing that?

AG: I'm not interested in curing anything. To use poetry to cure Reagan would be an abuse that would bring poetry down to Reagan's size. Poetry is about the vastness of the skies. It's the brilliance of the sun. It's an intellectual force.

We have imaginations. Reagan's got an imagination, I've got an imagination, you 've got an imagination; everybody's got their inner worlds that they're acting out, projecting, and constantly testing the limits of. So poetry is a way of making a model of your inner world and checking out the external, phenomenal world. That's Robert Creeley's idea.

The eminent poet Robert Creeley, this summer at the Naropa Institute lecturing, pointed out, using the word imaginal, that everyone actually has an imaginal world. And that is not a negligible thing because that is how an individual determines how they act to others. As Wall Street have their projection of what the world is like, the military people have their fantasy of that the world is like and the poets have their fantasy of what the world is like. So, if one says "Oh, the poets are just dealing with their imaginations," Yes, it's true, but oh, the Pentagon is just dealing with its imagination also.

So what is interesting is the boundary where poetry touches the actual world and defines it as the poet sees it so that he can formulate it and check it out and get some feedback as to what's real and what's not real, doing it in a very gentle way by making a verbal model rather than going out and cutting down the jungle and splashing Agent Orange all over everything and setting off an atom bomb, permanently changing everything just because of this fantasy that the communists are under the bed.

So the function of poetry is as big as the human mind. To make a model of the mind and communicate it to others so they can get some feedback, I guess.

JM: Which younger poets do you like?

AG: I like Antler, his poem "Factory" came out in City Lights. I like David Coate who has a book called *Quiet Lives.* I like Steve Kowit from San Diego. He's got a book, I forget the name of it but it's pretty interesting and very funny. It's influenced by the Portuguese epic twentieth-century poet Fernando Pessoa. I like an unpublished poet from Woodstock Andy Clausen among others. They are not so young, they are in their thirties.

Of the generation after mine, I like Ed Sanders and Anne Waldman, a lot of younger poets. Some poets have passed through Naropa I thought were interesting—Joe Ritchie and Sam Kashner, among others. Of women poets I like Anne Waldman and Diane di Prima.

Of my peers I like Philip Lamantia and Gregory Corso. Corso above all. He is the most gifted poet. There are Creeley, Snyder, and others. There is a great phalanx of people who were involved with the San Francisco Renaissance, in the New York School of the Beat school who have had tremendous survival power. They got stronger and stronger as they got older, like Snyder. Philip Whalen is now in a Zen training situation which will promote him to Zen Master within a year or so; the first American poet Zen Master. Michael McClure is now a solid playwright, the same with Sam Shepard. Burroughs is now finishing about three hundred pages of his third novel of the trilogy that began with *Cities of the Red Night. The Place of Dead Roads*, the second book of that trilogy is now at the printer. Robert Creeley has now put out his *Collected Poems*, Robert Duncan, Denise Levertov and all these folks are flourishing.

So we the fifties group made a tremendous jump forward and with it brought recognition to our teachers—William Carlos Williams, the Imagists, Charles Reznikoff. There has been a real change in the establishment of a kind of lineage of open form writing, firmly established and now with Naropa the establishment of some sort of linkage with the wisdom of the East—Tantric Buddhism, Vajrayana, Open Mind. So we have this healthy situation.

Mary Jane Ryals: I like how you say the older they get the stronger they are.

AG: Yeah, I think so.

MJF: There is a lot of ageism in the United States.

AG: Yes, there's quite a bit. I noticed that in the local newspaper article.

JM: Yeah, we noticed that.

MJR: Yeah, that's disgusting. It was an embarrassment.

AG: There is that stereotype. I think it was cultivated a good deal in *Rolling Stone* magazine. I notice it a lot in the rock 'n' roll world, just ignoring the fact that Shakespeare's best play was his last, *The Tempest.* Beethoven's best music was in his last quartets, like Schubert, Bach or Rembrandt, Cezanne, are all examples of growing. Even Bob Dylan is an example. Matisse, Picasso, Burroughs is a good example of that. Burroughs didn't even begin writing until he was forty.

So there's this consumeristic, shallow, typology stereotype of flash-in-the-pan which is appropriate for commercial writers but not for serious writers or artists.

MJR: Most media people leave the media by the time they're thirty, forty. They think they're burned out.

AG: They do, they do too much, so they project that image onto artists.

The other thing is that when artists burn out, they write about it and actually give an accurate account, like Kerouac. Or other artists do, like Cassady, so that it's visible, whereas insurance brokers, bankers, professors, and media people going out, it's a private scandal, no one talks about it. So you don't realize the attrition rate for insurance executives is greater than poets. The survival rate for poets is probably higher than insurance executives.

JM: That's what Jim Morrison said before he died, that rock singers don't have a higher early death rate than business men or anyone else.

AG: That's true. That's true.

JM: Do you have any comments on the change in generations from the beats to the hippies to the punks in the seventies?

AG: Well they seem like one continuation of Bohemia. I think in the beat generation, beginning in 1948 on, there was the introduction of a world transcending, apocalyptic view based partly on the realization of the possibilities of the bomb. That added a kind of dimension of seriousness. Then from the fifties on there was the introduction of literal Himalayan wisdom with Zen Buddhist roshis, teachers, Zen Masters coming to America, adding an element of wisdom that had been amateur before the Theosophists.

The sixties—the introduction of the Tibetan lamas, the *Tibetan Book of the Dead* and techniques of mind training that are really radical and interesting that were just guessed at in the West once the continuity of the old

Gnostics had been broken back during the Dark Ages. The East didn't go through the Dark Ages, through the destruction of the wisdom transmission principles and the West did have a breakdown.

MJR: The East didn't break down?

AG: No, I didn't say that. There was no breakdown of the transmission of the wisdom practices in the East. There is still some direct lineage back to Buddha and Chinese Buddhism in China and Zen Buddhism back to Japan. There is a direct lineage of teacher to teacher, from generation to generation, from Buddha's time to the present Zen Masters. Same with the Tibetan lamas. There is a direct lineage of unbroken transmission of mind training with the Tibetan Vajrayana Buddhists.

Whereas in the West, the old Gnostic schools that came from the same sources during the Dark Ages there was an inquisition. There was a breakdown of the transmission of Gnostic contemplative practices. In India there is the direct transmission of the ancient pronunciation and chanting in Sanskrit from generation to generation, unbroken. There is nobody who knows how ancient Greek was sung and chanted. There was a breakdown in that transmission both in the field of contemplative practice and in the field of poetic practice. So nobody knows how Homer was sung. Or how Sappho was sung. Whereas in the East there was no breakdown in the chanting of Sanskrit.

That's a really important thing. The accumulated wisdom, the tie-binding wisdom so characteristic of high civilization broke down in the West. So we got cut off from our roots, so to speak.

JM: Seems like a lot of people are returning to that today, poets doing music.

AG: Yeah, among many of the students who are out at Naropa. There is a lot of investigation of the ancient Greek meters and the inflections and pitches, up and down, in Homer and Sappho through Catullus and others in Latin. I'm sort of interested in that. Reconstituting and researching what were the old Greek dance music poetry practices. How did they do it. What where their modes. What were their chords, so to speak. What was a long vowel and what was a short vowel. What can be applied to Americanese in that basis.

That was something Ezra Pound started investigating back in 1905. The introduction of a classical quantity, the measure of vowel length as a measure in American poetry. He said that American poetry should begin to approximate that, or he hoped that American poetry would attempt to make use of that.

Do you know what that's all about? Or is this all gibberish?

JM: Some from reading Pound.

AG: The Greeks measured by long and short vowels, instead of stress. They also had up and down pitch, so that their spoken poetry had a lot of different inflections.

MJR: Their words had a lot of different meanings too.

AG: You are talking about another aspect. I am telling you about the measure, the length of the line that William Carlos Williams and Pound were interested in, as well as the element of music of poetry.

So that's the literary part. What other questions?

MJR: I want to ask about the difference I see in the fact that the lesbian movement is basically overlooked and the gay male movement is sort of sensationalized in the United States. Why do you think that is?

AG: I don't think that the lesbian movement is overlooked. The whole women's movement is fueled a lot by lesbian energy. In the poetic world there is a big lesbian movement in theater, in poetry, and in dance. There is an acute lesbian influence in the formation of groups, magazines that are very open about it, based on that question, particularly in the poetry world.

MJR: You mean people like Adrienne Rich and Robin Morgan and those people.

AG: Yeah, Marge Piercy, those people. Audre Lorde. Even Anne Waldman, who has a baby, still is involved with lesbian openness.

MJR: And Diane di Prima.

AG: Diane di Prima. At Naropa there are two lesbian poets, teaching, writing. I think it's been a really strong influence. There doesn't seem to be enough of a political alliance between boy lovers and girl lovers, lesbians and gays, because their sexual tastes are so different. It's sort of funny. In some respects mutually exclusive. But I just consider that a question of taste, between liver and Codfish. Some people like this, some people like Codfish, some people like meat. So there's this natural grouping together according to mutual tastes, but there should be more of a political alliance. There isn't now.

MJR: I agree.

AG: Another interesting thing is that Huey Newton in 1971 wanted to make an alliance with the gay minority groups and he did, but then the FBI intervened and began sending out poison pen letters—squawking angry Black brothers who were actually agents in disguise accusing Newton of being a fairy. In public that dubiousness was grassroots resentment but it wasn't. It was just set up by the FBI. I just saw those Freedom of Information Act papers on that particular case recently.

JM: Why is there so much antagonism between the artistic and political communities, why is there such a split?
AG: The split arose from the political community's rationalistic or hyper-rationalistic Marxists, out of a Marxist-Stalinist background, where they were killing poets like Mayakovsky or Yesenin, or suiciding them. The politicians have always been somewhat power hungry and short-sighted and rationalistic and poets have always been more ample-minded, more individualistic.

I think it was the fault of the political activists. They originally resisted grass and acid, although I think that it was acid that was the catalyst for the whole anti-Vietnam war movement, it was anathema to them. When it was discredited, driven off the market by the CIA and narcs, the anti-war movement diminished, slightly. The delegation of Chinese writers here last year had never heard of the relationship of teaheads and grassheads, acid heads and the anti-war movement, although that was quite strong.

The poets, the artists are more interested in freedom and their minds. The Marxist radicals have always been substituting the hyperintellectual system for another hyperintellectual system, resulting in the same authoritarian hyperintellectuality. Meanwhile they accuse the artists of being elitist intellectuals. So it's all these elitist Party hacks generally, that start wanting to restrict people's imaginations. A certain amount of restriction is natural, you know, even in the household—don't shit on the floor. But the humorlessness of the political radicals short circuited the growth.

That's what happened to the Communist Party. They got tied down to a very heavy ideology, lost all sense of humor and when the hip, or new consciousness came along they weren't able to adjust to it, either in Russia or America.

So now you have the New Left, and even the New Left was somewhat afflicted by the same sort of rigidity in mind. Kerouac's critique was very interesting. He talked about me, Jerry Rubin, and Abbie Hoffman in Chicago. He said: "These guys, these Jews, are creating new reasons for spitefulness," and it was quite true. Rubin finally said yes, it was all wrong to "Kill Your Parents."

So the political people who tend to be single-mindedly political, tend to create new reasons for spitefulness, get angry at their opponents and polarize things because they think in terms of fight. The old liberal thing— "Fight for Peace." They're still saying, "Fight for peace," not realizing that it is a contradiction in terms. You can manifest peacefulness, you can act with generosity, you can resolve conflict and polarization, but you can't fight for peace. You can fight for self-defense, but you can't fight for peace.

That was the experience of Chicago in '68. The first day in Chicago Leonard Woolf Lowenthal, working with Rennie Davis and Tom Hayden, set up a demonstration of karate and Japanese angry sort of snake dancing as their symbolic presentation of how they were going to defend themselves against the police. Now Woolf Lowenthal teaches Tai Chi and realizes that it was a big mistake, sending out the wrong signals, it was asking for trouble. They should have been rehearsing the Tai Chi, not the karate thing or rehearsing mantra. They were making believe they could challenge the police, defeat the police and it was just inviting a bloodbath. I remember being in Chicago before and trying to argue with then, saying: "Wait a minute, don't you realize what you're doing, you're sending off a signal that you're going to fight." We were supposed to be organizing a Festival of Life, not a festival of victory over the cops or something. "No, no, no," they said, "they're going to get us so we have to teach people how to defend themselves." So they brought, in a sense, new reasons for spitefulness there.

The left is still afflicted with that machismo. A lot of that got cleaned out during the seventies and early eighties when everybody realized that some kind of more feminine approach, peacefulness had to be evolved. That aggression that was so characteristic of US politics had to be infused with some delicacy and understanding .The gay liberation movement was good in that respect. The women's liberation movement was good in that respect. Trying to develop more feminine politics, or the female principle, to the extent that the female principle represents perceptiveness, thoughtfulness, softness, openness, generosity, comfort, sustenance, nurturing— so that men begin to develop nurturing faster.

Catching Up a "Bitter Buddhist": A Conversation with Allen Ginsberg

Thomas Gladysz / 1985

Red Cedar Review, Vol. 17, Issue 1 and 2, Spring 1985, 82–89. Reprinted with permission.

On February 11, 1985 I had the pleasure, the displeasure, the exhilaration, and the frustration of interviewing Allen Ginsberg. Ginsberg was at first "testy," giving crack-pot answers he later termed "poetic." But after a while, Ginsberg released his (public) persona, becoming a quite kind and humane man; battle became personal engagement.

This interview was conducted shortly after the publication of Ginsberg's *Collected Poems, 1947–1980* and prior to his February 14 reading at the Detroit Institute of the Arts. Ginsberg read "Many Loves," a poem written in 1956 detailing his first intimate encounter with Neal Cassady and now published for the first time in *Collected Poems.* Ginsberg also read new poems written while he was recently in China, as well as "White Shroud," an epilogue to "Kaddish." "White Shroud" talks of the conversation Ginsberg has with his mother after finding her living in a cardboard shack. She is a shopping bag lady and Ginsberg thinks to move in next to her. The poems from China and "White Shroud" reflect a new, more reflective, sometimes bitter voice in Ginsberg's poetry.

The following are excerpts from our interview.

Thomas Gladysz: What led you to bring out the *Collected Poems?*
Allen Ginsberg: I had nothing else to do—I was bored. I wanted to spend an afternoon doing something useful.

Gladysz: It must have took more than an afternoon?
Ginsberg: It took an eternity.

Gladysz: Do you feel at a particular junction in your career, making the time right to bring out the *Collected Poems?*
Ginsberg: Yes, I nosedived into heaven.

Gladysz: Through the seventies and eighties you have been working with music *and* poetry. What led you to merge the two forms?
Ginsberg: I had a visitation from the assembled spirits of Beethoven, Bach and Brahms, telling me to sing about the world in a new way, uplifting the Buddhist nature of reality.

Gladysz: Where does the merge of music and poetry lead to?
Ginsberg: It will go all the way back to Sappho and Homer, Sappho sang her songs and Homer his epics.

Gladysz: Do you feel that this merger of music and poetry is an outgrowth of American poetry?
Ginsberg: It is an outgrowth of American blues. Poetry and music have always been the same—like identical twins. It is only lately, since the devil invented the printing press, that the body got separated from the voice. It is the work of the devil—I kid you not—it is the work of the devil.
Ginsberg: What is your name?
Gladysz: Thomas Gladysz.
Ginsberg: You're calling from where?
Gladysz: East Lansing, Michigan.
Ginsberg: I read there in 1966. I had a terrible police problem. They had a very heavy police state. You couldn't sell my books; they had cops all over the place. East Lansing is where there was a professor who was working for the CIA secretly. Things were very complicated. (For the reading) they threw up every possible barrier they could. They didn't want me to read "Wichita Vortex Sutra."

Gladysz: During the 1950s and sixties when your poetry and the poetry of the Beats came under attack . . .
Ginsberg: What are the "Beats," a red vegetable or something? Do you know the names of any of the Beats? In China they know the names of the Beats; they aren't just a bunch of vegetables you boil in a pot. . . . Gary Snyder, the famous poet. Jack Kerouac, a writer. William Seward Burroughs the world-famous novelist. Michael McClure, poet and playwright. Philip Whalen,

Zen priest studying to be a Zen master, a distinguished poet. All respectable Americans, smarter than anybody else probably. Robert Creeley, Bob Dylan, the Beats—make into one color soup.

Gladysz: Do you feel that the American intellectual and literary establishment has come to accept the change that the Beats fostered?

Ginsberg: Half-and-half, they have done it in a half-assed way. They put me and Burroughs in the American Institute of Arts and Letters, yet they refuse to admit Gregory Corso, Robert Creeley, and Gary Snyder. In fact, the election came up yesterday and they voted in a bunch of *New Yorker* poets basically, or poets that are relatively academic compared to the early innovators. Gregory Corso never got a single literary prize in America—never got any money. While all sorts of inferior, second-rate, third-rate, fifth-rate poets are like pigs to the trough, seeing how much gruel they can get. Corso I think is the greatest poet. But I think it has always been like this, at all times, in all nations. The great poet is put down, while the second rate poet is a hero. Corso is a colossus of a poet, a supreme genius like Keats.

Gladysz: Why do you feel America waits till poets die to acknowledge them?

Ginsberg: Some poets are acknowledged—like Pound in an asylum, or some are half-dead, like William Carlos Williams after his heart attack. Sometimes they wait till they are paralyzed, like Whitman, fired when his book came out. Whitman was fired from his job—he had a job with customs. Sometimes they let them get to be famous—like Poe, who died alone in a gutter. Sometimes they get to be famous like me, but not have any money. I am "bitter," quote, unquote. I am a "buddhist," quote, unquote.

Actually, the reason I am so testy is that I am trying to get off dope. I am going through withdrawal symptoms from nicotine.

Gladysz: Could you tell me something about a record album called *Allen Ginsberg with Still Life?*

Ginsberg: Still Life is a band I work with when I am at Naropa Institute in Boulder, Colorado. I teach there in summers. We put out one record, a 45 called "Birdbrain." They selected poems to sing as lyrics to their songs; what you are actually hearing is cut-ups of my poems, except for "Capitol Air," which is not cut-up. But with the Gluons *Still Life* version the whole song is twenty verses like in the book. On the *First Blues* album there is a completely different set of verses than on the *Still Life* album.

Gladysz: Excluded from *Collected Poems* were twenty-two poems from the book *First Blues.* Why?

Ginsberg: My stress gave out. When we thought to add those, the book was nearly done. Anyway, it's always good to have something missing. It's also good for Full Court Press (publisher of *First Blues.*) They are songs, rather than poems.

Gladysz: Is there anything else excluded?

Ginsberg: Well, what I did is collect all the poems from anything that had been published, like letters, journals . . . everything worthwhile.

What I like best is "Many Loves." I thought that line, "and mine stuck out of my underwear" was so naïve and straightforward that it's poetry. It is so characteristic of somebody in that situation. That was the first time "Many Loves" was published except for a private printing.

What did you think of that poem?

Gladysz: I liked it.

Ginsberg: Were you offended?

Gladysz: No.

Ginsberg: I am always interested in people's reactions to what I write, especially a poem like "Many Loves."

Gladysz: You were recently in China, what were you doing there?

Ginsberg: I went to China at the invitation of the Chinese Writers Association along with Gary Snyder. They loved hearing Americans read. It was a really new experience for them and we were a big sensation, reading to audiences of more than five hundred.

They did have copies of my poetry over in China, some in books, some in different anthologies. They knew who the Beats were.

China is a beautiful country.

Gladysz: What lies in the future for Allen Ginsberg?

Ginsberg: Well, I recently had an exhibit of my photographs in New York, even managed to sell some.

I will also have six new books coming out. *White Shroud* will be a new book of poems. There will be *Selected Prose Essays—Assembled Proses* perhaps, as well as *The Journals of the '50s, Selected Correspondence.* I am also planning on doing an *Annotated Howl. The Annotated Howl* will have essays by a bunch of people who are mentioned in the book. For example, there is that line about a guy who jumped off the Brooklyn Bridge, that was Tuli Kupferberg.

Politics, Pederasty, and Consciousness: Interview

Robert F. Cunha Jr. / 1986

The Harvard Crimson, November 20, 1986. Reprinted with permission.

Allen Ginsberg sat down in Tommy's Lunch last Friday afternoon and ordered a raspberry-lime rickey. The foremost living American poet, in town to plug his new volume of poems, *White Shroud,* carried the several books and notebooks he carts from one poetry reading to the next. For a self-styled "post-beat modernist," he looked remarkably conservative: blue blazer, candy-striped shirt, and rep tie. The only hint of nonconformity was a small dried flower under glass which he wore as a lapel pin.

Ginsberg held court on a dizzying variety of topics, from poetry to television to his unabashed homosexuality. Clearly his favorite subject was politics; nearly every question was ultimately answered by his own inimitable brand of political analysis. In a deep, resonant voice, he switched subjects continually, drawing comparisons, and painting allegories that both illuminated and obscured his diatribe.

"My poetry's always been pretty accessible to everybody except pipe-bound academics and critics, at first. The reason is probably that I've been following William Carlos Williams' tradition in writing in the living American language and speech, writing in the living tongue, rather than an imitation of a literary tongue . . . It seems obvious. I don't know why other poets don't do it. . . . It's like poets do themselves out of their audience.

"Mostly [the poems in *White Shroud*] are about sex or dope or politics or meditation. Now that I'm sixty I'm looking at who I am as a public persona and a private persona and seeing if there's any difference. . . . Do [the poems] seem self-conscious? Awkwardly so?"

Are you the establishment now? "I've always been—from the point of view that Thoreau, Whitman, Williams is the American tradition. So that's one establishment, you might call it the hermetic establishment, the native establishment. Then there's an opposed, fake establishment that runs the money.

"Primarily my interest is in Buddhist meditation. . . . The Buddhist thing is if you see the Buddha on your path, kill him—if he gets in your way. Because if you get confused and get attached to the idea of it, cut it off, cut it down. Unlike the Moral Majority which would never cut down, never say their Christ is a stick of shit like Buddhists say Buddha is a stick of shit.

"I don't have an obsession with [aging]; it's an acknowledgment and a dealing with it. You know, Yeats had to deal with it, Eliot had to deal with it, we all have to deal with it. Everybody except idiots has to deal with it.

"As I get older, having very specialized sexual tastes, it gets harder to make out. . . . I like young boys. *Why?* Well, I'm not a young teenager. I'd have more chances at making out with younger guys if I were younger, dewier, dewy-limbed.

"[*White Shroud*] is the most graphic ever, except for one early poem called 'Please, Master,' which was super graphic. This is pretty clear, I think. Just the right moment in Moral Majority history to come out with something really graphic.

Is this a way of thumbing your nose at the censors? "No, it's a way of grounding my consciousness, and other people's consciousness, in the reality of erotic life when at this point Meese, the attorney general, wants to ban erotic life and persecute it, and get the Supreme Court on our backs over sodomy.

"Remember they were going to get the government off our backs? Now they even got them snooping in the bedroom. They want to turn the United States into a nation of informers, like Russia. The next thing you know kids will be informing on their parents for sodomy. Not merely just smoking a little grass, but sodomy.

"Fuck the American government. The American government is nothing but a bunch of second-rate poets and mass murderers—including our very popular president, who after all has a lot of karma bloodshit on his hands. He's hardly the one to be pointing a finger. Nor his wife.

"The whole government program on drugs is a lot of total hypocrisy to begin with, and why put up with that bullshit?. . . . There's nothing wrong with dropping a little acid or smoking a little grass. . . . They're a bunch of yapping dogs selling their own dope, double-dealing, corrupt, up to their ass with the Mafia, trying to get votes by denouncing poor, suffering junkies on the street. . . . The government can take its whole dope morality and shove it back up its own ass as far as I'm concerned, and the American public, too, if they're so stupid as to listen to the lies the government tells them."

Ginsberg ends White Shroud *with a poem called "Things I Don't Know."* "I just realized that there are a lot of things I don't know, that a lot of people don't know, but at least I don't know.

"[I did not] try to bring [*White Shroud*] to a triumphant, or untriumphant, ending. It's kind of an anticlimax. But I don't mind. Somebody's got to take on the anticlimax, or else everybody will be doomed to be afraid of the anticlimax. . . . Sometimes I can't come. That's pretty anticlimactic.

"[People] are always trying to make anybody who is dissident sound like a flake or a loser. It's exactly the same psychology they use in Russia. If somebody's a dissident, they call him a troublemaker, a neurotic. They even send him to a psychiatric hospital. It's a *Time* magazine-CIA-ex-Harvard con, that you're not really 'serious' like the businessman is 'serious.'

"That psychological consciousness . . . takes me in, it takes everybody in. Except every once in a while you wake up and realize—What did Walt Whitman say? 'I find no fat sweeter than that which sticks to my own bones.' Like, I'm bigger than the government, the government is a loser, the *government* is a flake, not me."

Has Ginsberg become more political? "It's not really so much political, unless you call Thoreau political. Thoreau, you know, did sit in jail rather than pay his war tax for exactly the same war we're fighting now [in Nicaragua].

Does Ginsberg pay his war tax? "I'm stuck with everybody else with that."

Is poetry the best way for Ginsberg to foment his "world revolution"? "It's the only way. Because ultimately it's a psychological revolution. . . . People are controlled by language, their thought patterns. He who controls language controls minds.

"The government itself is made of our words. So if you get in there with a jiu-jitsu in the language, you have the best chance of altering people's awareness or mind consciousness. It's sort of a psychedelic situation.

"Being vulnerable is being heroic—*not* being number one. Now we're supposed to be number one? From Nixon onward we're supposed to be number one. Not being number one is heroic. Being number one is cowardly, macho, S & M."

Allen Ginsberg: An Interview

Regina Weinrich / 1987

Five Points, Vol II, No. 1, Fall 1997, 31–46. Reprinted with permission.

This interview for WBAI radio took place on February 4, 1987, at 437 East 12th Street, Allen Ginsberg's East Village apartment. A rabbit warren of connected rooms, the place illustrated Allen's particular intermeshing of life and art, abustle, abang, and awhirr with plastering and painting by Allen's sometime musical collaborator Steven Taylor who was doubling as a carpenter that day. Our talk was interrupted several times by Peter Orlovsky, Allen's longtime companion, coming in and out.

Over ten years later, in this year of the poet's death, the transcribing of these words for the first time brings solace, his cadences Homeric, his phrasing thoughtful, his stating and restating, an unraveling of possibilities not finite sentences. He was our American underground unacknowledged poet laureate, who espoused nakedness in poetry and wore khakis for the GAP. World famous for "Howl" (1955) and "Kaddish" (1959), for his political stance, for his Buddhism, for accompanying himself on the harmonium, he was the Beat Generation's shining star and PR man continuing to champion the work of poets in his circle.

On one of several occasions when Allen came to read at The School of Visual Arts where I have taught courses on the Beat Generation since 1976, he read poems by Philip Lamantia, Gregory Corso, Philip Whalen, and Jack Kerouac. One would think he would read his own; the better to sell copies of his newly published *Collected Poems*, a large and important work. When asked why not a single Ginsberg poem, he replied, "What good is it if I'm famous in a literati of unknowns?"

Since the time of this interview much has changed, Harper and Row has become HarperCollins, for one thing, and has more recently put out *Cosmopolitan Greetings Poems 1986–1993* (1994); *Journals Mid-Fifties* (1995); and *Selected Poems 1947–1995* (1996). Other noteworthy books to appear since the late '80s include *Your Reason & Blake's System* (Hanuman, 1988); *Journals Early Fifties Early Sixties* (Grove, 1994); *Indian Journals* (Grove, 1996); and *Illuminated Poems*, illustrated by Eric Drooker (Four Walls, Eight Windows, 1996). Recordings since the time of the interview include *Hydrogen Jukebox*, music by Philip Glass (Elektra Nonesuch, 1993); *Holy Soul Jelly Roll: Poems and Songs 1949–1993*, produced by Hal Willner (Rhino, 1994); *The Lion for Real*, produced by Hal Willner (Mouth Almighty/Mercury, 1989, 1996); *Howl U.S.A.*, Lee Hyla score, Kronos Quartet (Nonesuch, 1996); *The Ballad of the Skeletons* with Paul McCartney and Philip Glass, produced by Lenny Kaye (Mouth Almighty/Mercury, 1996); *Jack Kerouac Mexico City Blues: 242 Poems*, read by Allen Ginsberg (Shambhala, 1996).

Allen Ginsberg admired the taped portion of Kerouac's *Vision of Cody* as a model of conversation transcribed, verbatim, with every pause and breath indicated. I have attempted to adhere to Allen's standard in the process of turning our words into text. Only an aside on the critic Norman Podhoretz and a lengthy interruption by Peter Orlovsky which did not pertain to the literary discussion were omitted here.

Most recently Allen Ginsberg was living in a new East Village loft, freshly renovated. I visited him there on October 31, and then saw him for the last time two days later on November 2, 1996, in Lawrence, Kansas, with William S. Burroughs. From the porch of Burroughs's modest red house, the two senior statesmen of American letters were waving goodbye.

Regina Weinrich: In the past few years we've seen several new books: *The Collected Poems* up to 1980, *White Shroud Poems 1980–1985*, and *The Annotated Howl*. Do you think the appearance of these books marks a new recognition for your artistry?

Allen Ginsberg: Well, it puts it out front for the public to see in a regular way, with a big company, with distribution, with pretty covers, an upper-middle-class artifact so the upper-middle-class then has to take note that it's a commercial artifact in their own sphere of economics from a company that has a big building office between Madison Avenue and Fifth Avenue, Harper and Row. The books are very coherently presented: the title of *Collected Poems* says 1947–1980 and a year later *White Shroud* says 1980–1985; it's a neat, clear presentation of a large body of work, so obviously people will take it as if it's real.

Weinrich: Well, there must have been a time when people didn't take the work as "real." Has the work always been recognized?

Ginsberg: It's been pretty much recognized around the world all along, from 1960 on for the last twenty-five years. It's only in the last three or four years since the *Collected Poems* came out that the semiotics of it, the terminology, the semantics of the situation have changed somewhat and people recognize and say that it is some kind of major work. But it has been all along. "Howl" has been in many schoolbooks and anthologies for the last twenty years and it's been translated into over twenty-two languages so that gives it a kind of popularity and intellectual credentials. It has been very much favored in Eastern Europe by the dissidents and intellectuals. It's a funny combination, but it all works well.

Weinrich: Is your work better known here or abroad?

Ginsberg: The recognition of literary quality, that it is high literature, is more common abroad. Now since Harper has published the books, the recognition is common here too, but it has taken longer for people to notice it was not just notoriety but there was also a question of literary quality, that the lineage that my poetry falls into has a lot to do with modern literature, classic literature, Oriental literature, and it has roots. It's not just finger painting out of the bug house.

Weinrich: Has that frustrated you over the years?

Ginsberg: Nah. I just keep writing poetry. I know what I'm doing. Maybe other people didn't quite know what I was doing, but I know what I'm doing. I mean I don't know what I'm doing any more than anyone else, but at least I know I don't know what I'm doing, and most people think they know what they're doing.

Weinrich: So you're not bugged by critics?

Ginsberg: I think about it. If a critic attacks the work and puts it down, there's economic loss somewhat, and I've been having enough problems making a living without having to be denied the normal prerequisite of any old second-rate academic, like an expensive professorship and trips for the USIA or Pulitzer Prizes or whatever they give out these days. But I still haven't been able to get enough money to live on. There was at first a financial problem. Then there is a problem of being read with sincerity rather than being read for the purpose of making fun, like there was a long period when people would read Whitman in order to make fun of him because professors or critics told them to do that so people didn't quite get it. Things seem to have settled down now. This problem wouldn't apply now to Gregory Corso or to Jack Kerouac. There is still an enormous resistance on the part of the academic world in that Kerouac was an exquisite writer in that he had an aesthetic scheme that was monumental. It's still possible for neo-conservative critics to attack him in the newspaper as if he were Errol Flynn or something.

Weinrich: Are you referring to this most recent attack by the critic Norman Podhoretz?
Ginsberg: Yeah, I saw it in the *New York Post.*

Weinrich: He managed to take a shot at you as well.
Ginsberg: In a way I was kind of grateful. My books had not yet been reviewed, and he mentioned them all over the country and talked about them in such a way that any sensible person would want to go out and read them, even though it was supposed to be an attack. I'm talking about his attack on Kerouac primarily. The stupid notion that Kerouac wasn't a great writer's writer. Most of the writers I know have learned an enormous amount from Kerouac's poetry. Just knowing him as a poet is important.

Weinrich: Let's go back to your work. One of the most interesting books to appear this year was the *Annotated Howl.* Whose idea was it to do this?
Ginsberg: I think it was Harper & Row's, Aaron Asher, the editor. I signed a six-book contract with them and one of the things they asked for was an anniversary edition of "Howl." I had saved all the manuscripts, so I had it in the back of my mind one way or the other. I had given explanations here and there, so it seemed possible to do and, therefore, inevitable. The book is a big thing and very pretty. The cover was basically designed by Harry Smith, the filmmaker, poet, archeologist, anthropologist, sociologist, recording engineer, and optics expert so that it is a very beautiful color blue with the gold sticking out into the eyeball. We tried to make the whole thing an artifact equivalent in aesthetic charm to the text, if that isn't boasting too much. John Clellon Holmes, a novelist, sent me the manuscript, which I had sent to Kerouac. I think it says up on the first page, sent by Kerouac to me August 30, 1955 JCH. He found it in his papers I guess about 1980 and sent it on to me, very generously.

Weinrich: And you thought it was lost?
Ginsberg: I thought I had given it to the lady who typed up the manuscript and she had lost it. So what the book consists in is a guide to the manuscripts, a Virgil taking you through the manuscripts, seeing what's

important. Then a dedication to Carl Solomon, a mysterious figure to most readers although he's a literary figure in his own right and well-known in the New York/San Francisco literary world as an essayist and book reviewer and prose poet. There's a section called *Carl Solomon Speaks,* with some of his essays reprinted and a little preface by him. Then there are forty to fifty pages of annotations line by line explaining every literary reference, background, literary echo, anecdotal reference like who jumped off the Brooklyn Bridge. That turns out to be in a disguised form about the poet Tuli Kupferberg, so Tuli wrote a little document about mistakenly trying to do away with himself as a young kid and a warning to other people not to try that. "Mohammedan angels staggering on tenement roofs" turned out to be old Philip Lamantia the poet who wrote a little document about a visionary experience he had in the fifties. So all the anecdotal material is now put into place so you can see the sources.

Weinrich: Did you find out anything new in working on this?
Ginsberg: Oh, all sorts of things: I had to do a lot of research. For one thing, I did find out that Tuli did actually jump off the Brooklyn Bridge and that he did hurt himself and wound up in the hospital with a cracked shoulder or hip. I had generalized with hyperbole a lot of gossip I had heard and made it into poetic truth rather than literal truth. This traces back to the literal truth of a lot of situations. The one I like most of all is, I ran into Lamantia who is a poet I really admire on May 25 in New Orleans at the Book Fair, and I asked him at the last minute could he make a footnote for his verse: "encountering Mohammedan angels fell upside down out of the clouds encountering Mohammedan angels illuminating the nimbus of the autumnal moon" or something like that. So he says:

> 1953 Spring aged 25 reading the Koran on the couch one night I was suddenly physically laid out by a force beyond my volition, which rendered me almost comatose. Suddenly consciousness contracted to a single point at the top of my head through which I was 'siphoned' beyond the room, space and time into *another* space and time which seemed utterly beyond any space and time before or since experienced. I floated toward an endless-looking universe of misty, lighted colored forms: green red blue and silver, which circulated before me accompanied by such bliss that the one dominant thought was: This is it, I never want to return to anywhere but this i.e. I wanted to remain in this Inevitable Blissful Realm and explore it forever—since I felt a radiance beyond even further within it and so, suddenly the outline of a benign bearded Face appeared to whom

I addressed my desire to remain in this marvel—and who calmly replied 'You can return, after you complete your work.'

So that's a very funny footnote and that explains the "Mohammedan angels staggering on tenement roofs illuminated" which is a verse in "Howl." So what I have done is given the background of anecdotes, background of literary references, historical background, tales of the tribe, so to speak. Younger people might not know what the topical references like "Fugazi's" are. So I explain that it was a bar on 6th Avenue in Greenwich Village in the early fifties, which was an alternative to the noisier place where the artists hung out, the San Remo on Bleecker and Macdougal. I even explain the rhetoric like a phrase "hydrogen jukebox": some end of the world or apocalyptic vibration was noticed by the subterraneans in the roaring of the jukebox, thus hydrogen bomb jukebox. I explain for anybody who didn't get the joke the hyperbole or simile or metaphor, the construction of the language.

Weinrich: Barry Miles, who edited the volume, makes a good deal about the fact that you actually did not get the title from Kerouac.
Ginsberg: I thought I did. I have a memory that he wrote me and said I received your "Howl." That letter is reported there, but Barry pointed out that I already had written it in the same blue pencil that I was making my other corrections on the original manuscript, so it must be "Howl" according to my own naming. I don't know. How do you remember after thirty years?

Weinrich: Does that disturb you? Does it make you think of the poem differently if you did or didn't title it?
Ginsberg: I was glad I thought of it myself. But I was also glad that Kerouac might have thought of it. Either way it's honorific. Which is better? Maybe we both thought of it at once. At least it gives something for scholars to figure out.

Weinrich: What about Kenneth Rexroth's role?
Ginsberg: Yes that's something I had forgotten. Ann Charters, Kerouac's biographer, who was around Berkeley in the mid-fifties and went to one of the early readings of the San Francisco Renaissance poets, Gary Snyder, Philip Whalen, Philip Lamantia, Michael McClure, myself, when we were all together with Kerouac, Cassady, Rexroth. She pointed out

that Rexroth had a really terrific poem which had a big impact about the death of Dylan Thomas, "You killed him with your Brooks Brothers suit, you dirty sonofabitch." An accusation against the middle class for having persecuted or ignored or not properly taken care of Dylan Thomas who died here in New York, heavy drinking, living at the Chelsea Hotel, visiting America. Died in St. Vincent hospital. Gregory Corso sneaked into his room while he was hovering between life and death in an oxygen tent, sat at his bedside for a while. Rexroth in his poem also used the word "Moloch." I probably picked it up from Rexroth. But I had forgotten that. I think that was a neurotic block out partly because I thought Rexroth's poem was too crude, too accusatory, negative in a sense. It was in a sense the classical beatnik poem, ingenious poem, right-minded and right-hearted, but it lacked an elegance that I wanted to see in my poetry or maybe I'm being too snobbish. Do you know that poem? Very famous. I think it was put out by City Lights as a pamphlet. What is it called? I've forgotten, but it was a big thing around San Francisco and in poetic circles at that time, and it's probably in his collected work, it made a big imprint on me, impression on me because it was even more bohemian than my bohemian or more beat than my beat. I wanted to say, "I'm with you in Rockland," not "I'm against you out there in the world." I wanted to accentuate the positive or do an alchemical job transforming lead into gold, so I think in order to accept guilt by association I recognize the Rexroth which really was the catalyst for "Howl," so I certainly should give him credit. I'm sorry I didn't in this book but that's another thing a scholar can amplify.

Weinrich: I can see the book leading to millions of articles, clarifying the poem, clarifying where other poets have taken off from it, because the poem has influenced a lot of people.

Ginsberg: Yeah, it influenced so many people I would like to demystify it and show the roots, make it really clear so there is no mystery about it, so people don't get misled, don't overidealize, don't use it to hype up their own egocentric resentments, anti-world thing. At the same time there's lots of information here critical of American society in the footnotes and the poem, about the military industrial hyper, hyperindustrialization of America and then we go on to literary matters. There's a whole section in the book of correspondence: my father's reactions, Kerouac's reactions, which are critiques, takes, but it also gives you an intimate history of a literary circle.

Weinrich: And also a process, and the whole beat fellowship that there was an interconnection, influence.

Ginsberg: And how does it relate to the outside, how does Trilling relate? What kind of reverberations from Ezra Pound, William Carlos Williams, Richard Eberhart, the more academic poets like John Hollander? The whole network of human relations is in the consequential literary situation, you get a picture of the network of human relations, and then you get an archetypal description of a poetry reading at the Six Gallery where "Howl" was first read from six or seven different angles as different people saw it and remembered it, then you have the whole legal history which repeats what's going on now. Reagan and Meese trying to turn this nation into a nation of informers like Russia. As Burroughs recently said, "Why don't we start rolling back on censorship and start censoring again." Now the Dead Kennedys are in the middle of a censorship battle, the rock band, and the literal phantoms of the Kennedys are probably involved in a censorship battle so that they don't know that the Mafia got them, the Mafia and the CIA murdered them or something. The congressmen's wives complain about the lyrics in rock music and a local DA in Los Angeles is trying to send a message to the entire rock world by suing them for peddling obscenities to a minor, there's a lot of book censorship going on via libel suits like Peter Matthiessen great scholarly exhaustive study of the FBI's misbehavior at Wounded Knee, the debacle where some FBI men shot each other probably and then Leonard Peltier was put in jail on a bum rap, Viking burned the book or chopped it because the FBI agent is suing him for reproducing information that was in newspapers and in courts. Peter Matthiessen is a very elegant, exclusive writer and this book which rips the mask off the FBI treating our American Indians like the accused Sandinistas are treating the Mosquitoes has now been burned. There is also a whole seamless web of repression and censorship recurring in the US trying to roll things back to the old. This book is sort of a stone in their way, sort of a mind bomb right now. So you have the legal history. And on a deeper level than the sociological what I've also made is a little tiny anthology, model text of earlier poems by now-classic writers, some well-known, some not, that influenced me and Kerouac and others all along, the precursor stylistics for "Howl." Everybody read T. S. Eliot, but if you scratch an English major you won't find that he's read Guillaume Apollinaire, a French poet of WWI times from whom Eliot took his syntax, collage style, montage style, punctuation style, basic poetic method. It's really amazing, although Eliot and Pound constantly talk about Apollinaire, very few of the academics who teach and study Eliot, very few go back to the root texts: Laforgue, Apollinaire, and others, so I have given Apollinaire's great poem "Zone," which is the equivalent of "The Wasteland," I have a whole anthology of poems by Mayakovsky, Kurt Schwitters, who provided me with the shape of the pyramidal litany of Part III of "Howl," and the same shape of a graduated litany that expands that I used in "Kaddish."

I found the text of "priimiittttiii" in *Dada Painters and Poets: An Anthology by Robert Motherwell* when I was in college. Schwitters, who was a Dadaist sound poet, was born in 1887. He got up in front of a whole bunch of Nazi generals before he fled Nazi Germany drunk and recited his sound poetry like that; everybody was too drunk to know what was going on. Then there is the great poem by Artaud, "Van Gogh: The Man Suicided by Society." It's very funny, it says that a sick society invented psychiatry to defend itself against the investigation of certain visionaries, whose faculties of divination disturbed it, so he accuses psychiatrists of being denim guerillas, Lorca's "Ode to Walt Whitman," which has the great line about Walt Whitman: "Not for one moment beautiful aged Walt Whitman have I failed to see your beard full of butterflies, nor your shoulders of corduroy worn down by the moon, your thighs of a virginal Apollo, your voice like a pillar of ashes ancient and beautiful"—I took a lot of that kind of language when I wrote "Howl," "Corduroy [shoulder] worn by the moon," putting the moon, a picture of the moon next to the shoulder as if the moon could wear down the shoulder, i.e. shoulder worn down by dream, disillusionment, falling apart of the body, is another way of saying it, whatever that means, putting those two together with such a distance between them is like hydrogen jukebox, putting things disparate and distant together, or the apt relation of dissimilar objects which was Aristotle's definition of metaphor.

Weinrich: Or is it perhaps an oxymoron?
Ginsberg: The oxymoron is when it clashes, but here it is a suppressed connective which is logical but is unstated unless you want to say that metaphor and oxymoron are identical. Think in the direction of Aristotle, he says the apt relation of dissimilars, though an oxymoronic aptness here.

Weinrich: With oxymoron when the two things in opposition come together they make a third thing. Like "bittersweet."

Ginsberg: Okay. I'll buy an oxymoron then. I'll have to look it up in my *Princeton Dictionary of Poetics* to see what I'm signing up for with these oxymoronics. So then I have a bibliography of all the different languages and an index so that people can look up their own names. Robert Duncan can look up his own name or Gregory Corso, but I would be ashamed to put out a historic book retrospective if I didn't at the same time have a collection of new poems to push further out into present and future. *White Shroud* was published the same time from Harper & Row. One or two poems I think are classic within my own canon of poetry, particularly the "White Shroud" poem which is a kind of epilogue to "Kaddish."

Weinrich: Yes, I heard you read it recently and I was transported, but I also kept thinking of "Kaddish" and your interest in mortality at this time.
Ginsberg: Why not? Everybody is interested in death. One's parents die, one's friends die, one will die oneself. It's a basic fact of life, if you don't know death, you don't know life, you think life goes on forever or something; you don't realize how precious it is. Unless you know death, you don't realize how life is sacred. And if you know death the wrong way you get to think that life is death. If you know the right way, you get to think that life is death also, but in any case it's a question of your attitude toward death. I'm not exploring death so much as an attitude toward death while you are alive.

Weinrich: Whitman was similarly preoccupied with death. I'm thinking of "Out of the Cradle Endlessly Rocking." The life and death are two parts of a pendulum swing.
Ginsberg: In this case it is more imagination. What it was is, my relation with my mother was incomplete and that's probably why I am gay. But there is nonetheless the weight and density of emotion of mother love that remains in the heart, not just mother love either but the weight and density of our relation with creation itself sometimes frustrated and sometimes blocked, but maybe the block from expression, the residue, the bulk of it is there in the heart or somewhere in the body or the mind there is this unexpressed completeness and the amazing thing is that I had a dream in which my mother who had been dead twenty-five or more years returned as an old bag lady in the Bronx and I was really glad to run into her on the street and said, "Gee now I could take up and I could take care of her like I should have when she was alive and I was alive," and we didn't quite manage to do that, so I reconstructed the whole broken connection with all the emotions that a younger son might feel at finally getting settled and

having a job and having enough money to finally be able to take care of his parents, and experienced it completely in the dream and when I awoke, I realized that all of my feelings were intact actually underneath; they hadn't been lost or dried out. It was actually all there. Everything that I thought was lost in terms of emotional fullness was intact and even though when I woke up, I realized no my mother wasn't here and it wasn't taking place, I was grateful to have the experience of the intactness of things, of emotion. Maybe that's the point of it. It related to something that William Carlos Williams said that influenced me very much when I was writing "Howl"— it's a phrase that I quote in my introduction about unworldly love that has no hope in the world and that cannot change the world to its delight but nonetheless Williams manifests that unworldly love because what he's saying is it's there even if it has no way of becoming practical or as a practical fact within us. It may be that having acknowledged the practical fact, acknowledged the emotion, the phrase was the matter is in objective acknowledgement of emotion, having once objectively acknowledged our own emotion, we might then find a way to relate it and to manifest it, but if we think that the emotion is gone or think it is not worthy or try to suppress it, avoid it or amnesia-yze it, it will come back to haunt us in other ways. So it is a matter of clarity or realization of your own heart and realization that the heart is not dead in anybody, even though they think so. People walk around thinking that they got dead hearts, and they might as well eat any excrement they can get along with, not realizing there's this whole reservoir of feeling inside themselves that comes out in dreams if nowhere else, and poetry in social form, if you are moving through, ransacking society or the community to find out where is this great reservoir of emotion, where are our feelings, the one safe place to manifest them, the one bank you can go to is the bank of art, poetry, painting, music, the whole otherwise unexpressed density of feeling and realization and understanding tears and laughter is all there intact or in our dreams, or some people have the ability to realize it in their bodies and careers and their fate, their lives, karma, destiny, and their social and human relations. They are fortunate, but for those who abandon their feelings, abandon themselves to make a living, for a bad marriage, mistaken gun heists in the Bronx in 1922. It's all there for us. What "Howl" is in its power is it resurrects all that feeling and manifests all that lost, abandoned, hopelessly denied feeling, unblocks it, undams it, expresses it in a clear way with an object, a friend in a jail or mental hospital suffering, gesture of sympathy saying I'm not going to reject you or myself or anybody else. Not reject.

You may have to deal with it, call limits, shrewd in relation, but you have to acknowledge the tragedy or the beauty or the fullness.

Weinrich: Let's talk about the unifying symbol on the books' covers.
Ginsberg: On the cover of all the books is a semi-triangular image of three fish made of three circles and a triangle designed by Pythagorean proportion of that particular design by Harry Smith, but originally it was an insignia I saw in Bodh Gaya, in India in 1963 at the place where Buddha was enlightened, Bodh Gaya, under the great Bo tree, there are a lot of statues of Buddha and mementoes and impressions. In the early days Buddha was not pictured as a human being but as someone who had "passed through" so they had a wheel or an umbrella or a tree or various other symbols, and there's a giant footprint, so there are some giant stone footprints, carved sculpture footprints like heels, some five feet long and two or three feet deep of old stone, maybe one thousand years old or fifth century or tenth century and on them is a triangle with an eye in it and then from each side of the triangle is the rounded body of the fish with the tail and fins. So I copied them in my notebook and I've been using it as a little sign, when I sign books, it takes a little time to do, to draw out, it requires patience so it's a little meditation exercise. So I gave the design to Harry Smith, and he reduced it to Pythagorean proportions so that it looks more like three turtles and three fish, then it's stamped in gold on all the bindings of the books. We have it on the covers. It makes it my own sign; after all I am a Buddhist, and my refuge name is Lion of Dharma, and my Bodhisattva vow name is Heart of Peace so my Buddhist signal is on the covers. So people are curious and they'll ask, so I go through this big explanation—why three fish? Well, there's the Father, Son, and the Holy Ghost, or the Buddhist equivalent of that will be Dharmakaya, Nirmanakaya, Sambhogakaya, or the world of ultimate reality, the world of relative reality and the intelligence that sees both at once, or form emptiness and the union of form and emptiness, the appreciation of inseparability, or life and death, and here we are discussing it so that makes three. The physics of one molecule clanking against another molecule isn't a fact of scientific data unless there is an observer: heaven/earth/man, ground/path/fruition, Father/Son/Holy Ghost, thesis/antithesis/synthesis—any way you want it.

Weinrich: It forms a kind of circle so it has a mandala effect.
Ginsberg: Extend it out you get a Jewish star. In hermetic design the ultimate proportions of it are Pythagorean. They reduce themselves to the archetypical like the Jewish star, or other designs. They all interlock ultimately.

Weinrich: I understand you will have a book of early photographs soon.

Ginsberg: I don't know which book will be next. Gordon Ball is working on my journals of the fifties which will include photographs, but I also have an invitation from Twelvetrees Press to put out a book of early photos so I may do that. As of February 1987, this month, I have my first museum show of thirty photographs at the Dallas Museum of Art going on now I just got back from there. I have simultaneously a show of thirty photos in Miami in Books and Books, a monthly show of photos. I have been visiting Berenice Abbott and my guru basically is Robert Frank. I show him my pictures and work with his printmakers, but I have been taking pictures for forty years.

Weinrich: The very best of the early beat photos are yours.

Ginsberg: I have the continuity of taking pictures of Burroughs or Kerouac or Peter Orlovsky or Herbert Huncke over forty years. I follow their faces which are sacred in a sense. Sacramental in a sense as in Kerouac's novels, a sense of community and a sacramental view of the other sentient beings, so that kind of interest or preoccupation leads to glimpses of people as they are among friends. A tender awareness as they are among friends. A tender awareness of each other's presence on earth together all at one time, just like Norman Podhoretz.

Weinrich: Have you ever photographed him, though?

Ginsberg: No but I think I should. I'll have to call him up and take my Rolleiflex to his office. The only way to approach him is through art. He gets it all tangled up, he gets his ethics and expression all tangled up and takes extreme positions.

Weinrich: What about music?

Ginsberg: I've been working with Steven Taylor for many years. We're going to do a record this spring and Hal Willner, who is the record producer for *Saturday Night Live*, and we have an angel who put up the money. He did some very good work with Berthold Brecht and with Sting and is doing a record with Marianne Faithfull now, so whatever new songs I've got including *White Shroud* with a string quartet background that Steven Taylor wrote and a version of "September on Jessore Road" with a string quartet that John Lennon suggested years ago at the John Sinclair benefit in Detroit in '71, suggested I try it like "Eleanor Rigby," so I'll be working with more music.

Weinrich: I understand you are teaching too.

Ginsberg: At the moment I'm distinguished professor of English at Brooklyn College conducting a series of lectures called *The History of the Beat Generation* as you are at NYU and at SVA and John Tytell at Queens.

Weinrich: What are your current political activities?

Ginsberg: At the moment my only avenue of political involvement is through the PEN Club's Freedom-to-write committee. I'm involved with the Dead Kennedys case and the Peter Matthiessen case as well as Irina Ratushinskaya's; we got her out. I put a lot of pressure a year ago in Moscow. I've been down in Nicaragua this year. Anne Waldman just got back. I am very sad about the deprivation of safety and goods there. They ran out of toilet paper in Managua, because of American embargoes and because all the money is going to defend themselves from Reagan's 100 million dollars, or whatever money is coming from the Saudis or the sultan of Brunei or Ollie North or General Secour. I also did a tour of Eastern Europe with Steven Taylor to Hungary, working with a rock 'n' roll band in Hungary putting out a record; I'm singing on two cuts. They are famous there, selling one hundred thousand records—I even get dollar money—four hundred dollars I made for my lyrics—that's more than I got from any American group. Then I went to the Struga Poetry Festival in August, to receive the Golden Wreath Award, yearly prize, formerly given to Auden and Neruda and others. It's a big deal in Eastern Europe; it's actual gold. Then I went to Poland and worked with Solidarity, stayed away from the government.

[Background noises, hammers and saws, sharply increase in volume.] What's going on in the background is life, someone smoothing out the plaster. All that noise is just the reconstruction of the yuppiehood of the Lower East Side, the landlord is sending people to renew the apartments though I've got an eviction notice here which has already been fought and won. My rent is cheap 'cause I've been here forever. They kept selling the building—it started at eighty thousand dollars and now it's worth nine hundred thousand dollars and it's been six years by real estate speculation, so the new landlord has put in a boiler and is reconstructing some of it. But he wants to get a lot of money for the apartments, but I've got rent control, so I'm safe for the moment. However, who knows? Funny thing is I've got this haunting dream constantly looking for my apartment in the megalopolis and not having an apartment, coming home finding that it is gone, it's in that dream comes back over and over again. It has to do with being dispossessed in one's body, inklings of what it feels like in the Bardo. That you don't know where you are supposed to be physically, when your body is gone your habitation has disappeared out from under you.

Weinrich: You seem so often disembodied. I wonder when do you have time to write?

Ginsberg: I write in bed in the morning or in the evening, I write fresh. If you write five minutes a day, that's more than anybody will want to read in a year. Two pages a day, that's seven hundred pages a year. Do you want to read seven hundred pages a year? Just write intensely despite all the noise around you; just focus your mind, fixed on whatever it is—you'll be all right in the middle of the megalopolis writing lyric poetry while the machines whine and scream about your ears.

A Conversation:
Ginsberg on Burroughs

Jeffrey Dunn / 1987

The Pennsylvania Review, Vol. 3, No. 2, Fall/Winter 1987, 39–51. Reprinted with permission.

Allen Ginsberg, poet and teacher, is the author of the groundbreaking poem, "Howl" (City Lights, 1956), among other writings, the most recent of which is *White Shroud: Poems 1980–1985* (Harper and Row, 1986). He is a member of the American Institute of Arts and Letters and cofounder of the Jack Kerouac School of Disembodied Poetics at the Naropa Institute in Boulder, Colorado.

William Burroughs, writer and recorder of space-time experiments, is the author of *Naked Lunch* (Grove Press, 1959) and most recently, *The Place of Dead Roads* (Holt, Rinehart and Winston, 1983). He is also a member of the American Institute of Arts and Letters.

Allen Ginsberg: Today is March 13, 1987, on the road between Seton Hill College and the Pittsburgh Airport. On Route, what, 30?
Jeffrey Dunn: That's correct. I am curious about your personal relationship with Burroughs and about the way in which your own writing relates to his.

AG: Well, I tend to follow the different topics that he picks up on or originates and imitate or readapt his ideas to my own use. He has always been a great source of ideas for me, and a teacher, particularly in copping attitudes. A teacher in copping attitudes is real good at copping attitudes. Then, the other thing is that we're both gay, and we have been lovers, the two of us, way back thirty years ago. So there is a kind of common humor and common experience and common sense of gossip and politics and cultural ethos that we exchange. And, as the younger person on whom he once depended—I served oddly as a kind of father figure to him, or son figure, I don't know what—but at one point he addressed a good deal of his writing to me, including *Junkie*, for which I was the agent, and *Naked Lunch*, for which I was the recipient for much of the epistolary routines, as he generated them and mailed them from Tangiers to San Francisco. And so I helped edit quite a bit, including *Yage Letters*, *Queer* (a new manuscript), and then there is a book of letters from him to me. Unfortunately, those were the letters that accompanied the fragments of *Naked Lunch*. The actual materials were not reprinted with that book. There are a few pamphlets that do have more of the material of *Naked Lunch* that wasn't used. And there is a very long, beautiful section that was never printed called "Interzone." That's going to be printed in the next year or so.

Q: How do you see the relationship between your work and his?
AG: Between my work and his is hard to say. Except for the fixed idea that the surface of the writing should be all concrete or specific or particular or visual things, "no ideas but in things," as Williams says, and not abstract drivel or generalization. That's certainly true with Burroughs, as well as with Williams and others. And then a nonjudgmental attitude in general, or a benevolent, indifferent attentiveness, which is his phrase. Or, a choiceless awareness is something I try to imitate, though I never get it. And so there is that attitude of tolerance, choiceless awareness, or benevolent, indifferent attentiveness, an attitude of inquisitiveness, which weighs or enters into whatever moral prejudice is brought to the situation and tries to look humanely at any situation and with some humor. Specifically, questions of junk, sex, and in certain rare cases even murder. As Dostoevsky looked on Raskolnikov's situation with a benevolent indifferent attentiveness, you might say, to some extent, and his point wasn't to punish the murderer, his point was to portray. So from Burroughs, out of that, you get tremendous black humor. A willingness to deal with what others will avoid. He goes into all sorts of territories like Chez Robert's restaurant menu, making a high-class restaurant menu so gross. Burroughs will gross out in all sorts of situations that other people would think would be untouchable to begin with. He not only touches them, but he grosses out on them and turns them into comedy so that what is created is that the attitude of everything is permitted, or at least as much is permitted in writing as is permitted by the mind in private. It is obvious when you read Burroughs that he or anyone could think of those things but why would anyone want to write about them? Well, because, anybody, everybody thinks of them and generally is scared unto death of really writing about them.

Q: Why would you say that is?

AG: Well, why did Christ get crucified? When I said scared to death, I meant it. When you start telling the truth, you find all sorts of private interests and concealed habits being aired and people get anxious and they want to protect their skin or their secrets or their vices or virtues, whatever, and begin to throw rocks at a person who starts confessing or starts talking openly about what everybody says you're supposed to hide, that's all. What if some student in a Catholic college began swishing and simpering their way through life? Everyone would get upset. Especially the fairies will get uneasy; maybe their secrets will get found out. Also, in Burroughs's case, a number of the secrets that he talks about are secrets that sustain power of repression in and among the police and in the military. Specifically, really, case in point, and really serious, and really astounding when you think of it, Burroughs has really exploded the myth of the dope fiend, as has been propagated by the police. He has pointed out that heroin is an illness and that the medical cure has been denied the junkie. He explained all this is the preface to *Junkie.* It has been a kind of conspiracy on the part of the cops, too. One, to create a bureaucracy of power because power is addicting. Two, to just enjoy repression, to enjoy being agents of repression. Three, to make money peddling dope, which is totally proven in every direction in the United States through inquiry after inquiry, commission after commission, such as the Knapp Commission, 1971, appointed by the governors that said, "Yes, the whole narcotics bureau of New York is on the make and is selling dope."

Q: We are talking about how repression is practiced against both the individual personality and individual writing. In terms of repression as it is used in a psychanalytic sense, I know that Burroughs used his own analysis as material for some of his writing. Can you tell us more about this technique?

AG: In Bill's case, he certainly had to suffer through sexual repression as a young St. Louis gent, hide his sensitivity all through Harvard, and probably came out late and had difficulty finding love partners or someone he could really talk to who could suffer or put up with his particular sexual tastes or respond to them. So, a good deal of his writing is exploring his own sexual position, rehearsing it over and over again, to sort of take it outside of himself, exteriorize it on the page and repeat it over and over again in different forms until his obsessive neurotic images lose their magnetic, hypnotic attraction or their conditioned attraction and become commonplace visions in the day. "Blue Movie" in *Naked Lunch* is one such repeated rehearsal of the feeling of helplessness of being hung, or being impaled, or submitting, losing control, abandoning control in order to have an orgasm. So, Burroughs realizes that everybody thinks such thoughts, not everybody, but enough people think such thoughts that those thoughts exist and, therefore, have to be represented, particularly if you've got this odd sense of black humor and his sense that he doesn't have to be responsible to a publisher, because he is not writing necessarily for publication. He's writing for his own pleasure and for friends and as a form for exorcising his own demons. So, that's one of the demons he exorcises, either the fear of loss of control or the obsessive lust to lose control.

So how does he deal with it? Well, in psychoanalysis you deal with it by talking to your doctor and airing it, acknowledging it, and examining where does it come from, and what is it motivated by, and what other habit patterns and mental patterns is it related to and is it paralleled by other mental patterns. Or do other things come from it or does it feed into other personal energies and repressions? As you begin to acknowledge and recognize the pattern, you can then alter the pattern or work with the pattern in some way or perhaps relate to the same pattern with less guilt. The whole pattern becomes transparent, and it becomes less of an obsession but more like play. But unless you are able to objectify it and maybe discuss it externally, it remains your own dark, unexamined secret and not really acknowledged.

Q: It seems to me that because Burroughs's writing is so original that it is difficult to locate him within a literary tradition. Could you do that for me?
AG: His specialty was all of Latin literature, Latin history. He knew all that in Harvard, and he constantly refers some uproarious anecdote of his own to Catullus and to Petronius' *Satyricon.* A lot of the pompous, worldly speeches by the bureaucrats come out of Caesar and Cicero, paraphrases and parodies. For later matters, Jonathan Swift's "Modest Proposal," like all of Swift's fantasy-parodies on human nature. He quotes Swift occasionally, especially in "Roosevelt at the Inauguration." He has such a mean opinion of mankind that he finally has Roosevelt, this outrageous monster, force all the cabinet to commit suicide or jack-off on the Capitol steps. He looked around for new worlds of degradation to conquer, and he has such a low opinion of mankind that he would sit there and say, "I'll make the bastards glad to mutate. I'll make it so tough that's why I'll make 'em glad to mutate." And that's very Swiftean, I'm sure.

So the element of black humor, and for the sort of racy prose, the racy vernacular, Louis-Ferdinand Celine, who Burroughs read very carefully and after a long time gave to me and Jack. For a certain aesthetic appreciation of opium, Jean Cocteau's *Opium*, for the panoramic montage, or jump cut, or collage, he has origins in Rimbaud and Eliot. Eliot's translation of St.-John's Perse's *Anabasis*—he quotes that quite often—"Came one who pressed bitter bay leaves in our hands." *Etranger. Qui suivit.* The stranger. Who passed—I'm sorry—*passait. Etranger. Qui passait.* [1] Or the very Burroughsean image of "the child with the smile sad as the death of apes." That's from *Anabasis* by St.-John Perse. [2]

There is also a tremendous affinity with Eliot. Both from the social cradle of the St. Louis aristocracy, as well as the sort of nostalgic perfume of their method, because, after all, Burroughs's *Naked Lunch* and later works are in a sense extensions of the method of *The Wasteland,* collage, decoupage, and as montage, juxtaposition of various literary and personal images, but the image is all boiled down to its most pungent and radiant and impenetrant as you have in the *Wasteland.* If you read a page of some of Burroughs's middle period work, like *The Ticket That Exploded,* "jacking off in the outhouse in St. Louis 1920, catfish, snowflake in the river," it's not very far from Eliot's recollection of St. Louis, "music down a windy street," I guess. "Wind hand caught in the door," is Burroughs, so actually Burroughs is T. S. Eliot applied to the novel. They have an obvious similarity of distinction, of distinguishedness, icy aloofness, impersonality, dry humor, super intelligence, blah, blah, blah, and all that.

They are very, very similar, even look alike a little bit. Have the same stature, same stoop though I think Burroughs was the more honest of the two and certainly wrote considerably more work. Eliot, you know, was really too timid to let go. I think Burroughs has a better sense of humor publicly, in any case.

Certainly he was influenced by Kerouac, a tiny bit influenced by me, but in the sense of enthusiasm for writing art, a writing path, a way of writing, writing as a sacramental way of life. He also was influenced by Spengler, by the sort of pompous veritablity of the English translation of Spengler's *Decline of the West*, the prefatory section, the fifty, sixty pages of preface by the English translator, or by Spengler, to the book, as it was translated into English. As Kerouac was influenced by that prose.

Kafka comes in often; the Kafkaean guards at the borders of countries in Burroughs are similar to Kafka's story about the guard standing at the gate. There is a guy who waits his whole life there but never goes through; and then, just as he's going way in despair, the guard asks why he's going away, and the guy says, "Well, you never let me through." He says, "Well, you never asked. You could've just walked through." Burroughs began with all sorts of funny border guards wiping their ass on the papers you brought 'em. Or, you know, jacking-off with their flies unbuttoned, which he observed in real life in Ecuador.

What else? We have Celine, of this century. Last century, Rimbaud, a little Baudelaire. In English, a bit of Tennyson he'll quote on and off. The world-weary "Ulysses" by Tennyson. You'll find scattered throughout his work quotations from Tennyson. "That's just we have, we have not now, but that which we are, we are."[3]

You'll see that often in Burroughs both in attitude and in direct quote because that reflects his St. Louis high school education. He can also quote a bit of Edward Arlington Robinson, and some earlier writing, and some Shakespeare, of course. He is a great master of quoting Shakespeare. So, that's quite a full bag of tricks, literary tradition.

Q: As well as his prominence as a writer, I also know that Burroughs has been heavily influenced by scientific investigations. What can you tell me about his interest in this area?
AG: From a scientific point of view, you remember, he actually did study anthropology. I think he got his M.A. in that at Harvard, which gave him a sort of analytic point of view for human folkways. He did study medicine for a year in Austria, I think, and so he's always had a sort of medical practitioner's eye. That's very obvious when you get to his parody of Dr. Benway.

Q: Isn't it true that he ran certain stages of his life as a scientific experiment? What sorts of experiments did he perform?
AG: That's what was always so astounding about him. One thing was testing what it felt like to cut off his pinky, of a joint off his finger. I think you'll read somewhere in his own writing where he talks about that.

Obviously, experiments with drugs were done and reported very precisely. I mean, he has been the great writer on drugs in this century, and he's the one great thememaster there. He had to invent the theme, in a sense, literarily. No one else was willing, though there was the book called *Opium* by Cocteau and a few other books. The experiments with cut-up and what they call now deconstruction of the word, was, in Burroughs's case, simply cut-up and deconditioning of the mind from the obsessive associations with language. Even in cut-up, even to the point of cutting out of language, his notion was all out of time-bound language and into space.

It's very close to Buddhists' views. It's not an eccentric Burroughsean direction of thought. It's actually a mainline direction, in both Buddhist and

Christian mysticism. So it's not that he's just experimenting in a little void of his own; he's just using much more modern means. If fact, he disapproves of what gets its effect, its results, without scientific means by sitting on your behind and shutting up instead of finding some way to stop the word, or virus, and thinking in terms of word in the beginning of the word was the word as a virus, linking those psychological or metaphorical notions as the notions of virus and space travel and what-not.

From the first time that I knew him he was experimenting with something. Beginning at the time he was being psychiatrized by Paul Federn, who was one of the disciples of Freud, so he got it really in the direct succession. Also by Dr. Lewis Wolberg who perfected hypnoanalysis, and, then, Burroughs found a whole succession of interior selves receding to the banks of the Yangtze.

Q: When I talked with Barry Miles in January, he told me about four personalities that he had worked out in what Burroughs calls routines.
AG: Yes, it might be seven or so. But he worked those out in routines.

Q: He listed four for me.
AG: Which ones?

Q: Let's see, the Southern, St. Louis aristocrat, the wild-west sheriff, the English nanny, and the silent Chinaman.
AG: Right, yeah. So those all became played out as literary routines. Then at the same time he was picking practical investigations into the theory of yoga called progress in relaxation, Jacobson, I believe. He taught that to me, and that's back in '44. Same time, progressive relaxation, you lie on your back and you relax everything from your scalp to your toes consciously. Not far from real yoga. Same time, he was interested in Korzybski's *Science and Sanity,* and he had studied with Korzybski in Chicago. That was one of the books he gave me and Jack in 1944, 1945. The big thick volume of *Science and Sanity* which separates words from the things they indicate. It cures most arguments over what this means and that means. You know the semantics theory of general semantics? So, he really went to the source of many things.

Later on he played with a certain amount of telepathy and did little experiments marking crosses and circles and squares. I remember there was a whole year we did that for fun. We would not see each other and match them every two days. Later he was in the experiment with Doctor

Dent's apomorphine cure. Then, when he was in England in the late sixties and the seventies, he went all the way through Scientology and became a "Clear." Then he turned around and denounced the organization as semi-fascist and praised the techniques and methods as used in the right hands as all right because they are very similar to his "Blue Movie." Take trauma and repeat it over and over and over and over again until it loses traumatic life, to clear the anxiety from the image. His use of drugs has always been very experimental and very purposeful. I mean not heavy-handedly purposeful because there was a lot of play and a lot of mistakes like Dr. Benway. Or, at least, there is as much scientism as there is in Dr. Benway, isn't here?

Q: I should hope so.
AG: Also in search of Yage, he went down there to experiment with a drug that was supposed to give you telepathic properties.

Q: Could you tell me something about Burroughs's interest in the orgone accumulator?
AG: Oh yes, a lot of Reichian interest. He's got an orgone accumulator. I inherited that, and it's sitting in my barn in the hay in New York state. I went to a Reichian myself back in 1947, and that was sort of an interesting thing. You know, all that Reichian stuff has evolved in to what we now know as shi-atsu massage and the holistic. It was not a will-o'-th'-wisp; it was a real thing. It's just now among the New Age people, a part of the health racket. Vitamin A he was interested in for keeping your weight down. He had a series of belly exercises. The book that went with that he lent me, and he lent Lucien Carr later. I forget the name of the author. At the moment, he's investigating cats and lemurs and the notion of interspecies communication. So I've been sending him all the material on lemurs I could find—you know, folk myths about lemurs or old *National Geographics* with lemur material.

Q: How exactly does Burroughs move the scientific experimentation in his own life into his writing?
AG: There was his interest in Mayan hieroglyphs. Also his interest in Scientology and progressive relaxation and psychotherapy and drugs were all predicated on the notion of something to do with expansion of consciousness, going beyond the limitations of language, or not being limited by language. The cut-up method in specific applications as cutting up words and sentences, or of cutting up sections of writing like *Naked Lunch*, and reassembling them at random sequence, has to do with loosening the mind

from preconceptions of form, or preconceptions of the sentence, even loosening the mind from being tied down to the material world and opening up the space where the "wind hand" can get "caught in the door," where you have an element of magic, where impossible things can meet and conjoin, such as in surrealism. So that by taking his own prose and cutting it up with phrases from Shakespeare and Rimbaud and *Time* magazine, he can have an impersonal text which speaks for the united voice for all three, with the images from all three juxtaposed and cut into the other or spliced genetically, so to speak, so that you have a genetic Frankenstein, basically, of Shakespeare, Burroughs, Rimbaud, and *Time* magazine.

It's a grafting of one virus on another or grafting one sentence on another. It's just like interspecies grafting or taking different opinions or thoughts or takes or images of your own mind and intergrafting them. You can produce poems, in a sense, scientifically, or you can experiment, at any rate, because I think that cut-ups are intended primarily as experiments rather than finished art products. I don't think he's so much interested in finished art products as he is in the process of experiment and what he will discover in the experiment.

What he is interested in is the different states of consciousness. So, specifically, the cut-up method, by changing the conditions and the habitual, accustomed, sequenced words and thoughts from its accustomed order, and breaking up the time logic, space logic, and the personal logic and any other logics, there are by the introduction of chance for aleatory means, a recombining of words and images using chance as the Dadaists have used it. Bring about an impersonal mixing of the elements that you have thought you have set in order, and the creation of a different order of reality than the one you could be able to think of or imagine so, and it will bring you an unimagined order of reality. Not an unimaginable one, but one that had not been imagined.

Like you could say two thousand years ago Caesar was the emperor, one thousand years ago the Middle Ages burned the manuscripts of Sappho, this century Russia and America had the bomb, so one thousand years ago Russia and the Roman empire had the bomb. Two thousand years ago, this century had the Roman empire. Well, now, actually this phrase makes sense—two thousand years ago this century had the Roman empire. I mean this century thinks of the Roman empire as two thousand years ago. So, you can make a number of permutations of those elements recombining them in ways you wouldn't be able to think of by simply doing it by chance and mechanically. That creates the new suggestion that suggests new combinations that make sense, but also suggests new interpretations of the old combinations and also suggests some kind of overlooking, humorous Over-Soul talking. It's like he is summoning up an Over-Soul to take up the language and themes that we are using and talk like the Cumaean Sibyl. Now, it makes a sort of Delphic or Sibylline author from utterances out of newspaper headlines. Like two thousand years ago this century had the Roman empire. That's kind of interesting, very Burroughsean, I just thought of it now. I was making it up.

Once you begin that you really get into this kind of Sibylline, curious, suggestive thing that goes across time, that breaks up our conceptions of time—which is exactly what Burroughs is after—"All out of time and into space." So, he is saying that the way we use language is so ritualized or accustomed it's like a virus; that it presets our notion of reality, but if you break up the verbal order of reality, you break up our apprehension of reality itself. Then, in that sense, the whole fabric of reality can rip and tear as it does in various moments in *Naked Lunch* and elsewhere where the technician gulps the bicarbonate of soda, and, suddenly, the time screen splits in half, and the invaders from the outer nebula rush in. Or when you break up the reality scene—no, the reality prop—and the boards and governors that set things up are invaded by the wild boys who are cutting through their time screens, which is nothing less, no different really, than what's happening now in IRANSCAM-gate. It's exactly the same thing where the scenario of reality written by all of Reagan's P.R. has of its own nature and stupidity split apart at the screen and all sorts of viruses are invading and all sorts of people come through. And, suddenly, the hero, Ollie North, looks like an awful neurotic when you see his shit-eating grin in the newspaper. It's the worst sort of neurotic baby, you know, the sort of kid that's in trouble in college all of the time. There is some superheroic, some larval entity inside of him like in Burroughs. So, Burroughs is very accurate in that way.

Notes

1. "Came such a one who laid bitter fruit in our hands. Stranger. Who passed," from St.-John Perse. *Anabasis*, tr. T. S. Eliot. London: Faber and Faber, 1959, 19.

2. "A child sorrowful as the death of apes—one that had an elder sister of great beauty—offered us a quail in slipper of rose-colored satin," from St.-John Perse. *Anabasis*, tr. T. S. Eliot. London: Faber and Faber, 1959, 35.

3. "We are not now that strength which in old days
   Moved earth and heaven, that which we are, we are,"—from Alfred Lord Tennyson, "Ulysses," lines 66–67.

A Conversation with Allen Ginsberg

The Monthly Aspectarian / 1990

The Monthly Aspectarian, Vol. 11, No. 8, April 1990, 43–49. Reprinted with permission.

The Monthly Aspectarian: Tell us about the tour you're doing with Philip Glass.

Allen Ginsberg: Well, the evening in Skokie is one of a series of things we put on together for various benefit purposes. It started with a Vietnam veterans group who asked Phil to work with me, setting to music "Wichita Vortex Sutra" which is a poem about the Vietnam war. It's found in a book called *Mind Breaths*, and it's also in my collected poems; it's dated around February 1966. So he wrote music to that and we do it as sort of a duet: me reciting poetry, sort of like an inspired oration, and him playing piano behind it. It's about an eight minute piece.

He's worked with a lot of poets in the past, and writers of all kinds like David Byrne and Suzanne Vega, and he's also worked with David Wang, a friend of his with *10,000 Airplanes*, an opera that he put on. And he's worked with Robert Wilson in *Einstein on the Beach*, another opera. And he's also worked with Doris Lessing. So he's done quite a bit of work with words, and both of us are Buddhist students and teachers, so we have that in common. I think that's sort of what brought us together to work together, aside from being neighbors. We both live near each other on the Lower East Side. We've known each other a long time, but we never did work together before last year, and that seemed to be very productive.

This benefit is for Gelek Rinpoche who has a Buddhist meditation center called The Jewel Heart. His main center is in Ann Arbor, and I've been out there several times. We made friends last year when we were introduced by Philip. He was an early student, side by side with my own Tibetan Lama teacher, Trungpa Rinpoche, who founded Naropa Institute. When both of those two Lamas were in India at the age of seventeen, they learned English together, or began learning English together. So I have sort of a heart connection with Gelek Rinpoche through my old teacher, who is dead now.

TMA: There's an explosion of interest in, you know, whatever heading you want to put on it, New Age or metaphysical . . .
AG: Well, we're more on a practical, grounded level of the art and practice of poetry and performance of poetry at Naropa. We're going to have this great summer session with William Burroughs, and I'll be there, and Anne Waldman, and Anselm Hollo and Bobbie Louise Hawkins. And then we're going to have a . . . Gary Snyder's coming this year, as well as Lawrence Ferlinghetti. So we've got a full house of poets.

TMA: A reunion.
AG: Yes, and on the basis of an interesting subject, which attracted Snyder, which is ecological poetics. So we're going to concentrate 1) on ecology 2) meditation and poetics—contemplative poetics, and 3) we're going to have a special week of Latin American poetry. So we've invited Nicanor Parra from Chile and several Nicaraguan poets and Salvadorian poets, and some specialists in Latin poetry. Some of our graduates, our ex-students, will be running the festival. And they've been spending quite a bit of time in Central America and South America: Argentina, Salvador, Guatemala, Honduras, and what-not. So some of our alumni have come back to help organize this festival of Latin American poetry. That will be all through July 1 through July 30. That should be quite a big jamboree. I think we've got a limited number of people we can accommodate for the summer. I think it's something like fifty or sixty, I'm not quite sure.

TMA: People who want to go better get moving on it.
AG: Yes, register and get with it. But it's quite a gang, because it will be myself, Snyder, Burroughs, Nicanor Parra, who's one of the greatest Latin American poets.
  We were talking about collaboration. Of course, the whole Buddhist thing is collaboration, which is what's going on with me and Phil. We're dharma students, and so we have a tendency to be attracted to each other's. . . . how each of us applies our dharmic meditative training to our art, and to presenting our art to society as an instrument of enlightenment or revelation of our own confusion or whatever. So I'm always curious how he relates his meditations and silences to turning outward toward the world. I

think he's curious how I do it too. So it's interesting to collaborate. But I've been working also with rock groups over the years, and jazz musicians.

TMA: Yes, I looked through this autobiographical piece and you've worked with just about everybody.

AG: I have a new record called "The Lion for Real," on Island Records. It's spoken poetry with music deliberately constructed for the poetry. And it covers . . . I recite my poetry, poems from 1952 to 1980, and a lot of good musicians that play at the Knitting Factory in New York. Some of them work with Tom Waits, some of them work with Marianne Faithfull. And the producer is a very intelligent guy, Hal Willner, who's also producing an album of Burroughs with strings that's almost finished. And it's out on Island Records. The Knitting Factory in New York is a venue where a lot of advanced jazz musicians play. There's Ralph Corney and Bill Frizell and Arto Lindsey and Lenny Pickett and Rebo. And G. E. Smith, who's playing with Dylan's touring band, and Steve Swallow, a quite refined bassist who's done a lot of work with Creeley's poetry.

So Willner had already produced the big Disney album with Sting and Ringo Starr and Tom Waits. He'd done an album with Marianne Faithfull, and he had already done an album of Kurt Weill's songs and Thelonious Monk music. So he's quite a professional. It's probably the best record I've done so far, as far as the spoken word. Because it's got . . . it's sort of upgrading the old jazz poetry stuff of the fifties. So that just came out, but it's very hard to get, it's hardly available in any of the stores, even though it's Island Records. I think they're going to put it out again when the Burroughs record comes out in summer, and package it for bookstores too. But the only way you can get it now, as far as I know if you can't find it in a store, is to write me.

TMA: Can you tell us a little bit about your Glasnost in the USA project?

AG: At the moment there's been an expansion of liberty in Eastern Europe and Russia. At the same time there's been a crackdown, a crescendo of censorship, here in many areas. One has been the Jesse Helms war on the National Endowment for the Arts: a neo-conservative attempt to stop government funding of individual artists. I think they want to go back to the elite funding just for symphonies and museums rather than a more democratic sense of funding for small groups and community groups, because they're afraid the community groups are all commie pinko homosexual eccentric black brown people of color. It's partly a racist . . . prejudice on the part of Jesse Helms. Because he was quoted in the *Times* as objecting to the

Robert Mapplethorpe show on the ground that it showed men of different races making it together. So I think he objects to the funding of black culture to begin with, much less allowing homosexuals to be funded along with heterosexuals. So there is a tremendous amount of chilling effect going on.

TMA: You've been dealing with censorship since the fifties.

AG: Yes, though I'm not so involved with the NEA, though I might want a grant later on. I just had a grant two years ago. But where it's really affecting me quite directly in an interesting way is that Helms also introduced a law in October '88 directing the FCC to ban all quote, indecent, unquote language twenty four hours a day. They never defined what indecent is, and it seems now to cover a huge range of literature from quotations in Tom Wolfe's *The Right Stuff*, to all of my major poetry that's in the anthologies that they use in colleges and high schools, to work by Kurt Vonnegut, Miles Davis, even James Joyce.

TMA: Anybody Jessie doesn't like.

AG: And of course Burroughs. But they don't define indecency. Now it's unconstitutional, the law, but to say for Pacifica or any listeners of a station to take it to court, as they have in the past and won, when they've been cited by the FCC, would cost them one hundred thousand to two hundred thousand dollars in legal fees. So what we've done is organize an appeal to the FCC which was holding hearings from . . . the formal end of the hearings was February 20—the date for submission of briefs, and March 20 for the submission of additional material. So a law firm in Washington representing Pacifica Network put in a very brilliant brief, which covered some of my work. And then we organized a consortium of lawyers in New York to represent the PEN Club, the American PEN Chapter, of novelists. Larry McMurtry is the president now, and Susan Sontag was our previous president, and before that it was Norman Mailer. So PEN Club and myself and William Burroughs and several others have participated, and were represented by the National Emergency Civil Liberties Committee. And handling that pro bono for any COC is the Rabinowits, Badine & Lieberman law firm in New York, and they're one of the best constitutional law firms.

TMA: That's great. There is a danger if they can outspend you.

AG: Well they can outspend us, definitely. No question, because they have the whole government on their side and they can rig the whole system that way. And then, in addition, there's the fundamentalist moral majority groups who have been organizing letter writing campaigns through Midwestern Television. There's a whole lot of groups, I've forgotten all of their names. But a lot of them are merging around the Heritage Foundation, which is behind some of the organization here. So the lawyers representing us, one of them is Ed DeGrazia, who is professor at the Cordozo Law School here at NYU, and he represented Grove Press in liberating Henry Miller's *Tropic of Cancer* and *Capricorn*, and William Burroughs' *Naked Lunch*, already three decades ago. So he's an old veteran of these kinds of censorship wars. He also represented Grove in "I Am Curious Yellow." He's a specialist in film censorship too.

In a previous lawsuit with the FCC, when the FCC on its own banned indecent language from six A.M. to midnight, we sued in 1987–88 and we won. Their excuse is to prevent children from being disturbed. But to do that, they're reducing the entire adult population to the level of minors during the major hours of the day. And now Helms is reducing all the adult population, all twenty-four hours of the day, to minors. So that's one area.

Then there's quite a bit of fundamentalist attempt to censor books in high schools and libraries. Then there is an attempt to isolate and label supposedly indecent language on phonograph records, which would include not only real outright porn or satanic or goofy stuff, but would also include high class poetry; like my record would not be able to pass without a label. Particularly because I have one attack on Czechoslovakian Marxist bureaucracy called "The King of May" on my record "The Lion for Real." And it has the line, "And when communist and capitalist assholes tango, the just man is arrested or robbed or has his head cut off, but not like Cabier. And the cigarette cough of the just man, in the bright clouds, is a salute to the health of the blue sky." So the word asshole would be called indecent even though it's in a political context.

Now what indecency is, they don't say. You see, the obscenity position in courts is that, if something is obscene it's protected as free speech if it has aesthetic value, like James Joyce's "Bloomsday" say, or "Howl," which had an obscenity trial. Or if it has social import or relevant social commentary. But the FCC is not counting that as an important element. And so, by calling it indecent, they shift the word away from obscene which has been legally chewed over, and they can start all over again.

TMA: Well all the way across the eighties there's been a rise of fundamentalism and oh, on a dark day, you could call it fascism.

AG: Well it's the same thing that's happening in Russia now with glasnost. Now you've got all these fundamentalists and anti-semites rising up out of the Russian unconscious, and you have the same thing in America too.

TMA: Do you care to comment on the drug war?

AG: Well that always seemed to be what Burroughs pronounced it in the *Midnight Cowboy* movie, some kind of excuse for setting up an international police apparatus. It's a fraud and a phony, the drug war. Because any real war on drug use would involve cure or treatment centers, and there are no treatment centers available now. You have to wait six months in New York to get any kind of treatment. So it's hypocritical. It costs more money to build jails and house people than treatment centers, and yet they're proposing billions for jails and very little for treatment centers. So that's already the first thing one can notice.

Secondly, Noriega and Bush and the administration, for a few years, were in cahoots in drug transportation and using profits from cocaine or heroin for off-the-shelf CIA and NSA operations, and that's pretty well known. Apparently Oliver North and Seacord and Bush's national security directory, Donald Grey, and various CIA agents that were working and operating in Central America, including John Hull, were all involved in the drug trade as a way of funding the Contra operations. You can read it in the average newspaper, the *New York Times*, that the State Department has known about Noriega's drug dealing for years, and the DEA was giving him letters of recommendation up to 1985. So there's an untold story there that casts suspicion over the entire sincerity of the highly touted advertised cover story of the drug war.

We don't know what Noriega knows about Bush; in fact, that's the big story about Noriega and Bush. You can even read that in the *Times*, people saying, "We wonder what Noriega knows about Bush's involvement with the drug business, with the Contras?" Bush was paying Noriega two hundred thousand dollars a year when Bush was head of the CIA, and Bush was sitting with Noriega and seeing his representatives when he was Vice President. So if I knew about it, he must have known about it. And Nancy Reagan can't say that she didn't know about it; she can't say she just discovered it yesterday; she can't be that dumb because it was in the papers—Noriega being a drug dealer. And it was in all the CIA reports; it was in all sorts of investigative journalistic books. So what's it all about? That's the big mystery. Nobody knows what it's really about.

The one thing it does seem to be about is extending police apparatus to patrol and dominate the underclass without solving the problems of the underclass that leads them to drugs. So they want to build more jails, they want to have more police, they want to have more draconian laws, they want to clobber women who have drug habits rather than . . . take their children away from them rather than giving them treatment, because there are no treatment facilities for addicted women. And they're now letting the CIA and army intelligence loose for domestic surveillance with the excuse of the drug war.

TMA: That's when it really starts to get chilling.

AG: That's where it gets very chilling. Historically it's always been un-American activity for the CIA to be doing domestic surveillance and for the army to be doing domestic surveillance.

TMA: Which they've always done, but now it's supposedly legal.

AG: Yes, it was considered against the law, but now the law backs it. So that's really a shift in ethos and a shift toward more and more Big Brother. And that's a curious contradiction, because the neo-conservatives who are behind the drug war, like Bennett, are the very ones who say, "Get the government off our backs." And yet they're putting more and more government on our backs. So it's a contradiction which makes you think that some of them looked at communists so long that they became what they beheld, in the words of Blake, "They became what they beheld." All the neo-conservatives stared at Stalin so much they've turned into Stalin, like Lot's wife turned to a pillar of salt. Then the other aspect is that they want to get more and more police and get the military involved. Whereas it's very widely accepted, historically, that narcotic bureaus themselves have always been saturated with corruption and dealing drugs on a federal, state and local level. That was proved in New York back in the seventies with the NAPP commission that said that drug dealing was epidemic in the narcotics bureau in New York City, which is the largest in the world. And when Ramsey Clark got to be Attorney General, he said he had to fire or indict forty-nine out of the eighty federal agents.

TMA: Well with profits like that . . .

AG: Obviously, as with prohibition, the profit motive is the main cause of the spread of drugs. And as long as you keep the profits high by keeping it in the black market you're always going to have this cash nexus as the motive as the spread of drug addiction.

Another element that should be borne in mind is that the government is constantly mixing up the soft drugs, which are not habit forming and are not lethal, with hard drugs—mixing marijuana and even LSD with speed, coke, and heroin. My recommendation would be to decriminalize marijuana and allow it as a cash crop for the small family farm, to save the All-American family farm, rather than the money being siphoned abroad; and maybe tax it. And then, for heroin, to send junkies to doctors to be cured or maintained as in any other country. And then, with psychedelics, give them over to Rabbis and Swamis and Priests and doctors and psychiatrists. More or less on the Swiss model. It is legal to do psychological and psychiatric experiments with LSD now. As of last year, LSD is legal for psychiatrists, for experimental therapy, in Switzerland for the first time. So there's been a big breakthrough finally in the total ban on the experiment, which is quite useful, and that might be a way of looking at LSD. That would leave the crack and coke and speed problem isolated as real difficult drugs that have problems. Those you'd have to be able to treat on a level with alcoholism, in the Alcoholics Anonymous model, and other models which are dealing with alcohol and violence would then come into focus or into some kind of perspective. I'm sort of proposing a resolution to the drug problem.

TMA: Well they don't really seem to be interested in helping people resolve things. They seem more interested in establishing a police state.
AG: Right. As Burroughs says, given all the information, it doesn't seem to be so much a war on drugs as a war on the underclass, and also a war on the sixties and a war on civil liberties. And along with the flag business, in an attempt to destabilize the constitution, and get a bigger Big Brother state like in Orwell. To lock all this drug discussion in, you have to have the bottom line, which is death statistics. According to the *Times*, about a half a year ago, twenty to thirty thousand people a year die from hard drugs, none from marijuana, none from LSD—or very rarely from LSD. Then one hundred thousand a year die from alcohol, and 385,000 a year die from heart attack and cancer and high blood pressure related to nicotine, tobacco.

Now the curious and interesting thing is that the Heritage Foundation, which is behind all this suppressive legislation and also the drug war too, is funded by alcohol: Joseph Coors. And Senator Jesse Helms, who is also behind a lot of the repressive legislation, is the tobacco cult senator from

North Carolina, who represents the tobacco lobby. Though he complains about spending taxpayers' money without asking them for art, he himself doesn't hesitate to spend taxpayers' money to subsidize tobacco agriculture in his state without asking the public whether they want to do that. The other one is that he throws his weight around as a member of the Foreign Relations Committee, trying to get Malaysia to buy and accept American cigarette advertising and buy American cigarettes. So it's a really interesting contradiction here, and it may be the key to why Helms is such a loudmouth, because he's got all that on his conscience and he knows he's guilty of being the main cancer peddler in the Congress.

TMA: Well this strategy seems to be backfiring on him too, because along with the already illegal drugs, the drug warriors are now talking about making tobacco and alcohol illegal.

AG: Well, it's pretty logical, because people began pointing out that the real drugs, the real drug damage, is from alcohol and tobacco, not from . . . the crime in the streets is caused, in a sense, by the police state on drugs and the repression and the creation of a black market or a criminal class. But the actual death statistics, and even social damage from alcoholism and cigarettes, is much larger. Except that the government propagandizes the dangers on the streets, quite rightly, of the crackheads and the speed freaks and the junkies. But they're out there robbing in order to get money . . .

One way of keeping one's head in the midst of all this glasnost in Eastern Europe, which is a great thing, and the hope of working for some kind of American glasnost. I think the American glasnost will come, as it came in Europe, from the tradition of the sixties, the openheartedness and the tolerance and the sense of humor that Vaclav Havel displays. And maybe some mixtures of meditative awareness.

TMA: It's on the spiritual level that it all works out.

AG: Well depending on what you mean by spirit. By spirit I'm getting back to the Latin roots, spiritus, meaning breathing. Where there's life there's breath—spirit.

The way it's commonly used leaves it so much up in the air there's a big mish-mosh it's unbelievable. I don't think it should be used in a general, generic thing like that, it's too much bullshit. It lets anything in from table rapping to Charlie Manson to crystal gazing to who knows what, and it doesn't focus on the ongoing process of breath which is the basis of meditation-awareness of breath which is the meditative process.

TMA: You've been involved with meditation for, what, thirty years?

AG: Well one way or another since I was in India, but I didn't really get down on my behind and sit regularly till about 1970. I started with Swami Muktananda, and then I began studying with Trungpa Rinpoche in 1972.

Allen Ginsberg in India: An Interview

Suranjan Ganguly / 1993

Ariel: A Review of International English Literature, 24:4, October 1993, 21–32. Reprinted with permission.

Allen Ginsberg's association with India began in 1962, when he spent over a year there with Peter Orlovsky, travelling and looking for a spiritual teacher. There were visits to the Himalayas with Gary Snyder and Joanne Kyger, to the caves of Ajanta and Ellora, to Buddhist shrines in Sanchi and Sarnath, protracted stays in Calcutta and Benares, and meetings with mystics, yogis, poets, writers, musicians, and religious leaders like the Dalai Lama. He also met, without knowing, Chogyam Trungpa Rinpoche, the Tibetan lama who would come to the US in the 1970s, set up the Naropa Institute at Boulder, Colorado, and become Ginsberg's teacher. In 1970, Ginsberg published the journals he had kept during his stay, and the following year he was back in India in the aftermath of the Bangladesh war. Now planning his third trip in 1994, Ginsberg gave this interview last July in the apartment he rents each summer in Boulder while teaching at the Jack Kerouac School of Disembodied Poetics at the Naropa Institute.

Suranjan Ganguly: So in February 1962 Peter Orlovsky and you arrived in Bombay with only a dollar . . .
Allen Ginsberg: Very little money. Did we only have a dollar? We went looking for mail, and there was probably some money waiting for us. We'd been out of touch for a long time, going on a boat to the Red Sea to Dar es Salaam and Mombasa and then to Bombay.

SG: Was there already the sixties craze to go East, to "spiritual India" and all that?

AG: I had already been to Europe and spent several years there and that was a traditional thing as in the nineteenth century and early twentieth century—the American in Paris. By 1961, I was more interested in going beyond the traditional expatriate role or voyage, of wandering out in the East, particularly India, the most rich and exquisite and aesthetically attractive culture. And also least expensive. . . . But at that time India was pretty well-unknown. There weren't that many people who went there. There were rare people, famous rare people who did that, but it wasn't a whole generation that took it on. It became a stereotype almost instantly when *Esquire* sent some photographer to take pictures of us and put out a fake cover with a guy who looked like me, and a piece on beatniks in India. And that apparently was a model for a lot of people going there. And then I published my Indian journals and that encouraged a lot of poor people to go looking for drugs. . . . But, then, I think it was a very valuable experience for many Americans. You will find any number of advanced Canadian and American practitioners who were there in the sixties and learnt Tibetan and who also translated major works and were interpreters for visiting lamas. So there was a whole network of understanding, of experience, of education that led ultimately to things like the Naropa Institute, to an institutionalization of the meeting of Eastern and Western minds.

SG: What did you associate India chiefly with?
AG: You know, it was thirty years ago and I don't remember very clearly except snake charmers and . . . I really didn't know what to ask for, but I had the idea of going there to look for a teacher. That was definitely the purpose. I had read the *Bhagavad Gita* and Ramakrishna's *Table Talk*, the *Tibetan Book of the Dead* and a lot of Buddhist writing. I had some idea of yoga but not much. Actually, when I was twelve years old I heard an American give a lecture on yoga in Paterson, New Jersey. I had read some Krishnamurti, some saint poetry, some Yogananda, a little of the *Mahabharata,* some of the *Vedas,* and translations by Isherwood and Prabhavananda of the *Upanishads.* I also read Lin Yutang's *The Wisdom of China and India.* Then on the ship I read *A Passage to India* and *Kim,* the Jataka tales and some *Ramayana.*

SG: What about the cultural scene—for example, did you see Satyajit Ray's films in New York in the fifties?
AG: Oh yeah, but not that many. I remember *Pather Panchali* and being very impressed by that. But on our way to India, at Mombasa, I saw a film which outdid Disney and would make millions of dollars if shown in

America. It was called *Sampoorna Ramayana,* and it was my real introduction to Indian mythology, to specific Indian attitudes. Boy! It was amazing! Ganesh was so pretty and amusing and sophisticated compared to the very heavy-handed, very serious Western regard for God—only one of them, watch out![1] An interesting, sweet and innocent film, probably more culturally wise than anything by Disney.

SG: Were you familiar with the Indian classical traditions in music and dance?
AG: I had seen Uday Shankar, an old man, dancing at City Center, New York, and there was some Shiva dance that he did that was absolutely astounding. I had never seen anything like that—such absolute and subtle control of the whole body so that a wave of energy could pass, beginning at the top of the skull and move down, go up the arm, and down to the belly, and from left to right. It was like a current of electricity. It was one of the most extraordinary and ecstatic artistries I had ever seen.

SG: Did the books you read provide a framework for such experiences?
AG: In the *Bhagavad Gita,* there is a visionary moment when Krishna shows himself with armies flowing from his mouth. That's a little bit like the high point of vision that you get in Dante's *Inferno* or some of Blake's "Last Judgment" or other poems, and to me it seemed immediately universal. . . . The *Gita* is really an universal poem, really archetypal. I had had some similar visionary experiences on my own—in the late forties they were related to Blake, and then in the early fifties I had some minor experience of psychedelic drugs—peyote, mescaline, the cactus, and then in '59 lysergic acid.[2] So I'd seen a lot of internal mandalas in my mind that reminded me of the pictures I'd seen in Tibetan Buddhism and of the universal form of Krishna in the *Gita.* So I was tuned into that kind of mythologic archetype as a real experience of consciousness, and I was looking for some way of making it more permanent, or mastering it or getting clearer about it in my own mind. . . . I was interested in what that older culture still had as a living transmission of spiritual and visionary energy because in the West there didn't seem to be one.

SG: Since you mention drugs, did you know about soma, a god and a hallucinogenic plant in ancient India, with roots in heaven?
AG: I was very interested in soma. I had met R. Gordon Wasson who had a lot of experience of mushrooms and who had a theory that soma was a

certain mushroom. So I was prepared to take that mythology a little more literally than most Westerners, as signifying something more literal on a spiritual level. There were realms of modalities of consciousness that were available and real, that were not within the Western psychological category except maybe in William James's *The Varieties of Religious Experience* or in the hermetic tradition of Blake.

SG: Was there a sense that the West had failed you in certain respects?
AG: Well, as I had written six–seven years before in "Howl": "Moloch whose fate is a cloud of sexless hydrogen." I had read Spengler's *The Decline of the West* in 1945–46 and was already anticipating the decline of empire which took a long time to happen, but in half a century it was almost gone, almost over. . . . So there was a realization that the West was impermanent, that the entire Western rationalistic, Aristotelean mind was causing chaos, and I was interested in Eastern thought, all summed up in that gesture—the very Indian gesture—when you ask, "Are you enjoying yourself?" and an Indian will shake his head . . . shakes his head. It could be either yes or no depending on the context, and I was interested in that context with its subtlety of expression rather than in a Western context. . . . Then there was something else I was interested in: the notion of the Kali Yuga.[3] I had read Vico's theories of the Golden Ages, Stone Ages, Iron Ages, and Bronze Ages, of the cyclical nature of things, so I was curious about the idea of eternal return and the cyclical evolution of *kalpas* and also, about the staggering number of *kalpas*.[4] That fitted in with my idea of the decline of empire, of an aeon being over. The scope of the cycles of consciousness and incarnation in Hindu and Buddhist mythology was very attractive given the smaller historical cycles of the American century.

SG: So after almost a year and a half in India, what did you find there that you had not found in the West?
AG: A more intimate awareness of the relation between people and God. Just the very notion of Ganesh with a noose in one hand and a *rasgoola* in the other, and his trunk in the *rasgoola*, riding a mouse. . . .[5] Such an idea of a god, such a sophisticated, quixotic, paradoxical combination of the human and the divine, the metaphysical and the psychological! You don't often get that in Christianity, except maybe in some esoteric Christianity. The idea of an entire culture suffused with respect for that mythology, that religion and its practices, that poor people could understand its sophistication and grant things that hard-headed Westerners are still trying to kill each other over.

That was a revelation: how deeply the sense of a spiritual existence could penetrate everyday relations, the streets and street signs . . . Naga sadhus walking around naked—people who would have been arrested in America[6] . . . or for that matter—I remember writing to Kerouac—everybody walking around in their underwear, in striped boxer shorts. What would seem outrageous or strange to Americans was just normal—it was hot and people wore very light cotton—it seemed so obvious. That showed me the absurd artificiality of some American customs. . . . And then just the notion of somebody being a businessman and then renouncing the world and being a *sannyasi* and going around with an intelligent expression looking for *moksha*, that was such a switch from the American notion of business, such a good model, but it doesn't work for even Indians now.[7] . . . And then the availability of ganja and its use in religious festivals and ceremonies was a great source of release for an American used to government dictatorship of all psychedelic drugs (even marijuana), to prohibitions, murders, beatings, corruption.[8] At least, in India there was some familiarity with what it was.

SG: But did you find the same kind of tolerance for sex, given India's notorious homophobia?

AG: In Bombay someone took us to a district where there were many transvestites, but whatever the situation, it was familiar, domesticated. . . . They don't have transvestite districts in America, of course! Although I was in India for a year and a half, I never had a love affair with an Indian. It was just that I was so absorbed in whatever I was seeing that I wasn't able to connect emotionally with any particular Indian. During our last days in Calcutta, somebody took me to a gigantic beerhall of a basement. . . . All homosexuals. I didn't realize it even existed. Maybe I didn't ask about it. I wish I had known.

SG: Since you mention Calcutta, were you, like most foreigners, overwhelmed by the city at first?

AG: I had no idea about Calcutta except I had heard of the Black Hole of Calcutta, but I didn't know what it was. I met Asoke Fakir there, who just appeared at my hotel one day and became my guide. He was both a fool and at the same time a devotional man, in some respects the most intelligent person I met in Calcutta, who knew what we wanted to see—low life, religious life, tantric life. I wanted to go to some place where people smoked a little ganja and were serious, so he took me on a walk along the banks of the Hooghly to Howrah Bridge and to Nimtallah burning ghat.[9]

SG: What was your experience of the burning ghats?

AG: I went there several times a week and stayed there very late at night. For one thing I was amazed at the openness of death, the visibility of death which is hidden and powdered and rouged and buried in a coffin in the West. To suggest the opposite, the openness of it is like an education which is totally different from the cultivation of the notion of the corpse as still relevant and alive and "don't kick it over." There they just lay it out and burn it and the family watches the dissolution; they see the emptiness in front of them, the emptiness of the body in front of them. So I had the opportunity to see the inside of the human body, to see the face cracked and torn, fallen off, the brains bubbling and burning. And reading Ramakrishna at the time: the dead body is nothing but an old pillow, an empty pillow, like burning an old pillow. Nothing to be afraid of. So it removed a lot of the fear of the corpse that we have in the West. And then I saw people singing outside on Thursday nights and other nights too. That was amazing, and the noise was rousing, very loud, and I would sit around, pay attention and listen, and try and get the words. I saw lady yogis meditating in the ash pit. I remember one lady who I thought was defenseless and poverty-stricken, so I offered her some coins and she spit on them and threw them back at me. And there was one very strange evening when I drank some *bhang*—it must have been mixed with *datura*—and went there with a completely screwed-up head, hallucinating.[10] And I thought I was in the used Vomit Market, everybody was so poor that they were selling vomit! Slept on a stone bench inside the temple all night and woke up and found my slippers gone. Pretty funny . . .

SG: In the journals, there are so many graphic details of bodies burning—as if you were getting high on death.

AG: I don't think I was. After all death is half of life. I was just describing life as I saw it.

SG: What did you think of the literary scene in Calcutta?

AG: We poets—Sunil Ganguly, Shakti Chatterjee, and others—met a lot in the coffee houses.[11] Peter and I were excited by the idea of there being a whole gang of poets like there were in New York and San Francisco, who were friends, and that we could communicate across the Pacific Ocean, and that East could meet West, and that they knew our work, and that we could interpret it more and show them poets like Gregory Corso and others they might not have heard of.

SG: If you were to go back to India, which cities would you revisit?

AG: I've a tremendous nostalgia mostly for Calcutta and Benares, and Benares particularly because I was very happy there learning a lot, and I had good friends. We had a beautiful house right above the market place and Dasaswamedh Ghat. There was a balcony looking down on the river and an alleyway that went down to the steps. That's where the beggars would gather. . . . And I remember getting really hung up on puris and potatoes.

SG: Now wasn't it in Benares that the Criminal Investigation Department of India got onto your backs?

AG: Yes. I don't know why. I think Blitz newspaper said that we were CIA spies. India was then at war with China over a border dispute, so. . . . Peter had a girlfriend, a mysterious Bengali lady, who was staying with us, and it was considered shocking by of all people secular Marxists, whereas her family was much more sophisticated, less questioning.

SG: Since you were living in a poor section of the city, how did you react to the squalor and human misery around you?

AG: The poverty was striking, but I don't know why we weren't repelled or angry. We were more interested in what we could do, how to relate to it, how to report it back to the Western world in a way that would rouse sympathy and action rather than horror. Peter was once an ambulance driver so he was not afraid of the homeless and the sick. Also, his own relatives had been in mental hospitals, so he was used to dealing with the mentally-disturbed. He was the heroic type, interested in attempting something. So I just followed Peter and he took utmost care.

SG: All this was thirty years ago. What did India give you that has mattered most, that has stayed with you and will always be there?

AG: The Indian influence was first of all on the voice itself and on the notion of poetry and music coming together. Pound had revived that notion and shown how for the ancient Greek poets song and poetry were one, even one with dance. The Greek choruses sang and danced and chanted, and Homer and Sappho sang with a five-stringed lyre. So India helped me to rediscover that relationship between poetry and song. I heard people singing in the streets, chanting mantras, so I began singing mantra too—"Hare Krishna Hare Rama" or "Hare Om Namah Sivaye."

SG: And you had never heard such chanting in America?

AG: I first heard it in India, not in America. I had never been to any Hindu temple here where people sat and chanted. I owned books that dealt with Buddhist mantras, but there was no place in America where there was mantra chanting or singing except maybe in the Vedanta temples. So it was not until I got to Bombay that I saw people singing together on the street; and in Calcutta, at Nimtallah burning ghat, people would gather, as I said, particularly on Thursday night, which was Kali night to sing amazing, beautiful choral stuff, and they would pass around a chilam and sing continuously, "Siya Rama Jai Jai Rama" or "Raghu Pati Raghav." But it was at the Magh Mela at Allahabad that I heard a Nepalese lady singing "Hare Krishna Hare Rama" and the melody was so beautiful that it stuck in my head, and I took it home to America in 1963 and began singing it at poetry parties, after poetry readings with finger cymbals first and later the harmonium.[12] And that began to develop into singing and chanting as part of my poetry readings and led to a deepening of my voice, which slowly began to fill up my body and resonate in the breast area (you might say by hyperbole, "heart chakra"), so that I could talk from there, and that reminded me of the voice of Blake that I had heard, as if my youthful apprehension of that voice was a latent resonance of my mature voice. So at public poetry readings I sang a great variety of mantras both Buddhist and Hindu, "Shri Rama Jai Rama Jai Jai Rama," "Hare Krishna," or "Om Shri Maitreya" or "Om Mani Padme Hum" or "Om" or "Gate Gate Paragate" which I sang quite a bit, the Prajnaparamita sutra. Then singing led to transferring my obsession with mantra to sacred song, to Blake, and I began making melodies from Blake's *Songs of Innocence and Experience* in 1968, and by 1969 I was writing my own folk songs and also recording the Blake songs I had set to music. In 1963, I met Bob Dylan and got interested in the new poetry that was in the form of song, influenced by the earlier Beat generation, by Kerouac and myself, and by 1970 I was recording songs with him. So things came together with the seed mantra planted. In that respect, India helped me to recover the relationship between poetry and music, offered me a model as well as gave me saint poetry in song.

SG: I notice when you sing you play the harmonium which is very popular in India. Any particular reason?

AG: Because I'm not a musician. I can't play anything. And this is like a child's instrument; it's so simple I can make out American chords and sing blues. It's actually a Western instrument, and oddly enough the larger harmonium, the foot pedal harmonium, the church organ, is probably the instrument that Blake used for his songs; so my first project in English was to set Blake to music.

SG: Why is it that at public readings you don't chant mantra that much anymore?

AG: In 1970, in America, I ran into Trungpa Rinpoche, the Tibetan lama who founded Naropa. I was showing him on the harmonium how I sang, and he put a paw on my hand, drunk, and said, "Remember the silence is just as important as the song." He then suggested that I not sing all the mantras for they would raise some kind of expectation or neurological buzz in the audience; but he didn't have any teaching to give to stabilize that or to develop it, and he suggested that if I were to sing in public, to sing "Ah," the mantra appreciation of the voice, or "Om Muni Muni Maha Muni Sakyamuni e Swaha" about the human Buddha of the Sakya family, a wise man, or "Gate Gate Paragate"—gone, gone to the other shore gone, completely gone, vacant mind, salutations—something which didn't require a structured sadhana or practice to have some effect and would not confuse people.

SG: I'd like to go back to something you said at the start of this interview— that you were looking for a teacher in India. Did you find one?

AG: No. Well, yes and no. I found teaching there and I found teachers there who really became my teachers in America. There is a photograph of Peter and I visiting a monk and it turns out that the young monk who showed us the altar was Trungpa Rinpoche. Then I met the Dalai Lama later at Dharamsala and had some teachings from him. And on a visit to Kalimpong, I met Dudjom Rinpoche, who was the head of the N'yingma sect of Tibetan Buddhsim. I was having a lot of difficulty with LSD—bum trips, hell trips, hungry ghost realms—so I asked him about it, and he gave me some very good advice, which was: If you see something horrible don't cling to it, and if you seem something beautiful, don't cling to it. Basically that's the essence of Buddhist teaching, and it has stuck with me all these years. It is still the seed. And I met others like Swami Sivananda, who said: "Your heart is your guru"; and Bankey Behari, who said: "Take Blake for your guru"; and Sitaram Onkar Das Thakur, an old Vaishnav, who said: "If you want to find a guru, eat certain kinds of food and die and repeat the mantra, 'Guru Gur Guru Guru Guru Guru' for three weeks."[13]

SG: Did you try it?

AG: Yes, sure, of course I did. I also met a lot of interesting yogis. Someone taught us *pranayam,* which was helpful for a while since it creates some kind of mental stabilization.¹⁴ But it wasn't until 1970 through Ram Dass—Richard Alpert—who was an old friend from the sixties that I met Muktananda, and he asked me if I had a meditation practice, and, since, as a matter of fact, I still didn't have one, he invited me to Dallas for a weekend and taught me a practice which I did for a year and a half until I met Trungpa, who suggested a more rounded form. So from 1972 I worked with Trungpa in the Tibetan Vajrayana style.¹⁵

SG: Shortly after you left India, you wrote "The Change: Kyoto-Tokyo Express" in Japan and it's widely regarded as a poem that describes what India did to you.

AG: Well, that's a little corny. It's a change from a sort of a preoccupation with the absolute to a preoccupation with the relative, accepting the body. . . . I renounce all forms of attachment—"in my train seat I renounce my power"—I will no longer be eternal or immortal or anything. I'll just be me. In a sense, it's a transition, but I don't think it's that well-expressed. People make a lot of it, but I don't think it's that good a poem because the references are too obscure, some of them like quasi-kundalini neurological buzzings or zappings. It's really a head trip with some emotion.

SG: What do you think of the rise of Hindu fundamentalism in India today?

AG: The greatness of India I saw was the absorption into Hinduism of all the gods—the Western ones and the Buddhist ones—and the open space, the accommodation to all varieties of human nature, and I would imagine the curse of India would be this exclusiveness.

Notes

1. Ganesh is a Hindu god with the head of an elephant.

2. In 1948, Ginsberg had a visionary experience in which he heard a voice—which he assumed to be Blake's—reciting "Ah Sunflower."

3. In Hinduism time is structured in terms of cycles, each cycle subdivided into four ages or yugas, the last of which is Kali Yuga, the age of discord.

4. In Jainism, time is also treated as cyclical, divided into recurring periods called *kalpas* or aeons. A *kalpa* has two phases, each of which consists of six eras.

5. A *rasgoolla* is an Indian sweetmeat made of ricotta cheese dipped in syrup.

6. The Naga ("naked") sadhus are holy men who do not wear clothes and belong to a sect that was originally militant.

7. A *sannyasi* is an ascetic who has renounced society and seeks *moksha,* which in Hinduism represents liberation from karma (one's deeds and consequences) and samsara (rebirth).

8. Ganja is marijuana smoked usually from a chilam, a clay pipe, passed around by smokers.

9. Hindus cremate their dead at Nimtallah Ghat on the banks of the Hooghly (as the Ganges is called in Calcutta).

10. *Bhang* is hemp mixed with almond milk, drunk usually during religious festivals. The seeds of the *datura* plant serve as an intoxicant.

11. Two distinguished contemporary Bengali poets. Sunil Ganguly is also a well-known novelist.

12. The Magh Mela is a fair held every year in January.

13. A Vaishav is a worshipper of Vishnu, the Hindu god who pervades the universe, holding it together.

14. *Pranayam* is a yogic breathing exercise.

15. Vajrayana is the school of Tibetan tantric Buddhism.

Public Heart: An Interview with Allen Ginsberg

Jim Moore / 1994

Hungry Mind Review, Issue 30, Summer 1994, 42–43. Reprinted with permission.

With the publication of "Howl" in 1955, Allen Ginsberg entered the public arena in America in a way no other poet has done before or since. "Howl"'s cry of anger and outrage against the complacency of the fifties became the central statement of Beat attitudes, offending and inspiring with its delirious plunge of language.

Performing his work widely in the sixties, Ginsberg agitated for civil rights, war resistance, psychedelic experience, and gay liberation. As a student and teacher, he has been connected since the seventies with the rise of interest in Zen in the US. The impact of his seemingly private vision on the American public psyche has been profound. People who have never read a word he has written have had their sense of America—its anguish and its pleasures—shaped by his words and presence.

On a recent visit to Minneapolis/St. Paul, Ginsberg was in a reflective mood, looking forward to the publication of a new book of poems, *Cosmopolitan Greetings* (HarperCollins), and to the release of several new CDs, critical to the presentation of his work which depends for much of its power on being read aloud.

Though Ginsberg responded to questions with a cranky liveliness and the frankness that is his trademark, I also felt a kind of tired reserve I hadn't expected. This disappeared entirely at the reading he gave that night, a sold-out benefit for Coffee House Press held on the campus of the University of St. Thomas in St. Paul.

Jim Moore: Thanks to your poetry and your presence on the American literary and cultural scene since 1955, the American story is a lot livelier than it would otherwise have been. How do you read the American story now, especially as it may have changed since 1955? What threads in the story particularly interest you?

Allen Ginsberg: In the 1940s and 1950s there was some sense of hope that there could be a big enough change to save the planet. There was, at least, a desire for that, a hope that people would strive for some sort of ideal America: democratic, conservationist, sexually open. Equal righteousness for blacks and for Jews, for gays and for women. Some of those things have come true and some have not. But maybe we're in a deeper hole than we were in the forties and the fifties. And maybe we're losing the planet.

The sexual revolution has done a good job of opening up people's minds. On the other hand, there's been an imposition of literary censorship on radio and television, which is the main marketplace of ideas. This is because of Jesse Helms's law, signed in 1988 by Reagan. This immediately kept almost all of my poetry out of commission between the hours of six A.M. and eight P.M.

One advance is the infusion of African American culture into white consciousness through rap, rock-and-roll, and blues.

On the other hand, the ecological devastation is so great and the militarization so expensive that it has dug a pit out of which I don't think America can ever climb again.

The addiction to fossil fuel has not abated. Rather than spending the money to find clean, renewable energy sources, we keep getting into giant Mideast wars with endless complications which have put a karmic hole in the middle of America's brain.

One change at least in the nineties: Bush and Reagan were sourpusses, depressing people. Clinton seems to be more cheerful. Even if he can't do much. The addiction to all sorts of poisonous products, services and habits is so great that we need something like an international Hazelden. But the United States is nowhere near bottoming out.

Moore: Where does the American poet fit into this story today? Is there a role for the poet? Or is poetry simply irrelevant for most people?

Ginsberg: Poetry's role is to provide spontaneous individual candor as distinct from manipulators and brainwash.

President Clinton went to Brooklyn College the other day, where I teach. You should read the Brooklyn College paper complaining about the whole visit as a theatrical setup. Everything was choreographed. Written out in advance. It had nothing to do with real communication.

Poetry is a saving grace as it was in Russia under Stalin. The whole renaissance of fifties, sixties Beat poetry, poetry slams as well as the transitional poetry of music from Dylan on through rap. There is this desire for candid, straightforward individual statement, as distinct from censored—literally censored—and packaged and manipulated newspapers and media.

Moore: It's such a different period now, and yet there is this interest, a sort of renaissance.
Ginsberg: It's not really that different now. Everything was canned then and stereotyped in the fifties, too.

Moore: But there's not that sort of sixties sense of possibility now.
Ginsberg: People had hope then, now they don't. It's a question of how you live with AIDS rather than how you die with AIDS or how do you get cured? The patient has AIDS. How do you live with that?

Moore: How do you live with it?
Ginsberg: It's a difference in attitude. Relation to the reality of the situation and trying not to create more suffering than already exists. Rather than resenting the situation and thrashing about, and cursing yourself and cursing the situation and making it harder for yourself and others to deal with.

Moore: Is your impulse now to write poems different from the kind of urgency that impelled poems like "Howl" and "Kaddish" into existence so many years ago?
Ginsberg: It's not so much an impulse; it's a method which is very specific. It's noticing my thoughts, noticing that I'm noticing, observing what's there, then realizing what is really there. Self-selecting. Being a stenographer of your own mind.

Moore: How is that any different from meditation practice?
Ginsberg: They intersect. You're scanning your mind and observing your thoughts, and what forms arise and flourish.

Moore: What makes you decide to write down what you're thinking at certain points?
Ginsberg: I notice it and catch myself thinking.
Moore: But every time you notice it you don't write it down . . .

Ginsberg: No. If I notice something that is really vivid enough to formulate, then I write it down. And that's somewhat self-selective so it's not a problem. If it's interesting, it's interesting, and if it's not, it's not.

I used to write occasionally out of irritability and anger. I have a big long poem I wrote this year about diet. "Come on pigs of Western civilization: eat more grease! Drop dead of heart attacks so the Chinese can take over with their tofu and stir fry and vegetables."

Moore: Thinking about your work as a photographer, does the impulse to take photographs come from the same place as to write?
Ginsberg: More or less, noticing the moment and space, the visual moment. Yes, it is very similar. I notice carrying a camera around habitually now, which I've done since 1984, I tend to write less in my pocket notebook. I take photographs of things that otherwise I would make verbal descriptions of.

Moore: But do you then come back to the photographs and try to write poems about them?
Ginsberg: I come back to the photographs and then I write captions, extensive captions on them; they're like haikus.

Moore: There's such a presence in the people that you photograph.
Ginsberg: We're friends. It's like family photos: they're really there. Out of one roll, there will be one genius photo, no matter who the amateur is. There's always something. If you gave it to a really good printmaker it could be something they could put in the Museum of Modern Art.

Moore: Is that true in poetry too? There's always one good poem?
Ginsberg: If you transcribe somebody's conversation, your grandmother's conversation, there'd be one or two passages that would be immortal. My father told a story about the horses his father used in order to run the family laundry business in 1914 or so. They got a horse from a locksmith, somebody who came from the same town in Russia, and they took the horse home and started working with it, but all of a sudden the horse fell down on the ground and they called the horse doctor who said, "His brain's turned over." Fifty years later I said, "What did that mean?" My father said, "I don't know. That's what they said in those days: 'his brain turned over.'" Anyway, the next horse was lame. Then the next horse was a very good horse, a very sturdy horse and actually quite good, but they discovered he was blind. But

he was a very talented horse and after they took him around a few times, he was able to do it without guidance. He knew where to go. So he was the best horse they ever had, this blind horse. My father used to jump off the laundry cart and run up three or four flights, deliver laundry and come back.

Those kind of family stories you also get in Charles Reznikoff. There were some maybe you might find occasionally in William Carlos Williams. I'm sure every family has stories. By isolating them and presenting them as poems, the stories survive. Nowadays there is quite a movement, a habit of younger kids—post-sixties kids—going back to their great-grandmothers or their grandmothers and taping their life stories, transcribing them, and publishing the elders. Maybe because the world is going faster and faster, unlike other centuries when there was some stability from generation to generation. This century, the world of our forefathers, is vanished.

Moore: As this century ends, what hopes do you have for poetry in the next century, American poetry?
Ginsberg: The same, always more of the same.

Moore: So poetry doesn't change.
Ginsberg: No, it comes from the bottom of the heart, expresses what is known universally and privately and hardly ever acknowledged in public.

Allen Ginsberg Interview

Harvey Kubernik / 1996

Initially published in *HITS* magazine in 1996. Reprinted with permission.

I interviewed Allen Ginsberg at length one late afternoon in Rhino Records' conference room in Westwood, California, in 1996 and by telephone from his New York City apartment.

This interview first appeared in 1996 in *HITS* Magazine and a shorter edited version appeared in *The Los Angeles Times* Calendar section on April 7, 1997 when the daily newspaper asked me to pen one of the tribute stories on Ginsberg when he died.

At the time of our *HITS* Magazine interview, Allen Ginsberg had just released a recording "The Ballad of the Skeletons."

In 2007 I wrote the liner notes to the first-ever CD release of Ginsberg's *Kaddish* for Water Records.

Q: Tell me about your new recording.
A: Well, the whole project has been a collaboration with a lot of geniuses, really. When you get Philip Glass and Paul McCartney along with (guitarist) Marc Ribot and (producer) Lenny Kaye and (mixer) Hal Willner, and David Mansfield. There's a seven minute version, as well as an edited, clean four minute version for radio.

Q: What was the genesis and development of "The Ballad of the Skeletons" poem and printed context?
A: It was published in *The Nation*. I started it because all that inflated bull shit about the right wing and ascend, and the family values, contract with America, Newt Gingrich and all the loud mouth stuff on talk radio, and Rush Limbaugh and all those other guys. It seemed obnoxious and stupid and kind of sub-contradictory, so I figured I'd write a poem to knock it out of the ring.

Q: Unlike most of the things you write, were there any inherent music or melodic rhythms in the poem when it was first written?

A: Yes. I had a riff, "Dum. Dum. Dum." "The *New York Times* . . ." I first thought of singing it, but then I thought better to speak it with that riff behind it. I had the riff. It got printed in *The Nation* with illustrations by Eric Drooker, and it came out in a book I did *Illuminated Poems*. The next stage was a benefit somewhere in a club at a reading I did with Amiri Baraka in New York and I ran into guitarist Marc Ribot there. I had worked with him before on an album, *The Lion For Real*. Mercury is bringing it out again. I asked Marc if he would accompany me and I sang him the riff. He added a little instrumental in between. But he made it dramatic. The next step was a benefit I did for Tibet House at Carnegie Hall that Philip Glass organized. I called David Mansfield, who I've recorded with before, with John Hammond, and he's a friend of mine. So, he was going to accompany me at Carnegie Hall, and Lenny Kaye was there with Patti Smith, and he asked Lenny if he could play bass, and he did a knockout job with David. And it was a big hit of the evening 'cause it was the one rocker, and Carnegie Hall was a benefit for Tibet House, and everything else was classical or softer.

Then I went to Princeton to give a reading by myself with my harmonium. When I got picked up by the limousine at the theater there was (director) Gus Van Sant. He had done a lot of work with (William) Burroughs and met him many times. When we got out of the hotel, he pulled out a guitar and I said, "Do you play guitar?" And he replied, "I have a band in Portland." So I said, "I don't have an accompanist tonight. Can you accompany me, after your lecture and during my reading?" So he said "Yeah." We rehearsed it and played it.

Then I had a gig at Albert Hall in London. A reading. I had been talking quite a bit to (Paul) McCartney, visiting him and bringing him poetry and haiku, and looking at Linda McCartney's photographs and giving him some photos I'd taken of them. So, McCartney liked it and filmed me doing "Skeletons" in a little 8mm home thing. And then I had this reading at Albert Hall, and I asked McCartney if he could recommend a young guitarist who was a quick study. So he gave me a few names but he said, "If you're not fixed up with a guitarist, why don't you try me? I love the poem." So I said, "It's a date." It was last November. We went to Paul's house and spent an afternoon rehearsing. He came to the sound check and we did a little rehearsal there, again. And then he went up to his box with his family. It was a benefit for literary things. There were fifteen other poets. We didn't tell anybody that McCartney was going to play. And we developed that riff really nicely. In fact, Linda made a little tape of our rehearsal. So then, we went on stage and knocked it out. There's a photo of us on the CD. It was very lively and he was into it.

Linda likes my photos and she likes Robert Frank, who is my mentor. And I had taken some photos of them in Long Island where they have a place and were saying goodnight to me when I was going back to New York. Good photos of them. We traded some photos. Paul was into poetry, and publishing his poetry. So he asked me to look at his poetry and critique it. We got onto haiku and Linda liked the form so she used those seventeen syllable forms for her book of photos. Paul is also a painter and had published a little book of his paintings. I also wrote haiku to a book of water paintings. One hundred and eight of them, to which I had written a haiku for each one, describing the painting. I showed it to him in Long Island and he was knocked out, and liked the form so he began working with that, also. So we had a rapport about technical things. I had done an album, recordings with (Bob) Dylan back in 1971 and the idea was that it was going to be put out by Apple (Records). But at that time, (John) Lennon had encouraged it and I paid for the thing, and they were going to pay me back but it turned out that I had made this album, paid for it myself, which was quite expensive. I had the money from poetry readings and actually it was a great idea because I had all the stuff with Dylan which later came out. In the late sixties or early seventies I visited McCartney in London. I was on TV that day, a "Pro Pot" rally in Hyde Park, and the cops had stopped me from playing a harmonium or talking on a microphone. So I came down from my ladder from where I was talking and gave the cop a flower. That was kind of a knockout for everybody in London at that time, rather than getting mad. And I was watching that on TV with Mick Jagger at McCartney's house. And McCartney was painting a satin shirt and he gave it to me as a "performance shirt." We talked a little. We met each other over the years and then we met again when he did *Saturday Night Live*, and he greeted me like an old lost buddy.

Q: Didn't you see The Beatles play, and there's some poem you wrote about the event?
A: Yes! I saw them in Portland, Maine. I was up there with Gary Snyder, probably 1965, 1966. In my *Collected Poems* it's dated by a poem describing The Beatles playing in Portland. I was with a couple of little children. I had gotten tickets and was sitting way out in the bleachers, and John Lennon came out and said, "We understand that Allen Ginsberg is in the audience. So three cheers. So now we'll have our show." He saluted me from the stage,

which amazed me and made me feel very proud with all these young kids at my side. Then I knew Lennon and Yoko Ono lived in New York and visited on and off. I was involved in some political things with them occasionally.

Q: What did Paul McCartney add to your recording of "Skeletons?"
A: He reacts to the words in an intelligent way. You can hear it on the tape. Like if I say on the recording, "What's cooking," all of a sudden he brings in the maracas to get that really funny excitement. When I say, "Blow Nancy Blow," he blows on the Hammond organ. He added a lot of enthusiasm and a lot of interpretation. And sometimes when I made a flub, he covered it. He left his lead sheet in his guitar case, so we had to share my lead sheet (at the gig), which was fun. Then I did the poem at Carnegie Hall for the Tibet House that followed the Albert Hall show. And then, Danny Goldberg, (President of Mercury Records), was in the audience at Carnegie Hall, called up my office and 'cause he heard it and liked it and said "Do you want to record it?" I got together Marc Ribot, who I had played it with first, Lenny (Kaye) and David Mansfield. And Lenny was the session-maker.

We made a basic track and McCartney had said, "If you record it, I'd like to work on it. It would be fun." So we did a twenty-four hour overnight mail to him, and he got it and listened to it after a few days. He spent a day on it. He put on maracas, drums, which was unexpected, which we needed, and organ, Hammond organ, trying to sound like Al Kooper. And a guitar which was very strong. Then the day it arrived, Philip Glass was in town and he volunteered because he thought it was my hit, so he wanted to do something with it. He added on piano, very much in his style, and fitting perfectly onto the rest of the tape. Then Hal Willner wound up mixing it and brought out McCartney's role and the structure that McCartney had given to it, 'cause he gave it a very nice, dramatic structure. I had planned that after "Blow Nancy Blow" you would have four consecutive choruses of instrumentals. McCartney and I had planned the breaks the first time and varied it a little, and I'm understanding the recording process more. I'm basically the poet. I have tunes I got up with. I have ideas but I still can't make a song with a bridge (laughs). As far as recording, I had to supervise my own recordings at first, and it was very simple-minded, the "William Blake's Songs of Innocence & of Experience Tuned by A.G." on MGM Records. I thought there were good musicians on it, and it may be coming out again. I've also done a new book of poetry from HarperCollins, and did a reading to celebrate it in New York at St. Mark's, which included members of Sonic Youth.

Q: You also did a rewritten version of "Amazing Grace" on "Skeletons" flip side?

A: About three years ago, Ed Sanders asked all of his friends to write new verses of "Amazing Grace" for one evening of "Amazing Grace" in St. Mark's. A lot of people from the Naropa Institute wrote. Anne Waldman, Tuli Kupferberg, and I heard of a Zen master who was working with the homeless, who had a sitting meditation on The Bowery with a lot of his students, including Anne Waldman. And they reported in mid-winter that it was terrible finding cardboard boxes to sleep in. The worst thing was that people would pass them by and not acknowledge their existence. Shutting them out. The sense of alienation and helplessness, and being ignored. No eye contact. People were scared of them. And that's what turned me on. Acknowledge them. That was the inspiration. Keep them in human contact. The verses I wrote seem to be full of heart, to the point, compassion.

Q: And now something you began as a poem, "Skeletons" has evolved into a recording collaborative. Do you consider the projected expanded audience?

A: Yeah, but when you write a poem like that, you run through in your mind, who is going to listen to it? President Clinton is going to hear this. I'll send it to Stephanopoulos, who I know. Dole will probably hear of it, or someone around Dole will hear it. Rush Limbaugh will probably hear it because it's me and it's nasty to him. Young college kids will hear it. I wonder what (Bob) Dylan will think? I wonder what McCartney will think? So all those people are present in my mind, inevitably, 'cause I know them. My father. My mother. My brother. What is Robert Creeley gonna think? What is Gary Snyder going to think? What is *People* magazine gonna think? What is God gonna think? What's Buddha gonna think? But literally, what will my Tibetan Lama teacher think? Is this too aggressive, or is this helpful? Things like that. I was fed up with the inflation of the right wing contract with America double-cross hypocrisy, basically. And it didn't seem to me that anybody was responding. *The Nation* asked me for the poem. I waited about a half a year and completed it. I originally called it "Skeleton Keys." Poet Carl Rakosi made some suggestions for me to edit and add "Ballad."

Q: Is there a reason you used skeleton as a metaphor throughout the poem?

A: I'm Buddhist, and you look at these issues through the grave, and also setting them up as skeleton puppets, setting up the military people, the advertising people, the network people, the talk show junkies, Big Brother. Setting them up as skeletons, as puppets. Setting them up as transparent phantoms, and looking at the issues out of the grave. The idea of putting all the present factions and seeing them from the grave as walking skeletons.

Q: Do you feel the music people are coming to your work now? Fans as well as musicians who have enjoyed your books and previous records?
A: All that, and a lot of these musicians have grown up on my poetry, or are younger and off set me now. So some, like Marc Ribot, once heard me read, and liked it. It's just an accumulation of experience with my poetry, and it seems at this point I'm able to work with any musician who I'd like to. I did a collaboration three months ago with Ornette Coleman for French television. They sent a limousine, and I did it with Gregory Corso and the late Herbert Huncke, and we went to Ornette's studio.

Q. Wait. Did Herbert Huncke check out?
A: Huncke died at the ripe old age of eighty-one. He died the way he wanted. He was surrounded by friends and he was full of morphine from the doctors.

It was a thing on the Beat generation. I read some poems and Ornette punctuated it with saxophone. We did a mono chordal chant ending in three chords. Ornette was totally great and listened. It has showed up in Europe already. Gregory would read a poem, would get up and make some comment, and Ornette answers with sax. They were talking back and forth.

Q: Lenny Kaye produced your latest recording that Mercury is distributing. Obviously, you have been aware of his production career and his twenty-five year collaboration with Patti Smith.
A: Lenny has worked with Patti, a poet, and he has worked with Jim Carroll, a poet, and John Giorno, a poet. So he's very literate and encouraging. And I didn't know if he'd pay attention to me, but at the Carnegie Hall benefit we all did together . . . when he stepped in, he was right on the spot, and helpful. Then we did it again at a benefit out in Ann Arbor, Michigan with Patti Smith. He (Lenny) was there and we did it again with a local bassist, and he played a fantastic solo. Since he knew how to get things together, and the people at the label, and he knew Danny Goldberg, who is a friend of Patti, so he was the natural person to take over.

Q: I've noticed some alternative and college radio stations will often pair you up with Patti Smith.
A: Patti is coming from the St. Mark's Poetry Project and Anne Waldman as a mentor, and Burroughs, who she loves a lot, so our paths have crossed

that way quite often. I think I first really saw her at The Burroughs Nova Convention in 1978, in New York. I really picked up on her there. Her improvisation on stage, and her vulnerability and her sort of informality and at the same time, her bravery. That was real interesting. And I've been watching her since. We've done a few shows together to raise money for a heart center. A big theater which holds four thousand people, and we filled it. We've done it three years. So she's inclined toward a Rimbaud kind of Buddhist thing, and I was interested in her Rimbaud connection and her Rimbaud behavior when she retired from the whole thing. That was very interesting, that someone could drop the whole theme and passion to take care of her children, and have a family, and come back renewed. And when she came back, she was friends with a friend of mine (an advisor), who had a t-shirt connection, and introduced her to Oliver Ray, who is now playing with her.

Q: What about poetry readings and performances? Is it different reading with a musician next to you or now a bunch of people sharing the stage?
A: I have to focus on my text. I'm still pointing toward the tornado.

Q: You still read from text on stage, from a book or typewritten. Do you ever read from memory?
A: I rarely read from memory. I sing from "Father Death Blues," and can sing "Amazing Grace" from memory, but I don't know what lines are coming, so I have to refresh myself. I'm not particularly interested in memorizing perfectly 'cause I think it's distracting from interpreting the text differently each time. I think you have to have all the dimensions at once, the book thing, the poetry thing, plus the performance, plus the musical accompaniment, and if you have all of them, and they're all in a good place, that's fine. But the reason I don't try to memorize, I guess I could, but I'm too busy, and I like to reinterpret the poem each time. Certain cadences are recurrent and certain intonations are recurrent, but on the other hand, if I don't memorize it, there's always the chance that somebody noticing something, and empathizing puts it a little differently, and bringing out meaning that I didn't realize before. So I prefer to have the score in front of me and interpret it new each time.

Q: Artists from new generations, alternative rock bands, still keep discovering your work and acknowledging your influence.
A: It's fun. You always learn from younger people. I learned a lot from William Carlos Williams, and the elders of my generation. People who were

much older than me when I was young. And that intergenerational amity is really important because it spreads myths from one generation to another of what you know, and all the techniques and the history. At the same time, Williams learned connection with Corso and myself and (Peter) Orlovsky. Renewed his lease, so to speak. And the advent of The Black Mountain Beat Generation Poetry Renaissance, San Francisco, really renewed his poetic life, in a sense, brought him out to the public and his mood of poetry . . . as the mainstream, rather than as the eccentric jerk from New Jersey. All of a sudden, with the phalanx of younger people following his lead, he became the sage that he was. And I think it gave him a lot of gratification to realize he had been on the right track, and that it wasn't in vain. And I get the same thing whenever I get to work with younger people. And I learn from them. I don't think I would have been singing if it wasn't for younger Dylan. I mean he turned me on to actually singing. I remember the moment it was. It was a concert with Happy Traum that I went to and saw in Greenwich Village. I suddenly started to write my own lyrics, instead of Blake. Dylan's words were so beautiful. The first time I heard them I wept.

I had come back from India, and Charlie Plymell, a poet I liked a lot in Bolinas, at a "Welcome Home Party" played me Dylan singing "Masters of War" from "Freewheelin' Bob Dylan," and I actually burst into tears. It was a sense that the torch had been passed to another generation. And somebody had the self-empowerment of saying, "I'll Know My Song Well before I Start Singing It." There's a young poet now, Jeffrey Manaugh, a senior at Chapel Hill (North Carolina), and he's about twenty, and he's a great poet, I think. I sent Ferlinghetti some of his pamphlets and Ferlinghetti asked him to send a manuscript to consider for City Lights. At the age of twenty, that's rare. So there's always, every generation, somebody comes along and knocks your heart open.

Q: Are you aware there's sort of a re-evaluation of Dylan's film, *Renaldo and Clara*? I mean, I first didn't understand a lot of it when I saw a rough cut before release, and later in limited release. Now it's garnering new acclaim in the US and around the Dylan collectors.

A: Dylan delivers. It's going to be a marvelous picture when people begin appreciating it. Well, first of all, it's Dylan extending himself to the extreme, and including all his friends and all his inspirers, and all his workable companions in a big circus going through America. A musical circus. His mother was along at one point. His kids were along at one point. His wife was along. Joan Baez's kid was along. So it was this great family outing trying to hit all the small towns, originally, like in Kafka's *Amerika*. The traveling circus in Kafka's *Amerika*. For me it was great, and to hear Dylan so often, I was able to hear backstage, in the audience, from the side, in the wings, and go out to the furthest seats with a pass. He was at a peak of musicality and energy and inspiration. Like "One More Cup of Coffee" and "Idiot Wind," which is one of my favorite lyrics. A national lyric with its great "Circles around your skull . . ." Really quite manic. It was great to see a band on a rock 'n' roll tour. Rolling Thunder Revue on a grand tour, and see all the work that went into it.

Renaldo and Clara was a great artistic film that was mocked when it first came out, although it was a hit in Europe, or it was very much appreciated in Europe. Now when people see it, I think people will realize it was a great treasure. At first people were screaming "Four hours! What a big egotist." But actually it's four hours of Dylan exploring the nature of identity of self, and pointing out there is no fixed identity. It was making a huge movie in an interesting way. I did an interview with Dylan for *Telegraph*. Dylan requested me to do it, and he explained the technique and construction and structure of the film. Specifically that they went through all of the footage and isolated everything that seemed to astound them. Then they divided it up into various topics, like marriage, rock and roll, children, God, poetry, politics, war, peace and all that. Then they made card files with those topics, and the primary colors, and the hooks in between, he composed it like a tapestry, not a linear composition, but a composition by artistic elements. You'll find the rose travels from hand to hand, throughout the film, along with the hat.

Q: With the release of your box set, the vinyl-to-CD reissues, new audio recordings by local and national writers, my own spoken word productions, as well as TV product advertising, utilizing beat slogans and phrasing(s), is this further proof of the literature living and breathing, and the era for once being displayed correctly, or at least an influence in commercial view?

A: The actual texts however, have not been rewritten, and are now coming up to more public notice like Burroughs' *Naked Lunch*, and Kerouac's new, unpublished poems, and for the first time, my actual voice available on a bunch of CDs, going all the way back to 1949 and stretching up to 1993, with the very first original reading of "Howl," which is sort of a standard anthology piece, that has never been heard, or a poem like "Sunflower Sutra" or "America," which was standard in the Norton anthologies in high school.

Q: I know that Burroughs introduced you to some key books in the mid-forties that were influential to your thoughts and writing, and Kerouac, around the same time, when you were attending Columbia University maybe around 1950, had been into some form of Buddhism and spontaneous prose, but an older generation of writers had an impact on your eventual voice. I joked when we were setting up the equipment as far as New Jersey goes, it's you, Bruce Springsteen, and Frank Sinatra, but you added, "William Carlos Williams," whom you met around age twenty.

A: I knew him from my hometown of Paterson, New Jersey. I'd seen him in 1948. He actually innovated the idea of listening to the way people talked and writing in that way . . . Using the tones of their voice and using the rhythmical sequences of actual talk instead of dat dat dat dot dot dot. "This is the forest . . ." Instead of a straight square metronomic arithmetic beat, there's the infinitely more musical and varied rhythmic sequences of conversation as well as the tones. 'Cause if you notice, most academic poetry is spoken in a single solitary moan tone that maybe doesn't have the variety of when you are talking to your grandmother or baby.

It happens every one hundred or one hundred-and-fifty years. It did in the days of Wordsworth, who in his "Preface to the Lyrical Ballads," suggested that poets begin writing in the words and diction of men of intelligence, or talk to each other intelligently, instead of imitating another century's literary style. So, I think what happened is that we followed an older tradition, a lineage, of the modernists of the turn of the century continued their work into idiomatic talk and musical cadences and returned poetry back to its original sources and actual communication between people. That was picked up generation after generation up to people like U2, who are very much influenced by Burroughs in their presentation of visual material, or Sonic Youth, or poets, like Thurston Moore and Lee Ranaldo are interested in poetry. I actually am working with them now.

Q: *Holy Soul Jelly Roll* is a very comprehensive survey of your recorded (audio) life. Poems, songs, musical collaborations.
A: It includes about a half hour of music with Bob Dylan, and songs of William Blake that I've set to music, some of it is uproarious and funny and very hilarious, joyful yodeling involved, in that, and a live cut with The Clash.

Q: I know you worked with The Clash on "Combat Rock." How did "Capitol Air" come together, incorporated in this box set? I debuted it on KLOS-FM when I did a radio interview two years ago on Frank Sontag's *Impact* shift and the phone lines lit up as if somebody won the lotto.

A: Well, it's an accident. I wandered into a place called Bonds, which at that time was a big (couple of thousand people) club in New York. The Clash at the time had a seventeen night run, and I knew the sound engineer, who brought me backstage to introduce me and Joe Strummer took one look at me and said, "Ginsberg, when are you going to run for President?" And then he said there was some guy that we've had trying to talk to the kids about Sandinistas and about Latin American policy and politics, but they're not listening. They are throwing eggs or tomatoes at him. "'Can you go out and talk?,' I said, "Speech, no, but I have a little punk song that I wrote that begins, 'I don't like the government where I live . . .'" So, we rehearsed it for about five minutes during their intermission break and then they took me out on stage. "Allen Ginsberg is going to sing." And so we improvised it. I gave them the chord changes. It gets kind of Clash-like good anthem, like music about the middle, but they trail off again. The guy who was my friend in the soundboard, mixed my voice real loud so the kids could hear, and so there was a nice reaction, because they could hear common sense being said in the song. You can hear the cheers on the record. I wrote "Capitol Air" in 1980, recorded with The Clash live in 1981 or '82. "Capitol Air" was written coming back from Yugoslavia, oddly enough from a tour of Eastern Europe, realizing that the police bureaucracies in America and in Eastern Europe were the same, mirror images of each other finally. The climactic stanza "No Hope Communism, No Hope Capitalism." Yeah, "Everybody is lying on both sides." We didn't play the whole cut because we didn't have enough time, but they built up to a kind of crescendo, which was nice when the whole band came in.

Q: Can we talk about record music executive, John Hammond Sr., perhaps the A&R man of the century?
A: I visited him in the hospital, on his deathbed, years ago, and our final conversation was about Robert Johnson and Bob Dylan. Well, I think I ran into him in the early sixties. He knew my poetry quite well. But it was around the Rolling Thunder Revue with Dylan that we got more intimate. I had already made one recording, William Blake's "Songs Of Innocence and Experience," in 1969 with some very good musicians, including Julius Watkins on French horn, Don Cherry, Elvin Jones and . . . used them. And also Herman Wright, a bassist that was suggested by Charles Mingus. Mingus encouraged me to do the Blake. So I had something to play.

I was on the Rolling Thunder tour, doing a little singing, and I had a whole bunch of new material I had done with Dylan in 1971. In 1971 Dylan and I went into a studio and improvised. I had forty minutes of music with him. So I brought that to Hammond in 1975, after the tour. I had a bunch of new songs and he said, "Let's go in the studio and make an album." I had some musicians who had been with me since 1968 or 1969 since the Blake. David Mansfield from the Rolling Thunder tour, and a wonderful musician, Arthur Russell, who Philip Glass has just put out posthumously on Point Records. Arthur Russell lived in my apartment building, upstairs, and had accompanied me across country on tours, and managed The Kitchen in New York. We had a good little group of musicians. Dylan made a record in the Columbia Studios. It was the first time I didn't have to pay! Then, Columbia wouldn't put it out because of dirty words, they said in those days. The anti-smoking, "Don't Smoke" poem. So things were in a stasis, but I continued recording myself in 1981, did a whole series of recordings with David Amram, by this time I was working with Steven Taylor, now the lead guitarist of The Fugs. He's also the lead guitarist for The False Prophets, a punk garage band.

So we got together at CBS Studios and did another forty minutes of music, and later, John Hammond put the two together. He had left Columbia and started his own label, John Hammond Records, to be distributed by Columbia. So he not only put out what he did with me, he put out a double album, and he got Robert Frank, who had done the (Rolling Stones) *Exile On Main Street* album cover, whose an old friend, to make a composite for our cover, and there was a really good playlist inside, and the text was a good deduction. However, the record didn't sell. Before I had a chance to rescue the further ten thousand copies they (Columbia) had, they shredded them, so they were gone and a rarity now. So what this four-CD box set is, is a summary of all the studio recordings I did, plus a lot of other stuff that was never done in a studio, but done in readings, plus another album with Blake, including Dylan on Blake, and a duet with Elvin Jones, including some work with Dylan out in Santa Monica in 1982 in his studio, the live Clash cut, and an excerpt from the opera I did with Philip Glass. So the range runs from a cappella up through folk, punk, dirty blues, classical, collaborations with Dylan, some rap, percussion and vocal with Jones. David Amram was on it as well.

Q: You know, I originally felt when you first started writing in the forties, there really wasn't any musical influence or instrumentation behind or around your words. Yet the first track on this box set recorded in the late forties in Neal Cassady's pad, actually has the radio playing in the background on the tape.

A: The first cut has a jazz background, because the whole atmosphere from 1940 and on was permeated with be-bop and (DJ), Symphony Sid.

Q: What does music and beat do to voice and text?
A: Well, a whole mish mosh. First of all, I grew up on all blues, Ma Rainey and Lead Belly. I listened to them live on radio station WNYC, back in the late thirties or early forties. So I have a blues background. There's some sort of Hebraic cantillation relation to the blues that I've always had. So the first thing on the collection is "When the Saints Go Marching In" that I made up a cappella when I was hitchhiking, and recorded in Neal Cassady's house a year later. Then things like my mother taught me. "The Green Valentine Blues." Just coming from everyone who likes to sing in the shower. Then there was the poetry and music, King Pleasure, and the people who were putting together be-bop, syllable by syllable, like Lambert Ross and Hendricks. I knew them in 1948. We used to smoke pot together in the forties, when I knew Neal Cassady, around Columbia when I was living on 92nd Street.

Q: Hey, I met drummer Freddie Gruber last week. Buddy Rich's main man. He told me you tried to hit on him once.
A: (laughs) I had a crush on Freddie. I saw him recently. Around 1944, '45, Kerouac and I were listening to Symphony Sid, and I heard the whole repertoire of Thelonious Monk, "Round Midnight," "Ornithology" and all that. I actually saw Charlie Parker, weekend after weekend a few years later at The Open Door. And in the sixties, went night after night to The Five Spot to hear Thelonious Monk, and actually gave Thelonious Monk "Howl," and got his critique on it two weeks later when I saw him again. "What did you think of it?" He said, "Makes sense." In 1960 I delivered some psilocybin from Timothy Leary to both Thelonious Monk and Dizzy Gillespie. And Monk said later on, "Got anything stronger?" Later on I spent an evening with him on what is now Charlie Parker Place around 1960. Also in San Francisco, in the mid-fifties, there was a music and poetry scene. Mingus was involved with Kenneth Rexroth and Kenneth Patchen. And Fantasy records documented some of that. The Cellar in San Francisco. By that time, I didn't know how to handle it, so I never did much of that myself 'cause I was more funky, old-fashioned blues. I couldn't cut the mustard with free jazz.

So then in the 1970s, I began turning on to Dylan. I knew him in the sixties. He taught me the three-chord blues pattern. So he was my instructor. I began singing in India, Mantra, and in the great sixties, I began transferring the sacred music idea to Blake, and began transferring that to folk music, and then got together with Dylan in the early seventies. Influences by Happy Traum and Rambling Jack Elliot, whom I've known since the forties, and Darrol Adams. So finally, the amalgam got together and it was very simple-minded blues, or adjective about a blues. Also, improvisation which was important. Finally, Hal Willner had the idea of going back to the old jazz poetry thing.

Q: What happens when the beat, or the music, collides with your words and voice?
A: Elvin has a very interesting attitude. He feels that he's not there to beat out the vocalist. He's there to put a floor under them. He's there to support and encourage, and give a place for the vocal to come in, not to compete with the vocal, but to provide a ground for it. He's very intelligent as a musician. We did it once together in 1969 on the "Blake" album; there was military-type drum, and then this recent rap song. I've got some other stuff we haven't put out with Elvin. I've rarely found opposition to the music because the musicians were very sensitive, and built their music around the dynamics of my voice.

Q: Subject-specific answer required: You write something on a piece of paper. Other people, musicians, come invited to participate and collaborate. Does the original intention become a different trip once there is music and other elements involved?
A: Well, it widens it into a slightly different trip, but the words are pretty stable, and they mean what they mean, so there is no problem. The interesting thing is adjusting the rhythmic pattern and the intonation to the musician's idea of what there is there. That's pretty good, because I'm good as an improviser, I can fit in, as you can hear on "Birdbrain." Where I can take a long line or a short line and fit in sixteen bars without worrying about spaces and closed places.

Q: Steven Taylor has been playing guitar on tours and recordings with you since 1975. What are his strongest assets as a musician, guitarist, collaborator?
A: He can play funky blues and can improvise. He was born in England, so he has this Beatles-Manchester . . . and came to America when he was ten. I invited him to the Hammond sessions in 1976. We toured Europe together with Peter Orlovsky and in 1982 we ended up in Dylan's studio in California

with David Mansfield. We played together at Woodstock around 1980. Ed Sanders saw us and said, "You've got a fantastic accompanist. Get yourself a band and go around the world." He's very supportive. Two years ago, he dropped out of The False Prophets to go to Brown University to get his PhD in ethnomusicology, influenced by the great ethnomusicologist, Harry Smith who he is very close to. Harry Smith, before he died, came out to Naropa where he was the resident ethnomusicologist and philosopher. He won a Grammy in 1991, the year he died. Harry recorded me for Folkways, which was edited by Samuel Charters. So for a blues pedigree, that's pretty good. "First Blues." It's still in print through the Smithsonian Institute.

Q: What kind of impact did FM Radio have on you as a writer and reader/performer?
A: By the time I got around to getting on the radio, it was actually an AM station in Chicago with Studs Terkel; recorded the complete reading of "Howl" in Chicago, later used for the Fantasy record. It was broadcast censored. '59. KPFA in the Bay Area then started broadcasting my stuff in San Francisco, a Pacifica station. Fantasy put out "Howl" and that got around. Then, Jerry Wexler at Atlantic, put out "Kaddish." It was radio broadcast from Brandeis University.

Q: Was there ever a conflict of written-page origin then into audio land?
A: We wrote, and we were in the tradition of William Carlos Williams spoken vernacular, comprehensible common language that anyone could understand, coming from Whitman through William Carlos Williams through be-bop. We were built for it. I can talk. I'm an old ham.

Q: Does the vision change once it leaves the paper?
A: No. It doesn't make much difference. The method of my writing to begin with is that I'm not writing to write something, is that I catch myself thinking; I suddenly notice something I have thought of when I wasn't thinking of writing, and then I write it down if it is vivid enough. And as far as the choice of what to write down or not, the slogan is vividness, is self-selecting. So in a sense, the method is impervious to influence by the audience because I'm just thinking to myself in the bathtub.

So even if it's the most private, it's the most public, because as Kerouac said in "Pull My Daisy," "Everybody is interested in their secret scatological doodlings in their private notebooks." I mean, what do people really think about?

Q: As far as performance and poetry readings, when you read before a house, aren't you trying to keep the same original birthplace word vision and not really expand or bring in heavy theatrical elements?

A: I like to stick to something that is grounded in anything I could say to somebody, that they wouldn't notice I was really saying it as poetry. Intense fragments of spoken idiom, with all the different tones of the spoken idiom, which is more musical than most poetry. Most poetry by amateur poets is limited to a couple of tones, a couple of pitches, instead of an entire range, so that the poetry we do fits with the music because it has its pitch consciousness. The tone reading the vowels up and down.

Q: You document by date. Page and performance dates, calendar time and year attached to the writing. I produced a poetry CD a couple of years back with the poet Harry E. Northup. Harry is a date freak like yourself. In the studio, on tape, he would read a poem written in 1989 but we were recording it in 1992. And we've just done a new recording in 1995 but we still listed the birth poem dates in the liners, but not on the tape this time. I'm in conflict about this exact documentation. He was reading things in 1994, written from five–ten years earlier. I'm still on the fence on this one.

A: Wouldn't it be interesting if you went to a concert by Dylan and he dated each piece. . . .

Q: Explain the use of chronology in the nineties, reading original work written and created decades earlier?

A: My background was William Butler Yeats. Seeing the sequence of his development, maturation and growth over the years was really interesting as a novel. How he began as a vague, misty-eyed young 1890's devotee of Irish Mythology and how he wound up this tough old guy who put a skin on everything he said. So I like the idea of seeing the development of the mind, or of the voice, or of the thought, or of the poetic capacity, and I want to leave that trail behind for other poets so they could see where I was at one point, or where I was at another. My oration, my pronunciation or my singing, my vocalization differs, and it builds.

As I get older it gets more interesting with more and more tones, and more and more breath, and deeper and deeper voice and higher and higher voice. But still the original rhythms and the original ideas are from the original text, so you've still got a chronology going. So people could see the development of the mind. I'm not writing about the external world. I'm writing about what goes through my mind. So, at a certain period I'm interested in this kind of sex, another period, this kind of politics, another period, this kind of meditation, and I like people to be able to dig there's a development, and not a static process.

Q: I'm still amazed at your readings, not just the impact you have on the audience, but your paper trail, book catalogues, albums, vinyl, first edition printings, out of print classics people want signed. Old money. New money. No money. It's like "This Is Your Life" on parade.
A: Not quite. It's my mind on parade. That's what the mind is for, to show other people.

Q: It's obvious that people want to be writers again. I feel that.
A: They want to express themselves. Not just to be a writer to be a writer, but they want to be able to say what they really think.

For years, and it's still evident today, there is still restriction on the radio airwaves, and a limited window when you can be heard. Six P.M. Most of the material on my four-CD box set might be banned from the air eight A.M. to six P.M.

Q: What do you want from FM radio?
A: I'd like for some FM station to play all four CDs one night, announced in advance so everybody could listen to it, and I think it would change not only heads, but expand people's emotional range. "All the time in eternity in the warm light of this poem's radio." That was 1953. So I was aware. I was laying out treasures in heaven, basically. I knew that after I was dead my stuff would slowly seep up, so I'm really glad I'm alive to put this (box set) recording together.

Allen Ginsberg: The Last Australian Interview

Stuart Coupe / 1997

The first time I set eyes on Allen Ginsberg was in the basement of the City Lights bookshop in San Francisco in the early 1980s when I was on tour with the Hoodoo Gurus. I thought of saying hello but figured he must get tired of that so in the same way that Jim Carroll used to follow Frank O'Hara around the streets of Manhattan during O'Hara's lunch break, trying to see what the great poet saw, I kept a distance as I trailed Ginsberg around the shop, looking at the books he was looking at. Early in 1997 I finally had the opportunity to interview Ginsberg. As it turns out it was shortly before he died so this is one of the last interviews he did. This is the full, unedited version of the piece which later appeared in various publications.

"He died several years ago, but I had a very interesting dream, a very brief dream," says Allen Ginsberg when asked about his early mentor, Carl Solomon, the man to whom his most famous poem, "Howl," was dedicated. Solomon originally wanted to publish the works of Ginsberg, William S. Burroughs, and Jack Kerouac before his New York publishers told him he was crazy. Like the young Ginsberg, Solomon was no stranger to the inside of a mental hospital.

Ginsberg was happily chatting at his New York apartment less than a month before his sudden, but not totally unanticipated, death aged seventy on Saturday April 5. He had suffered from chronic hepatitis that eventually led to cirrhosis of the liver.

A diagnosis of terminal liver cancer was made eight days before Ginsberg's death, with initial media reports suggesting that the poet and activist had between four and twelve months to live. Ginsberg slipped into a coma the day of the news. The day prior he had written about a dozen short poems, one of the last being entitled "On Fame and Death."

Ginsberg was no stranger to the media circus but had done few interviews with the Australian media over his career and had only visited the country once. In this encounter what had started out as a brief twenty minute interview to coincide with his musical performance "The Ballad of the Skeletons," which had recently been voted number 8 on the Top 100 songs of the moment as voted by listeners to youth radio network Triple J, turned into an hour and a half encounter with Ginsberg ranging over his poetry, the infamous Beat Generation, contemporary poetry, his feelings about Buddhism, Aboriginal musicians, Chinese politics, blues music, and his love life.

"I met him in the afterworld and I said, 'Well, how is it there?'" Ginsberg continued, speaking about Solomon in a manner which, in hindsight, seems rather prophetic. "And he said, 'It's OK, you get along just like in the mental hospital if you obey the rules,' and I said, 'What are the rules?' He said there are two rules: 'First, remember you're dead; second, act like you're dead.'

"And I woke up laughing. He said two years before he died 'I have life insurance but I'm dying.' It was a very courageous death, I must say. He was very much with it, even with his cancer. So we had a memorial service for him.

"The funny thing is that most of us are all together after thirty years. I see Gary Snyder, who has just finished a huge project that he'd begun working on some thirty or forty years ago, so we had a big banquet together in San Francisco. I saw McClure and Philip Whalen and I see Diane di Prima at Naropa, and Gregory (Corso) here and Kenneth Copeland and I have John Ashbery's job at Brooklyn College. Peter Orlovsky is just around the corner. We have supper every three nights. (John) Giorno is further downtown."

Aside from a vigorous social life, right until the end Ginsberg maintained an astonishing work schedule. A volume of *Selected Poems* was released earlier this year, as was his "The Ballad of the Skeletons" which was recorded with a variety of musicians including Paul McCartney and Philip Glass. This year has also seen a book called *Illuminated Poems*, Ginsberg's mid-1950's *Journals* and at the time of the conversation he was working on a book of essays from the sixties through to the nineties and was about to edit a collection of selected interviews. And as if that wasn't enough, Ginsberg was planning an *MTV Unplugged* musical performance to capitalize on the success of "The Ballad of The Skeletons."

"Next year they're bringing out 'The Lion For Real' from 1990," Ginsberg continued. "Then I have a book of photographs over the last ten years. There are a whole bunch of photos from India in 1962, the negatives of which were lost for many years and have now been returned to me. There's also a lot of fifties and sixties photographs that have never been seen. There's quite a lot of stuff to do. I'm working with Philip Glass. We had an opera out you know called *Hydrogen Juke Box.* There's also a new version of 'Howl' coming out with classical music accompaniment."

And it didn't stop there. After the interview Ginsberg was heading out to sign copies of his astonishingly large photo collection. In fact Ginsberg maintained arguably the most comprehensive literary archive of at least the last fifty years with some millions of photos, letters, journals, poetry, and paraphernalia sold two years ago to an American university for in excess of two million dollars.

If Ginsberg knew that his days were numbered it wasn't obvious. Certainly he'd had periods of illness over recent years but aside from his myriad of projects he was already committed to returning to Australia early in 1998 for the Adelaide Festival of Arts.

His last visit to this country had been for that festival in the early seventies when he did a variety of readings and performances including the one he recalled most where he appeared at the Adelaide Town Hall with a group of Aboriginal singers and musicians, something he appeared to remember with absolute clarity some twenty-five years later.

"I met (Russian poet) Yevgeny Yevtushenko in Adelaide and there were other poets from around the world but they had ignored completely Australian Aborigine song men," he said. "Some professors in Australian Aboriginal lore had invited a few Aboriginal song men to the university to sing in their class, to sing to the children and to see if the children would respond to the songs that they sang. But then the Aborigines didn't have enough money to get back home. So I said that I was happy to share my evening session at the Town Hall and they could have my receipts. That was so successful that we did another one at Port Adelaide Town Hall."

Surprisingly these readings were amongst the few things that weren't preserved in Ginsberg's archives, the poet being delighted when I offered to send him copies of the tapes I had of these occasions. There was a genuine delight that, albeit rough, these recordings existed and could be added to his collection.

It's an understatement to suggest that Ginsberg was the most influential American poet of his generation, perhaps of the last century, but something that separated him even further from fellow wordsmiths was that, like Burroughs, he was an astonishingly accomplished and powerful reader of his work. That's best heard on the four CD collection *Holy Soul*

Jelly Roll—Poems and Songs 1949–1993 which was compiled by Ginsberg and producer Hal Willner and released in 1994.

The collection contains many of Ginsberg's classic readings, but peppers them with lesser known performances, particularly a reading of "Howl" that, whilst suffering in quality by comparison with the original, completely impassioned version released in the late 1950s on Fantasy Records reinforces that Ginsberg was frequently very, very funny, something that's often not so apparent on the printed page.

"I don't read it that often, maybe one or two times a year when there is a special occasion," Ginsberg explained of his most famous work. "I have developed a certain technique and dynamics for its intonations so it's pretty interesting."

Equally amusing are early readings of such landmark poems as "Supermarket in California" and "America."

"Those are the very first readings of 'America' and 'Sunflower Sutra,' Ginsberg said of the performances on *Holy Soul Jelly Roll*. "And it's the very first reading of the complete 'Howl.' It's from a Berkeley reading just a few months after the first reading. The first time I read it I only read Part 1. Then we got together the same poets in Berkeley in a little theater and (Beat Generation historian and Kerouac's first biographer) Ann Charters was Peter Orlovsky's date. While there she met (blues historian) Sam (Charters). They got married after that. So that was a big day in our minds."

So did Ginsberg perceive the poems as being humorous?

"I thought America was humorous," Ginsberg continued. "Well, there is a kind of exuberance in poems like 'Sunflower Sutra.' When you say 'the cunts of wheelbarrows and the milky breasts of cars,' I mean, it's funny. It's sort of verbally surrealistic. But it has an exuberance and a kind of joy in it. The whole thing is about joy, about self-recognition . . . 'You were never no locomotive, Sunflower you were a sunflower.' The critics of the day dismissed it because they were so busy nit-picking about dirty words. And 'Howl' itself is very funny. You know, there's this kind of racy impetuousness. Also again that hyperbolic: 'Starving hysterical naked, starving hysterical naked, starving hysterical naked.'"

At the time when "Howl" was written Ginsberg was, with Jack Kerouac and William S. Burroughs, a third of the unholy trio that became known as the Beat Generation. They were intertwined with the likes of Neal Cassady, Gary Snyder, Gregory Corso, Herbert Huncke, Hal Chase, Lucien Carr, John Clellon Holmes, Michael McClure and an array of fellow travelers, some of them phenomenally talented, others grabbing on the coat-tails of what was not then but later to be perceived as a significant subgenre of American poetry and prose of the late 1940's and fifties.

Kerouac died in 1969, Corso's output is increasingly sporadic, Snyder became a committed Buddhist and maintained a low profile whilst the majority of others are notable predominantly for their presence in photos with The Big Three. Now, with Ginsberg gone, only Burroughs remains of the essence of the Beats. Until the end the two maintained an enduring friendship.

"I was with Burroughs a couple of times this year," Ginsberg said. "I stayed with him in his house. I cooked breakfast for him. We'd talk over the newspapers. Sometimes I'd take a lot of pictures of him and keep the tape recorder on for a couple of hours at a time. I see him all the time."

Given Ginsberg's candid approach to the conversation I decided to take a chance and ask about whether he thought Burroughs deliberately shot his wife Joan in the head in Mexico City. This infamous incident involved Burroughs supposedly displaying his marksmanship at a party, putting an apple on his then-wife's head, William Tell style—but ending up shooting her through the head.

"I don't know," Ginsberg hesitated when asked about Burroughs' possible premeditation in the killing. "It was just the gunshot—but she was very suicidal. I had been with them, with her, maybe ten days before. I spent about ten days with her and she was in a bad way, drinking and driving cars in a way that scared the kids and me in the back because we were all there, so there was already a kind of dread there."

Then there's Corso who I'd spoken to a year before in a belated attempt to get him to tour Australia with poet Anne Waldman. Corso was frightened about the length of the plane trip to Australia and wasn't in possession of a current passport. I'd suggested to him that I'd try and get Ginsberg to accompany him on the trip if it would make him more comfortable but even that wasn't enough to drag him out of his shared lower-East side abode in Manhattan.

"Oh, he's very busy," Ginsberg said. "He's been writing all these years but is neurotically refusing to clean it up and prepare it. I think he's the poet's poet."

In some ways, despite his lack of literary output, the other famous member of the Beats was Neal Cassady, a veracious writer of sub-Kerouacean prose (little of which has been published) and at various times the lover of both Kerouac (who made him, as the character Dean Moriarty, the hero of *On the Road*) and Ginsberg.

At the time, thinking about Cassady's personality and Ginsberg's ongoing involvement with rock 'n' roll (he recorded or performed with Bob Dylan, The Clash, Leonard Cohen, Phil Spector, and obscure punk bands the Gluons, to name but a few), I posited that there was possibly some implicit connection between the Beat Generation and the punk and post-punk generation that Ginsberg realized and had tapped into. I suggested that maybe there was a comparison between the restless spirit of Cassady (who died from heart failure alongside railway tracks in Mexico in 1968) and the suicidal Kurt Cobain of Nirvana. Ginsberg didn't totally buy the idea.

"I don't think Cassady was a suicide," he said. "And I don't think he was so pained as Cobain. Cassady was very exuberant and had a good time. The problem was towards the end . . . the LSD didn't do him any harm. He smoked grass very strongly but I think with all his all-night cross country driving with the psychedelic bus—(Ken) Kesey's (Merry) Pranksters—that he took a lot of amphetamine and he went down to Mexico to calm the nerves and went out walking. I think he passed a Mexican wedding where they plied him with some other things and the combination did him in. He was quite a vigorous guy but not so neurotic really.

"But Cobain was a marvelous singer. I hadn't heard much of him until towards the end of his life. I heard his unplugged version of that Lead Belly song and it was such a perfect vocal that I was really moved. It's one of my favorite songs but I only knew Lead Belly's version."

Ginsberg went on to reminisce about hanging out with Bob Dylan, meeting Phil Spector at his home in Los Angeles on a visit with Lenny Bruce and teaching the producer the Hari Krishna song which later evolved into George Harrison's "My Sweet Lord" and spending time with jazz great Thelonious Monk at the Five Spot club in New York. Throughout Ginsberg was totally unpretentious. His was simply a life lived in the spotlight and these were his friends, acquaintances, and inspirations. Nothing more, nothing less.

At the end of the conversation Ginsberg welcomed the option of continuing talking. We exchanged addresses and he asked how my love life was. I told him it was okay, thanked him for asking, and questioned how his was.

"My love life is OK too," he laughed. "I can hardly get it up but when you're seventy it's hard . . . unless you have somebody being helpful."

So was Ginsberg in that situation?

"I've found some younger chaps or lads quite helpful," he laughed. "There is life after sixty."

Index